# CIVIL WAR
## BATTLEFIELDS

# CIVIL WAR
## BATTLEFIELDS

WALKING THE TRAILS OF HISTORY

DAVID T. GILBERT

CIVIL
WAR
TRUST

FOREWORD BY

JEFF SHAARA

RIZZOLI
NEW YORK

New York Paris London Milan

# CONTENTS

# FOREWORD ✦ JEFF SHAARA

It started for me when I was 12. The place was Gettysburg, specifically the mile of open ground where Pickett's Charge took place. The guide was my father, Michael Shaara. Across those grassy fields, fence lines, and patches of corn, my father told the story of what happened there on July 3, 1863. But he was no historian. It was never about facts and figures. Michael Shaara was first and always a storyteller, and the story I heard was about the *people*, the men who made that charge and the men who waited for them along a ridgeline, a place we know today as the High Water Mark. To those who see this place through the eyes of the Confederacy, it was as far as those men would go. For those who think blue, it was the great stand that saved the Union. From that point on, the South's chances for winning the war diminished significantly. Even at the time, men on both sides seemed to grasp that.

Yet they continued to fight.

On the battlegrounds that spread from the Atlantic coast across the Mississippi River to Texas, horrifying battles had already been waged, and many more bloody awful tragedies were yet to come. By April 1865, more than 600,000 men would die in combat, and at least that many more would die of disease and lingering wounds. An exhausted nation—two nations—came together to heal the wounds as much as possible, and yet something amazing happened. Rather than obliterate the memories by obliterating the great battlefields, efforts began almost immediately to preserve that ground. In some cases, progress and growth made that impossible. But as time passed, and the wounds healed, the ground became something unique in this nation. It became hallowed.

My father toured Europe a great deal, and one observation he made was that "holy land" was all over the place. If there is any comparison to the United States, it is our battlefields. Over the past 150 years, we have embraced rather than destroyed a great many

of these lands, so that, even now, every person can find some value, some reason to take that marvelous walk.

The final result of my father's journey across the ground at Gettysburg was his novel *The Killer Angels*, the Pulitzer Prize–winning masterpiece told through the eyes of several pivotal characters who waged war during those few days in July 1863. Five years after my father's death in 1988, the book became the basis for Ted Turner's epic motion picture *Gettysburg*. Published in 1974, the book remains one of the most beloved and most widely read historical novels ever written. Today, the book has more than six million copies in print, and is now in its 114th printing, a milestone that most authors only dream of. All of that began with a walk on a piece of hallowed ground.

As I began to explore these stories on my own, the first step was research, and the first part of that research recalled my father's own journey across that amazing piece of ground. My first book, *Gods and Generals*, served as a prequel to *The Killer Angels*, and so my task was to explore the eastern campaigns, Lee and Jackson and Stuart pushing hard against McClellan and Hooker and Burnside. And so I began my own walks across many more pieces of ground.

The memories are vivid. At Fredericksburg, I climbed what had been the Confederate position on Marye's Heights, which is now, ironically, a national cemetery where only Union soldiers are buried. I happened upon a gravestone with a completely different appearance from the mass of the rest. Then I understood why. It was the grave of First Sgt. William Jones, Company A, 73rd New York Infantry. The gravestone showed in detail that Jones had been awarded the Medal of Honor. Standing before his grave was reward enough for that climb. Here was a true American hero.

A few miles south of Fredericksburg on I-95 is a sign that reads "The Stonewall Jackson Shrine." As

Gravesite of First Sgt. William Jones, 73rd New York Infantry, Fredericksburg National Cemetery, Virginia.

WILLIAM JONES
MEDAL OF HONOR
1ST SERG
CO A
73 NY INF

MAY 12 1864

curious as the name seemed to be, I ventured there, wondering if there would be something useful about Jackson that might help me tell my story. What I found was a shock. Close to the old rail depot at Guinea Station sits the remains of the Chandler Plantation. The "shrine" is in fact the small outbuilding where Jackson died. The preservation of the site includes the original blanket on the bed, medical equipment used to amputate his wounded arm, and the clock on the room's mantelpiece that marked the time of day when "Stonewall" stopped breathing. It was 3:15 p.m., Sunday, May 10, 1863. I am not necessarily a believer in ghosts, and I did not expect to be so profoundly moved by the experience of standing alone in that room. On that memorable day, Jackson's wife Anna, his doctor, and his aides were witnesses to the general's final words: "Let us cross over the river and rest under the shade of the trees." Those few moments gave me a visceral and dramatic feeling that this was a story I had to tell. And so, in *Gods and Generals*, the scene is described as it happened. And at the risk of sounding melodramatic, as I wrote those words, I couldn't hold back the tears. All of this because someone had the foresight to preserve a small nondescript frame building beside a long-gone plantation house.

The lesson was learned. In continuing to tell the story that became *Gods and Generals*, and in all the stories that followed, walking the ground became the first priority. Later on this journey, I visited the vast battlegrounds around Petersburg, Virginia, where Grant slowly strangled Lee's army in a siege that, by April 1865, ended that part of the war. I embraced every historical spot I could find, under the guiding hand of then-chief historian Chris Calkins. The Crater, Fort Stedman, Old Blandford Church, City Point: all are pivotal and dramatic sites where anyone can come to understand just why this place is so important. But it was an unexpected find that made an even greater impact.

Union Col. Joshua Chamberlain, already a legitimate hero for his actions on Little Round Top at Gettysburg (for which he was awarded the Medal of Honor), was severely wounded in fighting just below Petersburg. The only way I ever would have found that location, a crucial scene in my own book, was by following Chris to the unmarked location. It was smack in the middle of a subdivision. Today, the location of the site has been adjusted for further accuracy and is preserved

and marked so visitors don't require a skilled guide to find it. But the graphic comparison between the Stonewall Jackson Shrine and that nondescript piece of a housing development planted the seeds for my own dedication to the cause of battlefield preservation.

So many examples come to mind, examples that would certainly have special meaning to any student of the Civil War, or places that could grab and hold any tourist who is simply curious about what happened on a special piece of ground. As my writing career continued, I tackled a series of books that dealt with the war in the "West." That journey began with several careful examinations of the battlegrounds around Shiloh Church in southern Tennessee. I went there knowing nothing about what had happened there. But very soon, I began to understand that over a two-day period in April 1862 the armies bloodied each other to such an astonishing degree that the horrified citizens on both sides of the war were forced to understand that this was to be no brief gentlemen's spat. After learning of the 24,000 casualties at Shiloh, those on both sides of the conflict— who had boasted how their gallant boys would trample the rabble of their enemy—were now forced to accept that the enemy was just as capable of inflicting a brutal and bloody disaster on their boys too.

At Shiloh, there are as many poignant places to absorb as any field of the war. The enormous advantage of this place is that it is virtually original—untouched by massive development. As a result, it is extremely helpful to the storyteller who is trying to grasp the scope of the fight, and more importantly, to find those special places that add depth and emotion to the story. In this case, that storyteller was me.

Examples abound, including Bloody Pond, a small body of murky reddish water where dozens of wounded troops were brought, some for their last breaths. Legend states that the color of the pond comes from the blood of those troops (and countless horses) who lay close by. Also nearby is a peach orchard where Union troops took cover from repeated Confederate assaults. One of the most vivid accounts that I have read of any battle described how the storm of musket fire that sliced through the peach blossoms was so heavy that one soldier described the scene as though he were in the midst of a snowstorm.

Throughout the research that went into my stories, these experiences continued in nearly every place

Union Gen. Ulysses S. Grant's last line, Shiloh Battlefield, Shiloh National Military Park, Tennessee. The artillery along this ridge marks the final position of Grant's line on April 7, 1862.

I visited. And they continue still. At New Market Battlefield in the Shenandoah Valley, where young cadets from the Virginia Military Institute joined the fight against a Union force moving south, there is a field now known as the Field of Lost Shoes. One day I was walking in the footsteps of those cadets, and as had happened in May 1864, the rains had softened the ground. As though I needed a graphic explanation of why the field had such an odd name, I immediately understood. What that muddy ground had done to the cadets as they charged into battle had now happened to me. I lost my shoes.

Today, my writing journey through the Civil War has ended, at least for a time. It's on to other projects: Korea and Vietnam. But even through that research, the lessons remain, the value of the ground, of why it *must be preserved*. Museums are all well and good, and I support many of them. But as the zoo is not the jungle, so the museum is not the battlefield.

I live in Gettysburg now, barely a mile from the ridge where Union Gen. John Buford observed the rolling ground out to the west, astonished to see Confederate infantry marching toward his outnumbered cavalrymen. I walk those ridgelines often, and try to visualize that extraordinary scene through Buford's eyes. Nearly every day there are tourists on that ground, individuals and groups, some led by licensed battlefield guides. I truly hope that they understand the power of this place, what it meant to Buford and what it still means today. And passing often near the High Water Mark, I watch the people as they move out across the vast fields, walking in the footsteps of the 12,000 men who comprised Pickett's Charge. It digs deeply into me even now, those people making the same trek I did more than 50 years ago, when I see parents leading the young, and I smile to see that some of those children are barely 12 years old.

Field of Lost Shoes, New Market
Battlefield, Virginia.

# INTRODUCTION  DAVID T. GILBERT

There are many defining moments in our country's past, but few had a more substantial and significant impact on all citizens than the Civil War. The energy and effort still devoted to preserving battlefield sites, the ever-growing list of publications, the millions of visitors to Civil War sites every year, and even the contentious debates over enduring symbols of the conflict attest to the continued impact of the Civil War on our lives today. The profound constitutional changes brought about by the war were just the point of departure for a host of issues that still dominate our national conscience: the quest for legal and social equality for all Americans, debates over the proper role of the federal government, and never-ending efforts to reconcile differing cultural values held under a single national flag. As National Park Service historian John Henessey wrote in 2002, "The struggle to define America continues, and all paths to understanding that struggle invariably pass through the cauldron of America's Civil War."

An understanding of the battles and campaigns is crucial to understanding all other aspects of the Civil War. President Abraham Lincoln, in his second inaugural address, made this clear to a war-weary nation: "The progress of our arms, upon which all else chiefly depends, is as well known to the public as to myself, and it is, I trust, reasonably satisfactory and encouraging to all. With high hope for the future, no prediction in regard to it is ventured." He knew only too well that individual battles swayed elections, shaped political decisions, effected economic mobilization, brought women into the war effort, and influenced decisions to abolish slavery as well as to recruit former slaves as soldiers.

Glorifying the war by focusing solely on the mettle and bravery of its soldiers, however, misses a crucial point: the Civil War was a bloody, hateful conflict that not only pitted brother against brother, father against son, and neighbor against neighbor, but also left tens of thousands of mothers without sons, wives without husbands, and children without fathers. Civilians, too, paid a horrific price: the war left homes, farms, communities, and entire towns in ashes. Gaines Foster in his book *Ghosts of the Confederacy* admonishes us to take a deeper, more measured look into this national tragedy: "The rapid healing of national divisions and damaged southern self-image . . . came at the cost of deriving little insight or wisdom from the past. Rather than looking at the war as a tragic failure and trying to understand it, or even condemn it, Americans, North and South, chose to view it as a glorious time to be celebrated."

Culturally, we are still divided by basic disagreements about the meaning of the war, a division that often parallels, in uncanny ways, debates between individual rights and the reach of the federal government. The simple fact that slavery had become such a contentious issue in American politics in the 19th century—to the point where a new phrase, "the peculiar institution," became a common euphemism for the divisive word—offers a crucial message for our nation. Bridging deep, lingering divisions and finding common ground may be an essential component of a successful democracy, and is perhaps the salient message we should all take from the Civil War.

## The Second American Revolution

When the deep divisions and contentious debates erupted into civil war, both Northerners and Southerners believed themselves custodians of the legacy of 1776. As Civil War historian James McPherson has noted, "Every schoolboy and schoolgirl knew how [their Revolutionary forebears] had fought against the odds to forge a new republic conceived in liberty. . . . The crisis of 1861 was the great test of their worthiness of that heritage. On their shoulders rode the fate of the great experiment of republican government launched in 1776."

OPPOSITE: Artillery position on the Wilderness Battlefield, Fredericksburg and Spotsylvania National Military Park, Virginia.

FOLLOWING SPREAD: Confederate artillery position on Oak Hill, Gettysburg Battlefield, Gettysburg National Military Park, Pennsylvania. Fierce assaults by rebel infantry on the first day of fighting at Gettysburg drove Federal forces from this ridge.

The profound irony of the Civil War was that Confederate and Union soldiers interpreted the heritage of 1776 in opposite ways. Soldiers both North and South rallied to defend "liberty"—often intangible and abstract, but sincere and deeply felt. Corp. W. H. Williams of the 9th Alabama wrote on May 19, 1862: "I am engaged in the glorious cause of liberty and justice, fighting for all that we of the South hold dear." Union troops expressed the same passion. "This is not a war for dollars and cents," wrote Capt. James Goodnow of the 12th Indiana on January 11, 1863, "nor is it a war for territory—but it is to decide whether we are to be a free people—and if the Union is dissolved I very much fear that we will not have a Republican form of government very long."

Even the leaders on both sides cited parallels between 1776 and 1861 in their call to arms. Lincoln articulated Union war aims with words that resonate to this day: "Four score and seven years ago our fathers brought forth . . . a new nation, conceived in Liberty and dedicated to the proposition that all men are created equal." Likewise, Confederate President Jefferson Davis urged Southerners to "renew such sacrifices as our fathers made to the holy cause of constitutional liberty."

In the end, the second American Revolution of 1861–1865 radically changed America while settling two fundamental, festering issues left unresolved by the first Revolution of 1776: whether the precarious experiment of a democratic republic federated in a union of states would survive; and whether slavery would continue to mock the ideals of liberty upon which the republic was founded.

## "The Peculiar Institution"

Context helps explain each side's implacable commitment to the fight, and the irrefutable role that "the peculiar institution" played in tearing the country apart. Even a summary glance at the highly charged partisan and ideological debates that consumed the nation in the 1850s puts the issue of slavery front and center. The decade opened with the passage of the Fugitive Slave Act, which required that all escaped slaves were, upon capture, to be returned to their masters. The law galvanized citizens of free states who had long remained on the sidelines of the debate. It also influenced the 1852 publication of *Uncle Tom's Cabin*, which Harriet Beecher Stowe wrote to highlight the evils of slavery.

The Dred Scott Decision—the outcome of the 1857 Supreme Court case *Dred Scott v. Sandford*—added more fuel to the fire. The court held that "a negro, whose ancestors were imported into [the United States], and sold as slaves," whether enslaved or free, could not be an American citizen and therefore had no standing to sue in federal court. Northerners erupted in outrage. "All who love Republican institutions and who hate Aristocracy," warned the *Evening Journal* of Albany, New York, "compact yourselves together for the struggle which threatens your liberty and will test your manhood!" The *Richmond Enquirer* responded with equal vigor: "Thus has a politico-legal question . . . been decided emphatically in favor of the advocates and supporters of the Constitution and the Union, the equality of the States and the rights of the South, in contradistinction to and in repudiation of the diabolical doctrines inculcated by factionists and fanatics . . . The 'nation' has achieved a triumph, 'sectionalism' has been rebuked, and abolitionism has been staggered and stunned."

But perhaps no other event during the decade prior to the Civil War so galvanized the nation as John Brown's raid on the Harpers Ferry Armory and Arsenal in Virginia. In just three days—October 16, 17, and 18, 1859—Brown's attempt to incite a slave revolt struck mortal fear into the hearts and souls of all Southerners. According to historian Dr. Stephen B. Oates, Brown believed that even if he failed, was killed, or was captured and hanged, just his mere presence in Harpers Ferry—a bearded abolitionist with a gun, followed by a small band of raiders including five black men also armed with guns—would so polarize the country that it would surely ignite a sectional holocaust in which slavery would be destroyed. "He was a success, a tremendous success, because he was a catalyst of the Civil War," said Oates. "He didn't cause it but he set fire to the fuse that led to the blow up."

## Landscapes of Death

Confederates professed to fight for liberty and independence from a tyrannical government. Unionists fought to preserve the nation conceived in liberty from dismemberment and destruction. These conflicting impulses, which had propelled many volunteers into the armies at the war's beginning, became more intense as the fighting escalated. One of the greatest challenges when visiting Civil War sites today is to comprehend the grim and ghastly bloodshed that stained these battlefields. These places—now peaceful, serene parklands offering a quiet retreat from sprawling urban and suburban landscapes—were in many cases grim, godforsaken places that no soldier cared to remember or return to.

Robert Tilney, a veteran of the Fifth Army Corps, Army of the Potomac, perhaps said it best when he wrote: "How often the words 'Cruel War,' are uttered, and how glibly people beyond the reach of its influence talk of the misery caused by it . . . but not one thousandth part of the real misery is even guessed at by those who are not eye witnesses of its horrors." Other soldiers shared this profound and deeply felt sentiment, including a Confederate veteran of Shiloh who wrote, "O it was too shocking too horrible. God grant that I may never be the partaker in such scenes again. . . . When released from this I shall ever be an advocate of peace."

Meanings associated with routine places both picturesque and quaint before the Civil War became forever changed: Sarah Bell's Peach Orchard at Shiloh; D. R. Miller's Cornfield at Antietam; Joseph Sherfy's Peach Orchard and Wheatfield at Gettysburg. Other places gained grim new names: Bloody Hill at Wilson's Creek, Bloody Lane at Antietam, Bloody Pond at Shiloh, Bloody Angle at Spotsylvania—described by one Union officer as "a boiling, bubbling and hissing cauldron of death"—and Bloody Run at Cold Harbor.

Some names were unique, such as the Hornet's Nest at Shiloh, the Dead Angle at Kennesaw Mountain, and Hell's Half Acre at Stones River. Another name reappeared on battlefield after battlefield, in places that recalled the carnage in the slaughter pens of 19th-century stockyards. There was Slaughter Pen Farm at Fredericksburg, the Slaughter Pen at Gettysburg, and the Slaughter Pen at Stones River—where Sam Watkins of the 1st Tennessee Infantry wrote, "I cannot remember now of ever seeing more dead men and horses and captured cannon, all jumbled together . . . the ground was literally covered with blue coats dead."

Perhaps the most profound irony of the bloodshed and death left in the Civil War's wake was a somber warning by Gen. William Tecumseh Sherman, whose harsh "scorched earth" policies of total war left wide swaths of carnage across Georgia and South Carolina in 1864 and 1865. Sherman first learned that South Carolina had seceded from the Union in 1860 while he was serving as superintendent of the Louisiana State

OPPOSITE: Gen. William Poague's Confederate battery on the Widow Tapp Farm, Wilderness Battlefield, Fredericksburg and Spotsylvania National Military Park, Virginia.

FOLLOWING SPREAD: Sunrise on Saunders Field, Wilderness Battlefield, Fredericksburg and Spotsylvania National Military Park, Virginia.

Seminary of Learning and Military Academy. Reading the news, he exclaimed to a friend, "You people of the South don't know what you are doing! You think you can tear to pieces this great union without war! But I tell you there will be blood-shed—and plenty of it."

## Making Personal Connections

Historians estimate there were about 10,500 armed conflicts during the Civil War, ranging from major battles to minor skirmishes. While only a small percentage of these many thousands of sites have been preserved, including the 32 battlefields described in this book, hiking across these landscapes provides a crucial connection with the soldiers who fought there. By visiting these places and walking their trails, you're passing across the same fields and woods, hills and valleys, roads and rock outcroppings, and rivers and streams that significantly influenced the strategy and tactics of each battle.

Even deeper connections are made possible by reading the words of the soldiers who fought there— from their published letters and diaries, from interpretive signs along many of the trails, or even from the pages of this book. Stand in the Bloody Lane at Antietam Battlefield and read the description of the dead soldiers: "They were lying in rows like the ties of a railroad, in heaps like cordwood mingled with the splintered and shattered fence rails. Words are inadequate to portray the scene." Stand on Henry Hill at the very place where Gen. Barnard Bee pointed to Gen. Thomas Jackson's Virginia brigade and shouted, "There stands Jackson like a stone wall! Rally behind the Virginians!" Or walk the wooded trails at the Wilderness Battlefield and see for yourself why a soldier described the fighting as "bushwhacking on a grand scale."

Other connections may be much more personal. My own first visit to a Civil War battlefield was at Gettysburg when I was just 10 years old. Honestly, all I remember were the steep, rickety stairs of the metal observation tower on Culps Hill. But just a few years later, during a high school history class, I read about the "Battle Above the Clouds" at Lookout Mountain, Tennessee. It was an astonishing story and a stunning Union victory. How could this have happened? As it turns out, Confederate Gen. Braxton Bragg asked the same question in 1863. It was my first real connection with the Civil War, even though it was only from a

textbook. When it came time to pick a college, I chose to leave my home state of Connecticut and head south to Virginia, where there seemed to be more Civil War battlefields than in any other place in the country. And there, as it turns out, I made my second connection. My roommate, from Richmond, Virginia, derided me when I mentioned my interest in the Civil War and curtly corrected me: "You mean the War of Northern Aggression!" He was not angry, but quite firm. I wasn't in Connecticut anymore. To this day I'm still struggling to fully comprehend the Civil War: what happened, why it happened, and what it meant for our country. I did finally visit the Lookout Mountain Battlefield in July 2014. The landscape of the battle and view from the summit were every bit as spectacular as I had imagined.

Even more compelling connections are based on ancestors who fought in the war. My neighbor and battlefield hiking companion had two great-great-grandfathers who fought for the Union, which is strange since Winchester, Virginia—where I now live—staunchly supported the Confederacy. One ancestor, Thomas Spencer, served in the 5th New York Heavy Artillery from August 1862 to June 1865. He fought at the Battle of Harpers Ferry (1862), defended Maryland Heights during Gen. Jubal Early's invasion (1864), and fought three successive battles in the Shenandoah Valley at Third Winchester, Fisher's Hill, and Cedar Creek (all in 1864). My companion offered family stories and fascinating anecdotes as we hiked across both the Third Winchester and Fisher's Hill Battlefields, helping bring both places to life. His other ancestor, Franz Ludwik Heinrich Schultz, enlisted as Henry Schultz in the 1st New York Cavalry. He also fought in the Shenandoah Valley, mustered out of the service in August 1864 at Charles Town, West Virginia, and married Ann Roper in nearby Harpers Ferry in September 1864. This, of course, explains why my neighbor is a "Yankee" living in Winchester, Virginia.

## Preservation and Remembrance

The soldiers who fought the grim and bloody battles of the Civil War ultimately became the men who first preserved these places. In a wave of national healing and reconciliation, veterans spearheaded efforts in the 1890s to create the first five national military parks: Chickamauga and Chattanooga, Antietam, Shiloh, Gettysburg, and Vicksburg. "These Military Parks," the

veterans declared, "are not designed to commemorate either victory or defeat, but as monuments to the heroism of the American citizen soldier during the most trying period of our Nation's existence, and as object lessons of the struggles for the maintenance of the Union, and their cost."

Unfortunately, reconciliation came at a price, with the historic gains in legal, social, and political equality for African Americans pushed aside by government-sanctioned segregation. In establishing the Chickamauga and Chattanooga National Military Park on August 20, 1890, the House Committee on Military Affairs wrote, "The political questions which were involved in the contest do not enter into this view of the subject, nor do they belong to it. The proposition for establishing the park is in all its aspects a purely military project." The contentious, divisive issues that had brought both Northerners and Southerners to armed conflict were simply forgotten, as were the freedoms blacks had gained during the Civil War and Reconstruction. Instead, veterans now joined hands, "rejoicing that we now have a common flag that represents a common country." Listen to the words of President Woodrow Wilson on July 4, 1913, at the 50th anniversary of the Battle of Gettysburg: "We have found one another again as brothers and comrades in arms, enemies no longer, generous friends rather, our battles long past, the quarrel forgotten—except we shall not forget the splendid valor, the manly devotion of the men then arrayed against one another, now grasping hands and smiling into each other's eyes."

Reconciliation and remembrance of honor and valor also dominated the Civil War's 100th anniversary commemorations. It would not be until the first decade of the 21st century that Civil War parks began to engage in a concerted national discussion about the meaning of the war. Many park exhibits and interpretive programs not only teach the history of what happened at a particular battlefield, but also now explore the war's causes and consequences and tackle slavery as the principle issue dividing North and South in 19th-century America. Even the legacy of racism, which prevented African Americans from experiencing Lincoln's "new birth of freedom" for a century following Appomattox, is part of the difficult but vital discussion.

Civil War battlefield preservation was carried on by another generation of advocates in the mid-1920s,

OPPOSITE: Statue of Union Gen. Henry Slocum, Gettysburg Battlefield, Gettysburg National Military Park, Pennsylvania.

FOLLOWING SPREAD: Sunrise at Fort Stedman, Petersburg National Battlefield, Virginia. Confederate forces launched an all-out assault on the fort on March 25, 1865, hoping to break the Union siege of Petersburg.

when as many as 28 battlefield bills appeared before Congress. President Franklin D. Roosevelt's executive order of August 10, 1933, took the military parks from the War Department and placed them within the National Park Service of the Department of the Interior. The modern Civil War battlefield preservation movement is now spearheaded by the Civil War Trust, formed in 1987. Through 2016, the trust and its members have saved more than 43,000 acres in 23 states.

Connecting with these battlefields, with the stories they tell, and with the social, economic, and political events that swirled like a tornado around them is essential to understanding their legacy. The Civil War touched the lives of every American at the time, and it continues to do so today. The legacy forged by the war forms a seamless web of American values, traditions, and priorities. Spend time in one of these places, read a book about the events that happened there, and walk in a soldier's footsteps across a landscape once stained with blood. We should honor their commitment to battle by ensuring such a tragic war never happens again.

OPPOSITE: The Cornfield in springtime, Antietam National Battlefield, Maryland.

BELOW: Pyramid Monument near Prospect Hill, Fredericksburg Battlefield, Fredericksburg and Spotsylvania National Military Park, Virginia.

## Using This Book

*Civil War Battlefields: Walking the Trails of History* describes 32 battlefields at 25 sites in 12 different states. The book describes 124 battlefield hikes, from 0.2 miles long (Jackson Wounding Walking Tour Trail at Chancellorsville Battlefield) to 14 miles long (Cannon Trail at Chickamauga Battlefield). All hiking distances are approximate, based either on published material or my personal reconnaissance. Several sites include more than one battlefield: Manassas National Battlefield Park (First Manassas Battlefield and Second Manassas Battlefield); Fredericksburg and Spotsylvania National Military Park (Fredericksburg Battlefield, Chancellorsville Battlefield, Wilderness Battlefield, and Spotsylvania Court House Battlefield); Richmond National Battlefield Park (Gaines' Mill Battlefield, Malvern Hill Battlefield, and Cold Harbor Battlefield); and Chickamauga and Chattanooga National Military Park (Chickamauga Battlefield and Lookout Mountain Battlefield). Petersburg National Battlefield is a bit more complicated: there was the initial assault (June 15–18, 1864), a nine-and-a-half-month siege (June 18, 1864–April 2, 1865), a final breakthrough (April 2, 1865), and several battles in between. Descriptions of these actions and battles around Petersburg are accompanied by hiking trails at each location.

Because some sites include battles that were part of different campaigns, not all battlefields are described in chronological order, but rather in geographical order. This allows the visitor, for instance, to hike the Gaines' Mill Battlefield (Battle of Gaines' Mill, June 27, 1862) and the nearby Cold Harbor Battlefield (Battle of Cold Harbor, May 3–June 12, 1864) during the same visit to Richmond National Battlefield Park. To explore the Wilderness Battlefield (Battle of the Wilderness, May 5–7, 1864) and Spotsylvania Court House Battlefield (Battle of Spotsylvania Court House, May 8–21, 1864), which both immediately preceded the Battle of Cold Harbor, you will have to travel to Fredericksburg and Spotsylvania National Military Park several miles north of Richmond.

Always start your battlefield visit at each site's visitor center. There you will almost always find up-to-date trail information and detailed trail maps. Don't miss out on audiovisual programs, interpretive exhibits, or ranger-guided talks—each of these experiences will enhance your understanding of the site and make your battlefield hike much more meaningful.

Fort Sumter National Monument, South Carolina. The first shots of the Civil War were fired here on April 12, 1861, when Confederate artillery bombarded the Union garrison.

# CHRONOLOGY OF THE BATTLES

| NAME OF BATTLE | DATE(S) OF BATTLE | SITE NAME |
|---|---|---|
| **Battle of First Manassas** (First Battle of Bull Run) | July 21, 1861 | Manassas National Battlefield Park |
| **Battle of Wilson's Creek** | August 10, 1861 | Wilson's Creek National Battlefield |
| **Battle of Fort Donelson** | February 16, 1862 | Fort Donelson National Battlefield |
| **Battle of Shiloh** (Pittsburg Landing) | April 6–7, 1862 | Shiloh National Military Park |
| **Battle of Picacho Peak** | April 15, 1862 | Picacho Peak State Park |
| **Battle of McDowell** | May 8, 1862 | McDowell Battlefield Park |
| **Battle of Gaines' Mill** | June 27, 1862 | Richmond National Battlefield Park |
| **Battle of Malvern Hill** | July 1, 1862 | Richmond National Battlefield Park |
| **Battle of Second Manassas** (Second Battle of Bull Run) | August 28–30, 1862 | Manassas National Battlefield Park |
| **Battle of Harpers Ferry** | September 12–15, 1862 | Harpers Ferry National Historical Park |
| **Battle of Antietam** (Sharpsburg) | September 17, 1862 | Antietam National Battlefield |
| **Battle of Perryville** | October 8, 1862 | Perryville Battlefield State Historic Site |
| **Battle of Fredericksburg** | December 11–13, 1862 | Fredericksburg and Spotsylvania National Military Park |
| **Battle of Stones River** | December 31, 1862–January 2, 1863 | Stones River National Battlefield |
| **Battle of Chancellorsville** | April 27–May 6, 1863 | Fredericksburg and Spotsylvania National Military Park |
| **Siege of Vicksburg** | May 18–July 4, 1863 | Vicksburg National Military Park |
| **Siege of Port Hudson** | May 21–July 9, 1863 | Port Hudson State Historic Site |
| **Battle of Brandy Station** (Fleetwood Hill) | June 9, 1863 | Brandy Station Battlefield Park |
| **Battle of Gettysburg** | July 1–3, 1863 | Gettysburg National Military Park |
| **Battle of Chickamauga** | September 18–20, 1863 | Chickamauga and Chattanooga National Military Park |
| **Battle of Lookout Mountain** | November 24, 1863 | Chickamauga and Chattanooga National Military Park |
| **Battle of the Wilderness** | May 5–6, 1864 | Fredericksburg and Spotsylvania National Military Park |
| **Battle of Spotsylvania Court House** | May 8–21, 1864 | Fredericksburg and Spotsylvania National Military Park |
| **Battle of Pickett's Mill** | May 27, 1864 | Pickett's Mill Battlefield Historic Site |
| **Battle of Cold Harbor** | May 31–June 12, 1864 | Richmond National Battlefield Park |
| **Assault on Petersburg** | June 15–18, 1864 | Petersburg National Battlefield |
| **Siege of Petersburg** | June 18, 1864–April 2, 1865 | Petersburg National Battlefield |
| **Battle of Kennesaw Mountain** | June 27, 1864 | Kennesaw Mountain National Battlefield Park |
| **Battle of Monocacy** | July 9, 1864 | Monocacy National Battlefield |
| **Battle of the Crater** | July 30, 1864 | Petersburg National Battlefield |
| **Third Battle of Winchester** | September 19, 1864 | Third Winchester Battlefield Park |
| **Battle of Fisher's Hill** | September 21–22, 1864 | Fisher's Hill Battlefield Park |
| **Battle of Hatcher's Run** | February 5–7, 1865 | Hatcher's Run Battlefield (adjacent to Petersburg National Battlefield) |
| **Battle of Bentonville** | March 19–21, 1865 | Bentonville Battlefield State Historic Site |
| **Battle of Fort Stedman** | March 25, 1865 | Petersburg National Battlefield |
| **Battle of Five Forks** | April 1, 1865 | Petersburg National Battlefield |
| **Petersburg Breakthrough** | April 2, 1865 | Pamplin Historical Park (adjacent to Petersburg National Battlefield) |
| **Appomattox Court House** | April 9, 1865 | Appomattox Court House National Historical Park |

# EASTERN VIRGINIA

# FIRST MANASSAS
## BATTLEFIELD

VIRGINIA  Manassas National Battlefield Park

I N   E A R L Y   J U L Y   1 8 6 1 ,   J U S T   T H R E E   M O N T H S   A F T E R   C O N F E D E R A T E   F O R C E S had fired upon Fort Sumter in Charleston, South Carolina, people in the North clamored for military action. The *New York Tribune* had recently published one of the most influential editorials of the war, "On to Richmond." Many Northerners believed that a single heavy blow would open the way to the Confederate capital and bring a swift end to the Rebellion. Finally, on July 16, cheers rang out in the streets of Washington as Union Gen. Irvin McDowell began the long-awaited campaign to capture Richmond, Virginia, and end the war.

McDowell's army, 35,000 strong, was composed mostly of 90-day volunteers who had been summoned by President Abraham Lincoln after the startling news of Fort Sumter's bombardment. The new recruits, with just a few weeks of training, had little knowledge of what war would mean. Neither, for that matter, did most citizens on either side of the conflict. As the army marched west toward the key railroad junction at Manassas, Virginia, many citizens and congressmen with picnic lunches followed close behind. All were expecting a colorful show.

Waiting at Manassas Junction were 22,000 Confederate soldiers under the command of Gen. P. G. T. Beauregard, a West Point graduate and veteran of the Mexican War. Beauregard's troops were drawn up along an eight-mile front on the west bank of Bull Run, guarding the junction of the Orange and Alexandria and Manassas Gap Railroads. If McDowell could seize this junction, Union forces would disrupt Confederate communications with the Shenandoah Valley and stand astride the best overland route to Richmond.

Bull Run was just 25 miles west of Washington, but the inexperienced Union troops and their large supply column made slow progress. It took more than two days for the army to finally reach Centreville, a tiny village three miles east of Bull Run. Here most of the citizen entourage unfolded their blankets and unpacked

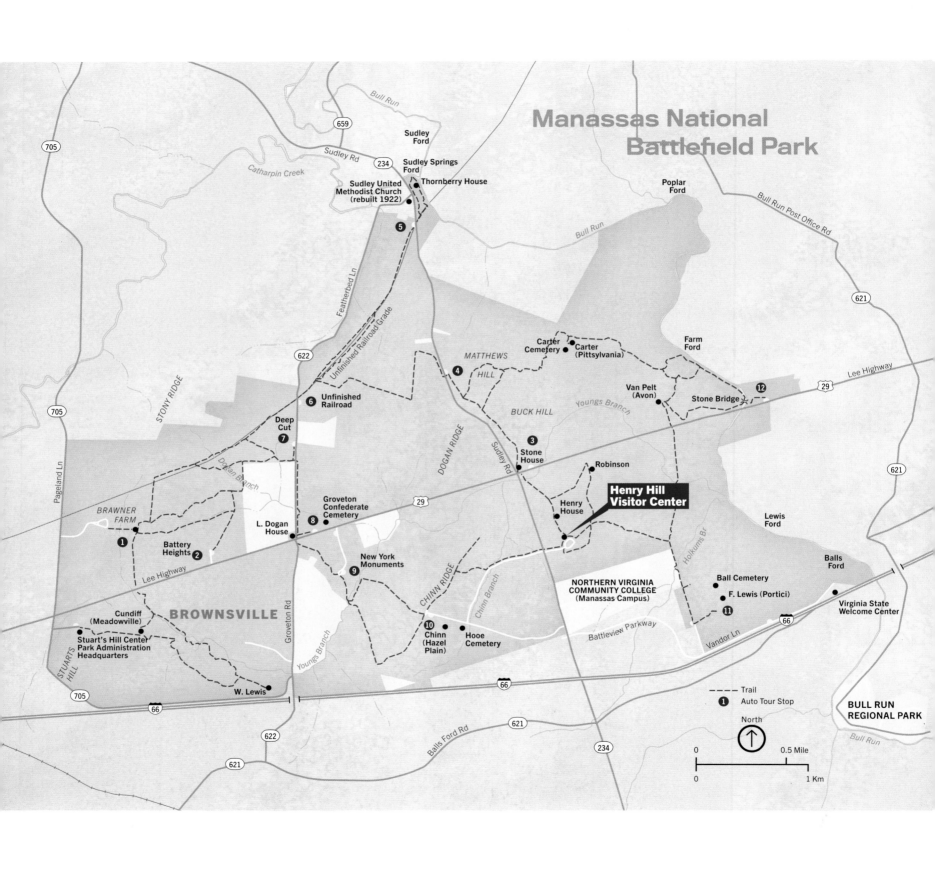

# Manassas National Battlefield Park

705
659
Bull Run
Sudley Rd
234
Sudley Ford
Sudley Springs Ford
Thornberry House
Sudley United Methodist Church (rebuilt 1922)
Catharpin Creek
Poplar Ford
Bull Run
Bull Run Post Office Rd
621
622
Featherbed Ln
Unfinished Railroad Grade
5
STONY RIDGE
705
6 Unfinished Railroad
Deep Cut
7
Dogan Branch
Carter Cemetery
Carter (Pittsylvania)
Farm Ford
MATTHEWS HILL
4
Lee Highway
29
Van Pelt (Avon)
Stone Bridge
12
BUCK HILL
Youngs Branch
621
DOGAN RIDGE
3 Stone House
Robinson
Henry Hill Visitor Center
Henry House
Lewis Ford
Groveton Confederate Cemetery
8
29
L. Dogan House
BRAWNER FARM
Pageland Ln
1
Battery Heights 2
Lee Highway
New York Monuments
9
CHINN RIDGE
Chinn Branch
Holkums Br
NORTHERN VIRGINIA COMMUNITY COLLEGE (Manassas Campus)
Ball Cemetery
F. Lewis (Portici)
11
Balls Ford
Virginia State Welcome Center
Cundiff (Meadowville)
BROWNSVILLE
Groveton Rd
Youngs Branch
10 Chinn (Hazel Plain)
Hooe Cemetery
Battleview Parkway
66
Vandor Ln
Stuart's Hill Center Park Administration Headquarters
STUARTS HILL
705
W. Lewis
66
622
Balls Ford Rd
621
621
234
--- Trail
1 Auto Tour Stop
North
BULL RUN REGIONAL PARK
Bull Run

0                    0.5 Mile

0                    1 Km

their picnic baskets for the pageant they expected to witness. After scouting the enemy positions, McDowell finally launched his attack in the early morning hours of July 21, 1861.

At about 2:30 a.m., McDowell sent two divisions—about 13,000 men—on a long march toward Sudley Springs, one of several fords along Bull Run. The crossing, which was beyond the north end of Beauregard's line, took Federal forces around the Confederate left flank. To distract the Confederates, he ordered a diversionary attack by another division at the Stone Bridge, which carried the Warrenton Turnpike—the main road from Washington—across Bull Run. At 5:30 a.m., a Union 30-pounder Parrott artillery piece shattered the morning air, signaling the start of the Civil War's first major battle. The Federal columns marching toward Sudley Springs again made slow progress as the men stumbled through the darkness along narrow country roads. By the time they crossed Sudley Springs Ford and deployed for their attack, it was after 9:30 a.m. Col. Nathan Evans, Confederate commander at the Stone Bridge, had already realized the attack on his front was only a diversion. Leaving a small force behind to hold the bridge, Evans rushed the remainder of his command to Matthews Hill in time to confront McDowell's flanking troops.

Evans's men put up a fierce fight, but his force of about 900 men was too small to hold back the Federals for long. Soon Confederate brigades under Gen. Barnard Bee and Col. Francis Bartow arrived at Matthews Hill, bolstering the thin line to about 2,800 men. Still, pressure was mounting as 20,000 Federal troops converged on the Confederate left flank. Shortly after 11:30 a.m., the Confederate line collapsed and the Southerners fled in disorder across the Warrenton Pike toward Henry Hill.

As the Confederates regrouped along Henry Hill, Gen. Thomas Jackson led five Virginia regiments, nearly 2,500 men, onto the battlefield. According to most accounts, Bee attempted to rally his 4th Alabama Infantry Regiment, pointing to Jackson's men and shouting, "There stands Jackson like a stone wall! Rally behind the Virginians!" But National Park Service historian John Henessey has uncovered several firsthand accounts that tell a slightly different story. Rather than rallying around the Virginians at noontime, the remnants of the 4th Alabama regrouped in the woods behind Jackson's line, where they awaited orders. When Bee finally got his infantrymen moving again, he spurred them to action with the instructions, "Come with me and go yonder where Jackson stands like a stone wall." Whichever account is correct, the name stuck, and "Stonewall" Jackson became one of the South's best-known generals.

Meanwhile, the Federals had stopped their advance to reorganize for a new attack. The lull lasted for about an hour, giving Beauregard enough time to reform his Confederate lines across Henry Hill. Confederate reinforcements also arrived on the field. Gen. Joseph Johnston had given a Union army the slip in the Shenandoah Valley. His 10,000 men, who had boarded trains in Winchester, Virginia, were rushed to the front from Manassas Junction. When the fighting resumed around 1:00 p.m., both sides attacked and counterattacked, firing away at one another for three hours in a bloody stalemate. Although McDowell had brought 15 regiments into the fight—outnumbering the Confederates two to one—no more than two were ever engaged at the same time. Around 3:00 p.m., a Confederate counterattack captured several Union cannon on the southern end of McDowell's line, helping

PREVIOUS SPREAD: Henry Hill and Henry House.

BELOW: March 1862 photograph of Sudley Church. As wounded soldiers stumbled back behind the lines during the First Battle of Bull Run, the Union army turned the church into a field hospital.

turn the tide of the battle. Around 4:00 p.m., two of Johnston's brigades crushed the Union right flank on Chinn Ridge, just west of Henry Hill. Beauregard ordered his entire line forward. McDowell's force crumbled and began to retreat.

What began as an orderly withdrawal soon turned into a rout. An overturned Union wagon blocked one of the bridges along the Warrenton Turnpike, and soldiers also found the road jammed with the carriages of citizens and congressmen who had come to watch the spectacle. Panic soon seized many of the soldiers. Still, the Confederates were too disorganized to follow up on their victory, and the defeated Union army found safety behind its Washington defenses the following day.

The Battle of First Manassas (or First Battle of Bull Run) had damaged both armies. Union casualties totaled 2,950; the Confederates lost 1,750 men. News of the contest was celebrated as a great victory in the South, while in the North hopes for a quick end to the Rebellion were dashed. Both sides, however, could now agree on one point: the road to victory would be a long, bloody fight.

ABOVE: Bull Run.

OPPOSITE: Stone Bridge over Bull Run. The original bridge, built in 1825, was destroyed during the First Battle of Bull Run.

# FIRST MANASSAS Battlefield Hikes

Manassas National Battlefield Park has more than 40 miles of trails, traversing key areas of both the First and Second Manassas Battlefields. Opportunities exist for both short and extended hikes. The hikes are easy to moderate, with steep climbs along the banks of Bull Run, and many include trailside interpretive markers describing the battle action that occurred at a particular spot. Hikers should begin at the visitor center on Henry Hill.

### First Manassas Trail (5.4 miles)

This extended hike leads visitors over the landscape where the newly formed Union and Confederate armies clashed for the first time. The trail begins at the visitor center and continues through forested areas and across a wetland, emerging at the Stone Bridge. The trail then follows Bull Run upstream before climbing up a steep hill and emerging onto the open crest of Matthews Hill—the site of the opening phase of combat. The trail descends into the valley of Youngs Branch and passes the historic Stone House (open seasonally). The building served as an aid station during both Battles of Manassas. After crossing Lee Highway (Route 29) at the pedestrian crosswalk, the trail heads up Henry Hill to the scene of fierce artillery clashes between the opposing armies. Caught in the middle was the Henry House, home of Judith Henry, an elderly widow who refused to evacuate her home during the battle and was killed by cannon fire (she is buried nearby).

### Henry Hill Loop Trail (1.2 miles)

The critical fighting at First Manassas centered on Henry Hill. This trail begins behind the visitor center, leads past Ricketts's Battery of Union artillery, and continues to the rebuilt Henry House. In the yard of the 1870 house is the grave of widow Judith Henry, who was mortally wounded by artillery fire and the only civilian killed during the first battle. Behind the house is an 1865 monument erected by Union soldiers in "memory of the patriots who fell at Bull Run." From the Henry House the trail continues north to the location of Imboden's Confederate artillery overlooking Matthews Hill, and then across the fields to the site of the Robinson House, where Col. Wade Hampton led his South Carolina troops into the battle. The trail loops back along the Southern line, where Gen. Thomas Jackson received his famous nickname, "Stonewall." The trail concludes at the site where Confederate infantry captured artillery from Capt. Charles Griffin's Union battery—a major turning point in the battle. This final stop faces Chinn Ridge where, late in the afternoon, a Confederate attack crushed Gen. Irvin McDowell's right flank and began the rout of the entire Union army.

## Matthews Hill Loop Trail (0.9 miles)

This trail explores the ground on which the opening phase of combat occurred and begins at the Matthews Hill parking area (Auto Tour Stop 4). The trail leads up the crest of the hill to Capt. William Reynolds's battery of Union artillery. From this vantage point, visitors can observe the landscape from Union artillery positions that overlook the historic Stone House and Confederate artillery positions on distant Henry Hill. Scenic vistas looking south and west give an excellent view of major portions of the battlefield. The trail descends down the front slope of Matthews Hill before turning east and entering the woods. Visitors will soon come upon the Stovall Monument, marking the approximate location where Pvt. George Stovall of the 8th Georgia Regiment was killed. The trail loops back by paralleling the Union battle line, with trailside markers indicating the approximate location of Federal regiments during the fighting.

## Stone Bridge Loop Trail (1.3 miles)

This trail begins at the Stone Bridge parking area (Auto Tour Stop 12) and leads down to the postwar Stone Bridge (Confederate troops destroyed the wartime bridge in 1862). It was here that Union forces deployed to divert Confederate attention from the main advance upstream. Upon crossing the bridge, the trail continues along Bull Run, with its picturesque displays of wildflowers in the spring and colorful foliage in the fall. The trail ascends a steep bluff to the overlook of Farm Ford, where Union troops led by Col. William Tecumseh Sherman crossed Bull Run on the day of the battle. Turning west away from the stream, the trail emerges out in the open fields of the wartime Van Pelt property. Visitors will pass the site of the Van Pelt home, Avon, used by Confederate Col. Nathan Evans as his headquarters. The trail cuts back over a watershed area with excellent birding opportunities from the wooden boardwalk through the marsh.

## Sudley Loop Trail (0.6 miles)

This trail starts across the road from the Sudley parking area (Auto Tour Stop 5). Visitors should use extreme caution when crossing busy Route 234 (Sudley Road). The trail parallels the historic unfinished railroad bed for a short distance before turning north along Bull Run. Visitors will pass the historic Thornberry House (not open to the public), one of only three prewar structures still standing in the park. The trail continues past the confluence of Bull Run and Catharpin Creek to the site of Sudley Spring Ford. More than 13,000 Union troops crossed Catharpin Creek at this site en route to the battlefield. The trail then follows the wartime Sudley Road trace back to the parking lot.

OPPOSITE: View across Henry Hill toward the Stonewall Jackson Monument.

ABOVE: Stonewall Jackson Monument on Henry Hill.

# SECOND MANASSAS
## BATTLEFIELD

VIRGINIA  Manassas National Battlefield Park

THE SECOND HALF OF 1862 WITNESSED A TRANSFORMATION OF THE CIVIL War, which became more contentious as Union and Confederate forces fought increasingly bitter, bloody battles. Union Gen. George McClellan was losing the confidence of President Abraham Lincoln. After McClellan's retreat from Richmond at the end of the Seven Days' Battles, Lincoln divided the Union forces in Virginia into two armies. He reluctantly left McClellan in charge of the Army of the Potomac, which had withdrawn to Harrison's Landing along the James River. But he stripped Gen. Irvin McDowell's First Corps from McClellan and combined it with the armies of Gen. John Frémont and Gen. Nathaniel Banks from western Virginia, forming the Army of Virginia under Gen. John Pope.

Confederate Gen. Robert E. Lee, satisfied that McClellan's army posed no further threat to Richmond, ordered Gen. Thomas "Stonewall" Jackson's wing of the Army of Northern Virginia to block Pope's advance toward Gordonsville and the Virginia Central Railroad. But Lee had larger plans in mind. Since the armies of both McClellan and Pope were now widely separated, he saw an opportunity to destroy Pope's forces before turning his attention back to McClellan. When he learned that McClellan's army was departing the Virginia Peninsula to join forces with Pope in early August 1862, Lee ordered Gen. James Longstreet's wing to join Jackson.

In a daring move, Lee ordered Jackson to execute a sweeping flank march across the Rappahannock River and around Pope's right on August 25. By sunset on the following day, the Confederates had completed a remarkable 55-mile march, striking the Orange and Alexandria Railroad at Bristoe Station in Pope's rear and subsequently capturing Pope's supply depot at Manassas Junction. With their line of supply in jeopardy, the Union forces abruptly abandoned their line along the Rappahannock and retreated north to pursue Jackson.

As the Union forces advanced on Manassas Junction—scene of the bloody First Battle of Bull Run the previous year—Jackson slipped away, deploying his forces along an unfinished railroad grade north of the Warrenton Turnpike near Groveton. Longstreet's column was just a day behind him. The two wings of Lee's army totaled about 55,000 men. Pope's Army of Virginia, composed of three divisions, totaled 51,000 men.

The Battle of Second Manassas (or Second Battle of Bull Run) began about 6:30 p.m. on August 28, 1862, as a Federal column advanced east along the Warrenton Turnpike near the farm of the John Brawner family. Jackson, concerned that Pope might be withdrawing his army behind Bull Run to link up with McClellan's army, ordered his men to attack. Savage fighting at the Brawner Farm lasted until dark, with neither side gaining an advantage.

Pope believed that Jackson was attempting to escape; he ordered his scattered forces to converge on the Confederate line along the unfinished railroad grade, where fighting resumed on August 29. He was certain he could destroy Jackson's forces before Lee and Longstreet could intervene. Throughout the day, in a series of uncoordinated attacks, Pope hurled his men against the Confederates. In several places the assaults momentarily breached Jackson's line, but each time the Federals were pushed back. During the afternoon, Longstreet's troops arrived on the battlefield and, unknown to Pope, deployed on Jackson's right. Lee urged Longstreet to attack the exposed Union left flank, but "Old Pete" demurred, arguing that circumstances did not yet favor an assault.

The morning of August 30 was quiet as Pope pondered conflicting reports on the enemy's disposition and intentions. Around midday, still convinced that the Confederates were retreating, the Union commander ordered his army forward in pursuit. The "pursuit" ended quickly. Skirmishers found Jackson's forces still ensconced along the unfinished railroad grade. Pope then ordered another assault against Jackson's line, sending Gen. Fitz John Porter's Fifth Corps, supported by Gen. John Hatch's division, against the Confederate right flank at the Deep Cut, an excavated section of the railroad grade. The Federals succeeded in breaking the Confederate line, but the Stonewall Brigade rushed in to close the breach. In one of the most notable incidents of the battle, two Confederate brigades

ran out of ammunition and began throwing large rocks at the 24th New York Regiment. Jackson's men, with support from 18 artillery pieces on high ground near the Brawner Farm, finally repulsed the Union assault, throwing it back with heavy losses.

At this moment, Lee and Longstreet seized the initiative and launched a massive counterattack against the weakened Union left flank. Longstreet's wing, nearly 30,000 strong, swept eastward toward Chinn Ridge. A brief, futile stand by the 5th and 10th New York Regiments ended in slaughter. In five minutes the 5th New York lost 123 men—the greatest loss of life in any single infantry regiment in any battle of the Civil War. Union forces on Chinn Ridge mounted a tenacious defense, which bought Pope enough time to shift troops onto Henry Hill and stave off disaster. At 8:00 p.m., Pope pulled his beaten army off the field and retreated eastward across Bull Run.

Estimated Union casualties from the battle were 13,830 killed or wounded; the Confederates lost 8,350 men. With Union forces in total disarray, Lee grasped the opportunity to launch his first invasion of the North, advancing across the Potomac River into Maryland during the first week of September 1862.

PREVIOUS SPREAD: Artillery position on Henry Hill.

OPPOSITE: Unfinished railroad bed. Confederate forces repulsed fierce Union assaults here during the Battle of Second Manassas.

BELOW: Artillery piece on Henry Hill.

FOLLOWING SPREAD: Stone House, which sheltered wounded soldiers as a Union field hospital during both Battles of Manassas.

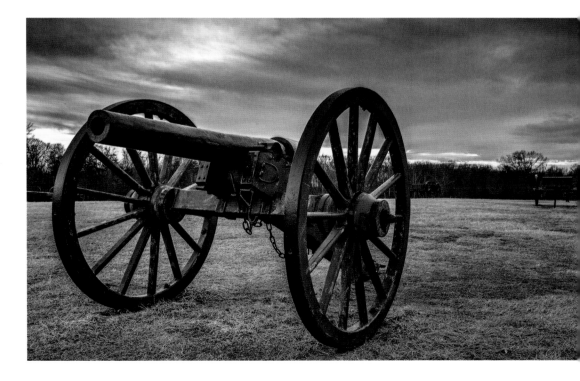

# SECOND MANASSAS Battlefield Hikes

Manassas National Battlefield Park has more than 40 miles of trails, traversing key areas of both the First and Second Manassas Battlefields. Opportunities exist for both short and extended hikes. The hikes are easy to moderate, with steep climbs along the banks of Bull Run, and many include trailside interpretive markers describing the battle action that occurred at a particular spot. Hikers should begin at the visitor center on Henry Hill.

## Second Manassas Trail (6.2 miles)

This walking trail leads visitors through the climactic stages of the Battle of Second Manassas (Second Battle of Bull Run). The trail begins at the visitor center and heads north past the Stone House (open seasonally) to Buck Hill, where Gen. John Pope established his headquarters. From Matthews Hill, visitors can look west to the area of the unfinished railroad where Gen. Thomas "Stonewall" Jackson placed his Confederate forces. The trail continues along this unfinished railroad bed, leading to a clearing at the Deep Cut—the scene of a bloody battle where Jackson's troops turned back a major Union assault. The trail then turns south and passes the Lucinda Dogan House (one of three surviving Civil War–era structures in the park). Moving across the road, the trail winds uphill toward New York Avenue. Monuments mark the site where the 5th and 10th New York Regiments were slaughtered in a massive Confederate counterattack that swept eastward toward Chinn Ridge. After touring the Chinn Ridge area, the trail leads back to Henry Hill, where the last fighting of the three-day battle occurred.

## Brawner Farm Loop Trail (1.6 miles)

This trail begins at the Brawner Farm parking area off Pageland Lane (Auto Tour Stop 1). It crosses historic farmland and the scene of some of the deadliest fighting during the opening day of the battle. The trail follows a paved path down to the Brawner Farm Interpretive Center (open March to November) and then continues east along the Union battle line. A short side trail leads up to Battery Heights, where Capt. Joseph Campbell unlimbered the cannon of the 4th US Artillery, Battery B. The trail loops back via the Confederate position, following the battle line once occupied by the Stonewall Brigade.

## Chinn Ridge Trail (1.0 mile)

This trail begins at the Chinn Ridge parking area (Auto Tour Stop 10). The paved path, which is wheelchair accessible, traverses an area that witnessed heavy fighting on August 30, 1862. Interpretive signs tell the story of Union troops who made a desperate stand on Chinn Ridge and blunted Gen. James Longstreet's massive Confederate counterattack. Near the conclusion of the trail, visitors pass a monument dedicated to Col. Fletcher Webster of the 12th Massachusetts, killed in action on Chinn Ridge. He was the son

of noted orator Daniel Webster. The paved trail returns to the parking lot via the same path.

### Deep Cut Loop Trail (1.2 miles)

This trail, which starts at the Deep Cut parking area (Auto Tour Stop 7), passes through the unfinished railroad bed to a clearing at the Deep Cut—the scene of a bloody battle where Gen. Thomas "Stonewall" Jackson's troops repulsed a major Union assault on August 30, 1862. It was here that the Confederate brigades of Col. Bradley Johnson and Col. Leroy Stafford ran out of ammunition and resorted to throwing large rocks at the men of the 24th New York Regiment, prompting some of the surprised New Yorkers to throw them back.

### Unfinished Railroad Loop Trail (1.2 miles)

This trail begins at the Unfinished Railroad parking area off Featherbed Lane (Auto Tour Stop 6). It then heads northeast along the unfinished railroad bed, where Gen. Thomas "Stonewall" Jackson placed his Confederate troops. Interpretive markers discuss the bayonet charge by Gen. Cuvier Grover's Union brigade on August 29, 1862, which briefly punctured the Confederate defensive line. Before looping back to the parking lot, hikers have the option of continuing down the railroad bed via the Sudley Connector Trail to Sudley Church. The Sudley Church area served as the Confederate army's left flank during the Battle of Second Manassas.

OPPOSITE: Deep Cut, which was the scene of some of the fiercest fighting on the Second Manassas Battlefield.

ABOVE: Henry Hill and Henry House.

# FREDERICKSBURG
## BATTLEFIELD

VIRGINIA  Fredericksburg and Spotsylvania National Military Park

GEN. AMBROSE BURNSIDE INHERITED COMMAND OF THE ARMY OF THE Potomac on November 7, 1862. His predecessor, Gen. George McClellan, had succeeded in stopping Gen. Robert E. Lee's invasion of Maryland at Antietam in mid-September 1862. But McClellan, ever cautious, had shown neither the resolve nor the aggressiveness that President Abraham Lincoln demanded in pursuing Lee's army. After much prodding by Lincoln and General in Chief Henry Halleck, Burnside proposed a late-fall offensive. In a plan that relied on quick movement and deception, he would move his entire army from its camps around Warrenton, Virginia, to Fredericksburg, 40 miles to the east. The maneuver would place the Army of the Potomac on the direct road to Richmond, and ensure a secure supply line from Washington.

With the president's approval, Burnside launched his army eastward on November 15. The blue-clad veterans began arriving at Fredericksburg on November 17, deploying along Stafford Heights on the northeast side of the Rappahannock River. The Federals had indeed gotten the jump on "Bobby Lee," forcing the Confederate commander to act quickly to shift his own scattered forces to defend the city. But already Burnside's plan began to unravel. The Federals could not move south without first crossing the Rappahannock—the largest of several river barriers that flowed across their path to Richmond. Through a combination of miscommunication, military bureaucracy, and poor weather, the pontoon bridges Burnside had ordered didn't arrive until November 25, giving the Confederates enough time to occupy the high ground southwest of Fredericksburg.

The Confederate forces of Gen. James Longstreet were deployed along a series of rises known as Taylor's Hill, Marye's Heights, Howison Hill, and Telegraph Hill (subsequently known as Lee's Hill) just west of Fredericksburg. Gen. Thomas "Stonewall" Jackson, whose army had been encamped around Winchester,

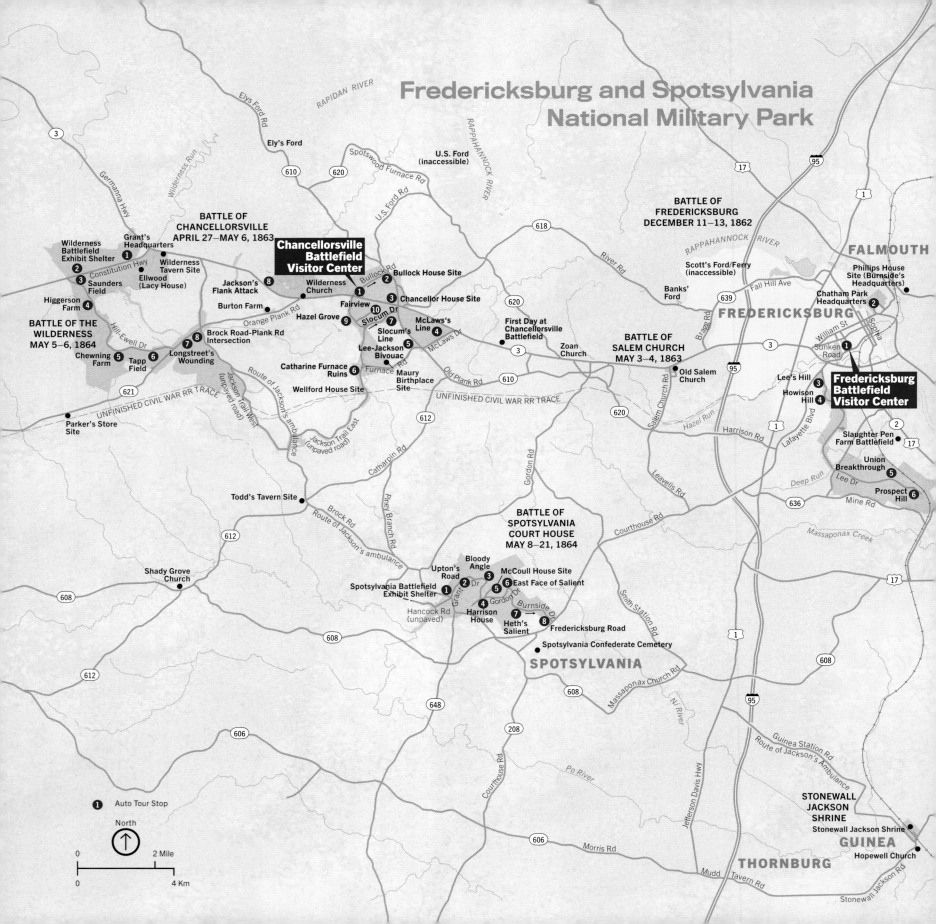

# Fredericksburg and Spotsylvania National Military Park

RAPIDAN RIVER

RAPPAHANNOCK RIVER

Elys Ford Rd

Wilderness Run

Ely's Ford

Spotswood Furnace Rd

U.S. Ford (inaccessible)

U.S. Ford Rd

Germanna Hwy

**BATTLE OF CHANCELLORSVILLE**
APRIL 27–MAY 6, 1863

**BATTLE OF FREDERICKSBURG**
DECEMBER 11–13, 1862

FALMOUTH

Wilderness Battlefield Exhibit Shelter ❶
Grant's Headquarters
Constitution Hwy
Wilderness Tavern Site
Ellwood (Lacy House)
❷
❸ Saunders Field
Higgerson Farm ❹

Jackson's Flank Attack ❽

**Chancellorsville Battlefield Visitor Center**

Bullock Rd
Bullock House Site ❷
❶

Wilderness Church

Scott's Ford/Ferry (inaccessible)

Banks' Ford

River Rd

Phillips House Site (Burnside's Headquarters)

Chatham Park Headquarters ❷

FREDERICKSBURG

Fall Hill Ave

**BATTLE OF THE WILDERNESS**
MAY 5–6, 1864

Burton Farm
Hazel Grove ❾
Orange Plank Rd
Fairview
Slocum Dr ❿
❼ Slocum's Line
❸ Chancellor House Site

620

First Day at Chancellorsville Battlefield

**BATTLE OF SALEM CHURCH**
MAY 3–4, 1863

Bragg Rd

Sunken Road ❶

William St

Sophia

Hill-Ewell Dr
Chewning Farm ❺
Tapp Field ❻
❼ ❽ Longstreet's Wounding
❽ Brock Road-Plank Rd Intersection

McLaws's Line ❹
McLaws Dr
Lee-Jackson Bivouac
❺

Zoan Church

3

Old Salem Church

Salem Church Rd

3

Lee's Hill
Howison Hill ❸
❹

**Fredericksburg Battlefield Visitor Center**

621

Parker's Store Site

Catharine Furnace Ruins ❻
Furnace Rd
Maury Birthplace Site

Old Plank Rd

610

UNFINISHED CIVIL WAR RR TRACE

Lafayette Blvd

Hazel Run

Harrison Rd

1

Slaughter Pen Farm Battlefield

17

608

Jackson Trail West (unpaved road)

Route of Jackson's ambulance

Jackson Trail East (unpaved road)

Wellford House Site

Catharpin Rd

612

UNFINISHED CIVIL WAR RR TRACE

Leavells Rd

Deep Run

Lee Dr

Union Breakthrough ❺

Prospect Hill ❻

Mine Rd

636

Massaponax Creek

17

Todd's Tavern Site

Brock Rd
Route of Jackson's ambulance

Piney Branch Rd

Gordon Rd

612

Shady Grove Church

**BATTLE OF SPOTSYLVANIA COURT HOUSE**
MAY 8–21, 1864

Courthouse Rd

608

608

Upton's Road
Bloody Angle
McCoull House Site
Spotsylvania Battlefield Exhibit Shelter ❶
❷ Dr ❸ ❺ ❻ East Face of Salient
Hancock Rd (unpaved)
Harrison House ❹
Gordon Dr
Burnside Dr
❼ Heth's Salient
❽ Fredericksburg Road

Smith Station Rd

Courthouse Rd

1

608

606

648

208

Spotsylvania Confederate Cemetery

SPOTSYLVANIA

95

Massaponax Church Rd

Ni River

Po River

Jefferson Davis Hwy

Guinea Station Rd
Route of Jackson's Ambulance

**STONEWALL JACKSON SHRINE**

Stonewall Jackson Shrine

606

Morris Rd

Mudd Tavern Rd

THORNBURG

GUINEA

Hopewell Church

Stonewall Jackson Rd

❶ Auto Tour Stop

North ↑

0 ___ 2 Mile
0 ___ 4 Km

Virginia, in the Shenandoah Valley, didn't arrive until November 29. These troops were deployed across Prospect Hill south of Fredericksburg, guarding a long stretch of the Rappahannock River where the Federals might attempt a crossing. With both wings of his army in place, Lee commanded nearly 85,000 men along a seven-mile front. Burnside's army totaled 120,000 men in three grand divisions. The Right Grand Division was commanded by Gen. Edwin "Bull" Sumner, the Center Grand Division by Gen. Joseph Hooker, and the Left Grand Division by Gen. William Franklin. No other Civil War battle featured a larger concentration of soldiers.

Burnside was convinced the Confederates had weakened the left and center of their line to concentrate against him on their right (downstream or south of Fredericksburg). He decided to cross the river directly at Fredericksburg, writing to Halleck on December 9, "I think now the enemy will be more surprised by a crossing immediately in our front than any other part of the river. . . . "

In the foggy predawn hours of December 11, 1862, Union engineers began assembling and deploying their pontoons in the river. Much to their consternation, they came under fire from the Mississippi brigade of Gen. William Barksdale hiding in the cellars of houses not far from the riverbank. Union artillery was ordered to dislodge them, and 150 guns mounted on Stafford Heights "vomited forth their terrible shot and shell into every corner and thoroughfare," according to an eyewitness. The bombardment continued for nearly two hours, but had little effect on the well-concealed Southern sharpshooters. Finally, Union landing parties, crowded into small pontoon boats, ferried themselves across the river. One hundred thirty-five infantrymen from the 7th Michigan, 19th Massachusetts, and 20th Massachusetts Regiments engaged the Confederate marksmen, pushing them back from the riverbank block by block in a rare example of street fighting during the Civil War. After dark, the bridge builders finally completed their work.

It took the Army of the Potomac the next two days to complete its river crossing into Fredericksburg. Burnside finally issued his attack orders early on the morning of December 13. They called for an assault against Jackson's corps by Franklin's Left Grand Division, to be followed by an assault against Longstreet's line on Marye's Heights by Sumner's Right Grand Division. But Burnside's instructions were vague and ambiguous, reflecting either a lack of confidence in his plan or a misunderstanding of his opponent's disposition—or perhaps both.

PREVIOUS SPREAD: Union cannon at Chatham on Stafford Heights.

BELOW: Battery D, Fifth US Artillery, on Stafford Heights.

When Franklin was told to attack the Confederates with "a division at least," he designated Gen. George Meade's division to spearhead the assault, supported by the division of Gen. John Gibbon. The two divisions totaled 8,000 men—just a fraction of the 60,000 men in Franklin's command. Meade's men began their advance at 8:30 a.m., with Gibbon following close behind. At around 10:30 a.m., the morning fog began to lift from the battlefield. Confederate shells from a 14-gun battalion hidden in the trees on Prospect Hill ripped gaping holes in Meade's ranks as they closed within 500 yards of the Confederates. Still, the assault found a 600-yard gap in Jackson's line, and Meade's Pennsylvanians fixed bayonets and charged into the Southern defenses. But the breakthrough was temporary. Confederate reserves counterattacked, slamming into the exhausted and outnumbered Federals and driving them back to the Richmond Stage Road. According to one Federal soldier, "The action was close-handed and men fell like leaves in autumn. . . . It seems miraculous that any of us escaped at all." Gibbon's attack also suffered heavy casualties and failed to support Meade's temporary breakthrough. Fighting in this part of the battlefield, now known as the Slaughter Pen Farm, came to a close.

According to Burnside's plan, the advance through Fredericksburg toward Marye's Heights would not commence until Franklin's assault began rolling up Jackson's corps. By late morning, the Union commander decided to wait no longer and ordered Sumner's Grand Right Division to move forward. The Confederate position here was formidable. To succeed, the Union forces had to advance out of the city, descend into a shallow valley bisected by a canal with just three narrow bridges, and ascend an open slope 400 yards wide to reach the base of the heights. Confederate artillery on top of the hills thoroughly blanketed the Federal approach. Artillery commander Edward Porter Alexander assured Longstreet that "we cover that ground now so well that we will comb it as with a fine-tooth comb. A chicken could not live on that field when we open on it." Across the base of Marye's Heights, along a 600-yard portion of the Telegraph Road where years of wagon traffic had worn the roadway down into a sunken ditch, a brigade of 3,000 Georgia infantrymen were ensconced behind a formidable four-foot stone wall. This deadly ground soon became known as the Sunken Road.

Sumner's first assault began around noon, followed by a ghastly series of futile attacks that continued, one after another, until dark. As each assault was repulsed with appalling losses, Burnside stubbornly ordered the attacks to continue. Around midafternoon, he ordered Hooker's Center Grand Division to join the attack. All told, seven Union divisions were hurled at Marye's Heights and the "terrible stone wall." Casualties on the Union side totaled 8,000 men, while the Confederates lost just 1,000 men. As darkness fell across the battlefield, not a single Union soldier had reached the Sunken Road. Longstreet later stated the obvious: "The charges had been desperate and bloody, but utterly hopeless."

Total losses for the day were 12,600 Union soldiers killed, wounded, or missing—almost two-thirds of which fell in front of the Sunken Road. Lee lost 5,300 men—about half of the Union total. On the evenings of December 15 and 16, Burnside withdrew the remnants of his shattered army back to Stafford Heights, dismantling the pontoon bridges behind him. Six weeks later, he was relieved of command.

# FREDERICKSBURG Battlefield Hikes

Several loop trails and point-to-point trails explore key parts of the Fredericksburg Battlefield. Many of these hikes include trailside interpretive markers describing the battle action that occurred at a particular spot. Visitors should start at the Fredericksburg Battlefield Visitor Center on Lafayette Boulevard near downtown Fredericksburg, where hiking information and trail maps are available.

### Sunken Road / National Cemetery Loop Trail (0.9 miles)

This hike starts at the Fredericksburg Battlefield Visitor Center. The trail follows along the Sunken Road, and then climbs up Marye's Heights to the National Cemetery. It was along this ground, on December 13, 1862, that Union troops poured out of Fredericksburg to attack Confederate forces ensconced behind a stone wall and along the heights. For eight hours Federal forces repeatedly charged the Confederates, only to be slaughtered by devastating musket volleys and artillery fire. Although the town of Fredericksburg has encroached upon the battlefield, visitors can still visualize the commanding ground the Southerners occupied in repulsing the Union assaults. Wayside exhibits along the trail provide details and photos of the battlefield carnage. Bullet holes are still visible in the walls of the historic Innis House.

### Lee's Hill Trail (0.25 miles one way)

This hike starts at the Lee's Hill parking area (Auto Tour Stop 3). The high ridge nearby, called Telegraph Hill before the battle but now known as Lee's Hill, served as Confederate Gen. Robert E. Lee's headquarters during the battle. Throughout the afternoon of December 13, 1862, Lee and his generals watched uneasily as Union forces repeatedly attacked Southern troops in the Sunken Road. It was on this hill that Lee uttered one of his most famous quotations, telling a colleague, "It is well that war is so terrible, or we would grow too fond of it." The hike to the top climbs about 110 feet.

### Bernard's Cabins Trail (0.9 miles)

This hike starts at the Bernard's Cabins parking area on South Lee Drive. Arthur Bernard owned the Mannsfield Plantation here in 1862. The path, also called the Mannsfield Slave Cabins Trail, leads to the site of Bernard's slave cabins. The dwellings, which are now gone, were home to as many as 35 slaves. During the battle, the Confederates posted artillery around the cabins. Union artillery bombarded the site, ravaging the Confederate batteries and leaving the homes of Bernard's slaves a shambles, never to be rebuilt.

### North Lee Drive Trail (2.7 miles one way)

This trail follows the line of Confederate trenches along North Lee Drive between the Howison Hill parking area (Auto Tour Stop 4) and the parking lot near the intersection of South Lee Drive and Lansdowne Road.

### South Lee Drive Trail (2.3 miles one way)

This trail traverses the woods and high ground behind Gen. Thomas "Stonewall" Jackson's line along Prospect Hill. The hike starts either at the parking lot near the intersection of South Lee Drive and Lansdowne Road or at the Prospect Hill parking area (Auto Tour Stop 6).

### Slaughter Pen Farm Trail (1.7 miles)

Over this ground two Union divisions under Gen. George Meade and Gen. John Gibbon launched their assault against Gen. Thomas "Stonewall" Jackson's forces holding the southern part of the Confederate line at Fredericksburg. Despite suffering enormous casualties, Meade's men were able to temporarily penetrate the Confederate line along Prospect Hill, and for a time represented the North's best chance of winning the Battle of Fredericksburg. The fighting on this portion of the battlefield, later named the Slaughter Pen, produced 5,000 casualties and five Medal of Honor recipients.

OPPOSITE: Innis House along the Sunken Road.

ABOVE: Dilapidated farmhouse on the Slaughter Pen Farm. This part of the Fredericksburg Battlefield has been preserved by the Civil War Trust.

# CHANCELLORSVILLE
## BATTLEFIELD

VIRGINIA  Fredericksburg and Spotsylvania National Military Park

AT CHANCELLORSVILLE, GEN. ROBERT E. LEE WON HIS GREATEST VICTORY, but lost his legendary general Thomas "Stonewall" Jackson. The campaign that resulted in Jackson's death emerged from the fallout of the Union defeat at Fredericksburg in December 1862. On January 26, 1863, President Abraham Lincoln replaced the author of that debacle, Gen. Ambrose Burnside, with Gen. Joseph Hooker. With the change, Lincoln admonished his new general: "Beware of rashness, but with energy, and sleepless vigilance, go forward, and give us victories."

Within weeks, Hooker restored the health and morale of his troops, whom he proudly proclaimed "the finest army on the planet." Lee's army, despite its recent victory and high morale, still lacked adequate clothing and supplies. Food was so scarce that Lee dispatched Gen. James Longstreet with two divisions in February 1863 to forage for supplies in southeastern Virginia. This left Lee with 60,000 men at Fredericksburg. The Army of the Potomac, totaling 130,000 men, was camped just across the Rappahannock River.

"Fighting Joe" Hooker, as the press had labeled him, crafted a brilliant plan that he expected would compel Lee to abandon his Fredericksburg entrenchments and force him back to Richmond. He would send most of his infantry 40 miles upstream to ford the Rappahannock and Rapidan Rivers beyond the Confederate defenses and sweep east against Lee's left flank. The rest of "Fighting Joe's" army would cross the Rappahannock at Fredericksburg and menace the Confederate front as the second blade of a great pincers. "My plans are perfect," boasted Hooker, "and when I start to carry them out may God have mercy on General Lee, for I will have none."

On April 27, 1863, Hooker commenced the campaign, sending three corps totaling 40,000 Union troops west toward Kelly's Ford. Eleventh Corps, commanded by Gen. Oliver Howard, led the way, followed

by Twelfth Corps under Gen. Henry Slocum, and finally Gen. George Meade's Fifth Corps. The Confederates faced a serious dilemma. Conventional military wisdom counseled Lee to withdraw his outnumbered army and retreat south to escape Hooker's trap. Lee instead chose to meet the Federal threat head-on. Digesting reports from Confederate skirmishers and Gen. J. E. B. Stuart's cavalry, Lee deduced that the primary threat was from the west, where Hooker's three corps were concentrating around the country crossroads at Chancellorsville.

By the afternoon of April 30, Hooker's force was bolstered by Gen. Darius Couch's Second Corps and Gen. Daniel Sickles's Third Corps, which crossed the Rappahannock River at the U.S. Ford. Union forces, now totaling 50,000 men and 108 artillery pieces, rendezvoused at the Chancellorsville crossroads. "This is splendid," exclaimed Meade. "We are on Lee's flank and he does not know it."

Then, to the astonishment of his corps commanders, Hooker sent orders to stop the advance, break off contact with the enemy, and fall back to positions around Chancellorsville. Meade exploded: "My God, if we can't hold the top of a hill, we certainly cannot hold the bottom of it!" Slocum was even more furious: "Nobody but a crazy man would give such an order when we have victory in sight!" Debate over Hooker's stunning reversal began at once. His own explanation, given weeks later to a friend, was simply, "for once I lost confidence in Hooker."

Lee and Jackson, on the other hand, were only too happy to seize the initiative. Lee dispatched the divisions of Gen. Richard Anderson and Gen. Lafayette McLaws west toward Chancellorsville, where they fortified a prominent ridge covering the Orange Turnpike and Plank Road. Around 3:00 a.m. on May 1, Jackson roused his Second Corps, leaving Gen. Jubal Early with a division to protect Fredericksburg while marching the rest of his troops west.

Lee and Jackson conferred near the intersection of the Orange Plank and Furnace Roads on the evening of May 1. Around midnight, Stuart, Lee's cavalry commander, joined the two generals. The Union right flank, he reported, was "in the air"—unprotected by any hill, river, swamp, or other natural feature. With this information, the two generals concentrated their entire attention on how to attack that flank. Jackson's

cartographer, Jedediah Hotchkiss, produced a hastily sketched map showing a circuitous route that would get the Confederates around the Union army. Jackson's corps—about 30,000 troops—would make the march while Lee, with the remaining 14,000 infantry, would occupy a position more than three miles long and divert Hooker's attention during Jackson's risky trek. Once in position, "Stonewall" would smash the unsuspecting Federals.

Counting Early's division back in Fredericksburg, this plan divided Lee's army into three pieces, any one of which might be routed if Hooker resumed the offensive. But Lee was counting on Hooker's caution, and Jackson's troops were put in motion around 7:00 a.m. on May 2. Jackson's column snaked its way along uncharted trails barely wide enough to accommodate four men abreast. Although spotted by Union scouts, Hooker interpreted the march as a retreat, confident

PREVIOUS SPREAD: Union artillery piece at Fairview.

OPPOSITE: Early morning mist along the Hazel Grove-Fairview Trail.

BELOW: An 1865 photograph of the Chancellor House ruins. This structure served as the headquarters of Union Gen. Joseph Hooker during the battle.

that his own bold maneuver had succeeded in forcing Lee to abandon Fredericksburg.

Jackson's daring 12-mile march ended about 3:00 p.m., when he began deploying his troops across the Orange Turnpike. Two hours later, the Confederate front extended nearly two miles across the flank of the unsuspecting Union Eleventh Corps. Although several reports warned of Jackson's approach, Howard's headquarters dismissed them as frightened exaggerations from alarmists or cowards. Finally, at 5:30 p.m., Jackson ordered his troops forward. Confederates erupted from the woods and sent the astonished Federals reeling.

Howard's troops fought bravely, hastily forming up battle lines across Jackson's path. Sgt. James Peabody of the 61st Ohio Regiment later wrote that while his brigade was playing "draw poker," the "bullets began whistling over our heads along the flank. . . . and by the time we had gotten into line and taken arms, they had crowded us so much from the right as to turn me 'right about.'" The Union forces were overwhelmed, and the retreat turned into a rout. By dusk the Confederates had rushed forward more than two miles. Still, Jackson had to halt the advance as many of his brigades had become intermingled and disorganized. He summoned Gen. A. P. Hill's division to the front, determined to renew his attack despite the darkness.

While Hill brought his brigades forward, Jackson rode ahead of his men to reconnoiter. When he attempted to return, a North Carolina regiment mistook his small party for Union cavalry. Two volleys burst forth in the darkness, striking Jackson three times and shattering his left arm. He was taken to the rear, where his arm was later amputated. Shortly afterward a Federal shell struck Hill, incapacitating him, and command of the corps fell to Stuart.

Despite his misfortune on May 2, Hooker still held the advantage at Chancellorsville. Sickles's Third Corps occupied the high ground at Hazel Grove, dividing the Confederates into separate wings two miles apart. Aggressive action could defeat each wing in detail and carry the day. Instead, Hooker ordered

PREVIOUS SPREAD: Union artillery position near the Chancellorsville crossroads.

RIGHT: Site of Gen. Thomas "Stonewall" Jackson's flank attack on the Chancellorsville Battlefield.

Sickles to abandon Hazel Grove and fall back to Fairview, an elevated clearing closer to his lines around Chancellorsville. Once again, he had surrendered the initiative to the Confederates.

On the morning of May 3, Stuart immediately placed 30 cannon on Hazel Grove. Confederate gunners pounded Fairview with a spectacular bombardment. Stuart then launched brigade after brigade against entrenched Union lines on both sides of the Orange Turnpike between 6:30 and 9:30 a.m., resulting in the bloodiest fighting of the battle. Confederate pressure was relentless, and Union troops were slowly pushed back to the Chancellor House, site of Hooker's headquarters.

In the midst of the violence Hooker himself was put out of action when a Confederate artillery round shattered a column he was leaning against on the Chancellor House porch. Before relinquishing command, Hooker instructed the army to assume a prepared position in the rear, protecting the bridgehead across the Rappahannock River. Stuart pressed forward, first to Fairview and then against Hooker's remaining units at the Chancellorsville crossroads. Lee's wing advanced simultaneously from the south and east. The Bluecoats receded as thousands of Confederates poured into the clearing around the Chancellor House, now engulfed in flames.

Intent on maintaining the initiative, Lee prepared to pursue Hooker and seal his stunning victory. But a courier bearing news from Fredericksburg forced a change of plans. Gen. John Sedgwick's Sixth Corps had driven Early's division from Marye's Heights and now menaced the Confederate rear. Lee assigned Stuart to watch Hooker's army and sent McLaws eastward to deal with the threat. Sedgwick engaged the Confederates four miles west of Fredericksburg at Salem Church, but a powerful counterattack stopped his advance. The next day, May 4, Lee shoved Sedgwick back across the Rappahannock River at Banks Ford and once again focused on the main Union army now dug in north of Chancellorsville.

Hooker, however, had seen enough. Despite his formidable defensive position and some 75,000 troops

Site of Gen. Thomas "Stonewall" Jackson's flank attack shrouded in morning mist.

still at his disposal, he ordered a withdrawal across the river on the evening of May 5. By 9:00 a.m. on May 6, virtually all of Hooker's men were on the north side of the Rappahannock River. National Park Service historian A. Wilson Greene wrote that "this decision may have been Hooker's most serious blunder of the campaign." Greene contended that Lee's impending assault on May 6 might have failed and completely reversed the outcome of the battle. By the end of the fighting, Hooker had suffered more than 17,000 casualties. Lee's own casualties totaled 13,000, a significant number considering the relative size of the two armies.

Lee's victory stunned the North. Faced with another battlefield disaster, Lincoln exclaimed, "My god! What will the country say?" The Confederate victory, however, was tempered by the loss of Gen. Thomas "Stonewall" Jackson. On May 5, Jackson was taken to a small house near Guinea Station south of Fredericksburg. Lee sent him a message: "Tell him to make haste and get well. . . . He has lost his left arm, but I have lost my right." Five days later, on May 10, Jackson died of pneumonia as a result of his wounds.

BELOW: Site of Gen. Thomas "Stonewall" Jackson's flank attack on the Chancellorsville Battlefield.

OPPOSITE: Union artillery position at Fairview.

# CHANCELLORSVILLE Battlefield Hikes

Several trails crisscross the Chancellorsville Battlefield. Hikes are easy to moderate. Many of these hikes include trailside interpretive markers describing the battle action that occurred at a particular spot. Visitors should start at the Chancellorsville Battlefield Visitor Center on Virginia Route 3, where trail maps and guides are available.

### Chancellorsville History Trail (4.0 miles)

This hike is comprised of two loops. The first loop (0.5 miles) skirts a line of Civil War earthworks along the western edge of the battlefield. The second loop (3.5 miles) traverses portions of the battlefield where fighting occurred on May 3, 1863. Highlights include the Chancellorsville crossroads, Chancellor House site, Bullock House site, lines of both Union and Confederate trenches, and the apex of Gen. Joseph Hooker's last line. The Chancellor House served as Hooker's headquarters until victorious Confederates swarmed over the ground on May 3, pushing the Union line north to the intersection of the Bullock and Ely's Ford Roads. Blue blazes on trees and mowed paths in clearings mark the route. This hike begins at the large battle painting outside the Chancellorsville Battlefield Visitor Center.

### Jackson Wounding Walking Tour Trail (0.2 miles)

This short trail also begins at the large battle painting outside the Chancellorsville Battlefield Visitor Center. Hikers can follow the trail in a loop around the back side of the center to see the site of Gen. Thomas "Stonewall" Jackson's reconnaissance and wounding, and to visit monuments to Jackson and to an unknown Union soldier.

### Hazel Grove-Fairview Trail (1.4 miles)

This trail begins across the road from the Hazel Grove parking area (Auto Tour Stop 9) on the Chancellorsville Battlefield driving tour. On the morning of May 3, 1863, the Confederates concentrated 30 cannon on Hazel Grove, opening a spectacular bombardment on Union artillery positions at Fairview. This hike follows the Confederate advance from Hazel Grove to the Union battle line at Fairview. Combat here, described by one historian as "the most intense and concentrated few hours of fighting in the entire war," resulted in more than 17,500 casualties on both sides. The trail descends and climbs about 75 feet in each direction.

### McLaws's Line Trail (1.1 miles)

This trail begins at the McLaws's Line parking area (Auto Tour Stop 4). The site, acquired in 1997 by the Central Virginia Battlefields Trust for the National Park Service, saw action on each of the three major days of fighting during the battle. Visitors will learn about the Union forces who briefly held the ridge here on May 1, 1863; the Confederate forces whose tactics diverted Union attention from Gen. Thomas "Stonewall" Jackson's daring flank march on May 2; and the Confederate assault toward the Chancellorsville crossroads on May 3.

### First Day at Chancellorsville Battlefield Trail (3.0 miles)

A series of interconnected trails crisscross the First Day at Chancellorsville Battlefield. The complete trail, forming a loop, is about three

miles long, but hikers may opt to take one of the shorter loops. The battlefield, which is owned by the Civil War Trust, is three miles east of the Chancellorsville Visitor Center on Virginia Route 3. It was here, on May 1, 1863, that the Battle of Chancellorsville took a dramatic turn. When Gen. Joseph Hooker's Union column, 70,000 strong, began advancing eastward against Gen. Robert E. Lee's flank, his lead elements encountered Confederate troops here. Fighting raged for three hours, causing 500 casualties on both sides. Rather than hold his ground, however, Hooker ordered his troops to abandon their advance and fall back to the Chancellorsville crossroads. He had surrendered the initiative to Lee on the first day of the battle. Union Gen. Henry Slocum later wrote, "Our movements up to the arrival at Chancellorsville were very successful & were well planned. Everything after that went wrong, and Fighting Joe sunk into a poor driveling cur."

OPPOSITE: First Day at Chancellorsville Battlefield along Virginia Route 3 east of Chancellorsville.

ABOVE: Site of McLaws's Line on the Chancellorsville Battlefield.

# WILDERNESS
## BATTLEFIELD

VIRGINIA  Fredericksburg and Spotsylvania National Military Park

ON MARCH 3, 1864, PRESIDENT ABRAHAM LINCOLN PROMOTED ULYSSES S. Grant to lieutenant general, giving him command of all Union armies. Grant's resume of victories in the Western Theater was impressive: Fort Donelson (February 16, 1862), Shiloh (April 6–7, 1862), Vicksburg (July 4, 1863), and most recently the Battles of Lookout Mountain and Missionary Ridge at Chattanooga (November 23–25, 1863). Grant traveled east to Washington, DC, meeting with Lincoln to devise a strategy of total war against the Confederacy. He soon established his headquarters with Gen. George Meade's Army of the Potomac in Culpeper, Virginia. Although Meade retained command of the army—inherited from Gen. Joseph Hooker after the Battle of Chancellorsville—Grant was now calling the shots. His instructions to Meade were clear: "Wherever Lee goes, there you will go also."

The 1864 Overland Campaign commenced on May 4, when Union forces advanced south across the Rapidan River to find and engage Gen. Robert E. Lee's Army of Northern Virginia. Fifth Corps led the way, marching into a dense, forbidding woodland known as the Wilderness. Meade intended to push through the Wilderness, wheel his army to the right, and attack Lee's forces, which were camped around Orange, Virginia. Both armies entered the spring campaign brimming with confidence. The Northerners were refitted, well supplied, and led by a new commander who had won now-legendary victories in the west. The Confederates were equally optimistic, once again defending Virginia soil under their own legendary general, and anxious to avenge their defeat at Gettysburg. But Lee's 62,000-man army was vastly outnumbered and outgunned: the three Union corps led by Gen. Gouverneur Warren, Gen. John Sedgwick, and Gen. Winfield Hancock, and the independent Ninth Corps under Gen. Ambrose Burnside, totaled 120,000 men.

The Confederates easily spotted the Federal advance from their signal stations, and Lee immediately ordered his army to march east and strike its opponent in the Wilderness. Here Grant's superior numbers would be neutralized by the inhospitable terrain. Gen. Richard Ewell's corps advanced along the Orange Turnpike, while Gen. A. P. Hill led his men along the parallel Orange Plank Road a short distance to the south. Gen. James Longstreet's corps had to make a much longer march from around Gordonsville and wouldn't reach the battlefield for several more hours.

On the morning of May 5, 1864, Warren received word that Confederates were approaching his column on the Orange Turnpike from the west. He dispatched a Union division to investigate the report. Around noon, the 140th New York Infantry pushed across Saunders Field, a patch of rare open farmland in the Wilderness, where they found Ewell's Confederates already dug in west of the field. A sheet of musket fire from the Southerners exacted a heavy toll in casualties. An officer in the 140th New York recalled that the Confederates "gave us a volley at long range, but evidently with deliberate aim, and with serious effect." The Battle of the Wilderness had begun. As Warren hustled additional troops toward Saunders Field, the fighting expanded across a mile-wide front. The battle ebbed and flowed, often dissolving into isolated combat between small units confused by the bewildering forest. One participant called it "bushwhacking on a grand scale." By nightfall both sides dug in, with neither side having gained an advantage.

Shortly after Warren's men had spotted Confederates on the Orange Turnpike, Union Gen. Samuel Crawford, at the Chewning Farm, observed another enemy column headed up the Orange Plank Road toward its intersection with the Brock Road. These were Hill's troops, and they posed a serious threat. If the Confederates gained possession of this vital intersection, they might drive a wedge between Warren's Fifth Corps and Hancock's Second Corps, threatening the entire Union line. Meade ordered a division of Sixth Corps to seize the crossroads. Around 4:00 p.m., Gen. George Getty's division attacked, and, with help from Hancock's men, halted the Confederate advance. Fierce close-range fighting continued until nightfall, when darkness and exhaustion ended the day's combat.

Lee expected Longstreet's corps to relieve Hill on the Orange Plank Road that night. Hill, also anticipating Longstreet's arrival, made no preparations for renewed Union attacks in the morning. This mistake proved nearly disastrous to Lee's army. At 5:00 a.m. on the morning of May 6, Hancock ordered 23,000 men from Second Corps forward. His Union troops overwhelmed Hill's unprepared divisions. Lee faced a crisis. But just as the Confederate line began to collapse, the Texas Brigade from Longstreet's corps arrived on the battlefield. These troops, along with others from Arkansas, Georgia, and Alabama, charged the Union line and halted Hancock's advance. Longstreet, using an unfinished railroad cut for cover, then launched a counterattack on the Union left flank, rolling up Hancock's surprised troops "like a wet blanket." The Federals streamed back toward the Brock Road.

In the wake of his splendid achievement, Longstreet trotted eastward on the Orange Plank Road to prepare a final assault against the fleeing Northerners. But just

PREVIOUS SPREAD: The Milky Way brightens the night sky above an artillery piece on the Wilderness Battlefield.

OPPOSITE: Old railroad cut, site of Confederate Gen. James Longstreet's flank attack on the Wilderness Battlefield.

ABOVE: An 1866 photograph shows skeletons of unburied soldiers in the woods on the north side of the Orange Plank Road.

as the Confederates seemed on the brink of victory, Longstreet was hit by an errant volley from his own troops. His wound took him out of the battle, and it was now up to Lee to organize the final assault against the Union line. The delay and confusion caused by the sudden change in command gave Hancock enough time to construct earthworks just beyond the Brock Road. When Lee finally attacked, his troops were repulsed with heavy losses. The Union line had held. At the other end of the battlefield, just beyond Saunders Field, an attack was launched on the unprotected Union right flank by Gen. John Gordon near sunset. Gordon's Georgians captured two Union generals and routed the Federals in the woods. Gen. Alexander Shaler, one of the captured generals, recalled that "the enemy moved against us in front, on the flank, and in the rear, completely enveloping us in fire." But the attack had come too late in the day, and Grant was able to reform his battered brigades in the darkness.

On May 7, both sides dug in and awaited attack. But Grant demurred, realizing he could make no further headway in the Wilderness. The battle had ended in a stalemate. The Federals pulled out of their trenches after dark and marched east toward another crossroads at Spotsylvania Court House. Grant had suffered some 18,000 casualties—nearly twice as many as Lee—but his troops were not dispirited. When they realized that the army was not retreating but advancing, they cheered their new leader. They finally had a general who was determined to march on Richmond.

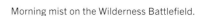

Morning mist on the Wilderness Battlefield.

# WILDERNESS Battlefield Hikes

Several trails explore pivotal engagements of the Wilderness Battlefield. Hikes are easy to moderate. Many of these hikes include trailside interpretive markers describing the battle action that occurred at a particular spot. Visitors should start at the Wilderness Battlefield Exhibit Shelter on Constitution Highway (Virginia Route 20), where exhibits provide an overview and orientation to the site.

### Gordon Flank Attack Trail (1.9 miles)

This hike starts at the Wilderness Battlefield Exhibit Shelter. The trail follows the path of the May 5, 1864, Union attacks across Saunders Field that initiated the battle, passes through the tangled woods and along the trenches where Union and Confederate troops became locked in a stalemate, and crosses the path of Gen. John Gordon's devastating flank attack on the evening of May 6, which almost broke the Union line. Only the timely arrival of Federal reinforcements and darkness halted the Confederate advance. According to Gordon, if his assault had occurred earlier in the day, "it would have resulted in a decided disaster to the whole right wing of General Grant's army, if not in its entire organization."

### Wilderness Crossing Trail (1.4 miles)

This hike begins at Ellwood, a historic home built around 1790. The house sits off Constitution Highway (Virginia Route 20) just south of Grant's Headquarters (Auto Tour Stop 1). In 1825, Revolutionary War hero Marquis de Lafayette dined here during his triumphant tour of America. Gen. Robert E. Lee camped here in June 1863 on his way to Gettysburg. Union Gen. Gouverneur Warren and Gen. Ambrose Burnside made Ellwood their battlefield headquarters during the fighting in the Wilderness. Gen. Thomas "Stonewall" Jackson's amputated left arm is buried in the family cemetery. The trail follows old roads through the Wilderness, including the historic Orange Turnpike and Germanna Plank Road, before reaching the former site of the Wilderness Tavern. On May 5, 1864, Union troops marched south and east on these roads before encountering the Confederates.

### Chewning Farm Trail (0.5 miles)

This hike starts at the Chewning Farm parking area (Auto Tour Stop 5) on the Wilderness Battlefield driving tour. The old farm road leads to the ridge where the Chewning House once stood. Wayside exhibits discuss the farm's tactical importance and its occupation by both Union and Confederate armies during the battle.

### Tapp Field Trail (0.7 miles)

This hike starts at the Tapp Field parking area (Auto Tour Stop 6). The trail traverses Tapp Field, where wayside exhibits describe the critical fighting that occurred here on May 6, 1864. The Army of Northern Virginia and its commander, Gen. Robert E. Lee, faced disaster when a powerful Union attack swept Gen. A. P. Hill's Confederate divisions from the woods along the Orange Plank Road. Only the timely arrival of Gen. James Longstreet's reinforcements saved the Confederates from defeat. At a desperate moment during the battle, Lee attempted to

lead a charge of the Texas Brigade across the field, prompting a cry from the entire battle line, "Go back, General Lee! Go back! We won't go on unless you go back!" With reluctance, Lee yielded and rode to the back of the line. A Confederate staff officer later wrote, "I have often seen Gen. Lee, but never did I see him so excited, so disturbed—never did anxiety or care manifest itself before so plainly upon his countenance."

### Vermont Monument Trail (0.5 miles)

This hike begins at the Brock Road-Plank Road Intersection parking area (Auto Tour Stop 8). The trail leads through a part of the battlefield that one soldier called "a wilderness of woe." The intersection of the Orange Plank and Brock Roads was critical to both armies

during the battle as each struggled to maneuver through the tangled forests. As vicious charges and countercharges swept through the woods here, fallen soldiers littered the ground while fires scorched the forest, consuming dead and wounded alike. The Federals were able to hold the crossroads, repulsing several determined Confederate assaults on May 5 and 6, 1864. The Vermont Brigade monument honors 1,234 casualties of Vermont's "Old Brigade," which defended the crossroads.

### Federal Line Trail (3.5 miles one way)

This hike starts at the picnic area on Hill-Ewell Drive. The trail follows the Union line that extended north-south between the old Orange Turnpike (Virginia Route 20) and the Orange Plank Road (Virginia Route 621) on May 5, 6, and 7, 1864.

OPPOSITE: Tapp Field on the Wilderness Battlefield.

ABOVE, LEFT: Ellwood Manor. The Battle of the Wilderness swirled around this manor house for three days in May 1864.

ABOVE, RIGHT: The arm of Gen. Thomas "Stonewall" Jackson, amputated at a field hospital at Wilderness Tavern during the Battle of Chancellorsville, was buried in the small family cemetery at Ellwood Manor.

# SPOTSYLVANIA COURT HOUSE
## BATTLEFIELD

VIRGINIA  Fredericksburg and Spotsylvania National Military Park

ON THE MORNING OF MAY 8, 1864, GEN. GOUVERNEUR WARREN'S UNION troops approached an open plateau on the road to Spotsylvania Court House, just a few miles southeast of the Wilderness. Warren's scouts saw the Confederate cavalrymen of Gen. Fitzhugh Lee defending the ridge near a place called the Spindle Farm. When a war correspondent later confused a nearby house called Laurel Hill with the farmland on this ridge, the name stuck. Laurel Hill became the first battleground at Spotsylvania.

The armies of Gen. Ulysses S. Grant and Gen. Robert E. Lee were both racing for the vital crossroads at Spotsylvania Court House, through which the road to Richmond ran. By wedging the Army of the Potomac between Lee's army and Richmond, Grant hoped to lure the Confederates into battle on ground more favorable than he had found in the Wilderness. If Lee's cavalry could hold Laurel Hill, they could block Grant's army from reaching the crossroads.

Warren, confident his infantry would have no trouble dislodging the Southern horsemen from Laurel Hill, called for an attack. The Maryland Brigade led the Yankee charge, but when they were within just 50 yards of the Confederate line, they instead found the infantry brigades of Gen. Richard Anderson's First Corps. The Federals were repulsed with sheets of artillery and musket fire. Lee's army had won the race to Spotsylvania.

Both armies flowed onto the battlefield during the rest of the day. At Spotsylvania, Lee's soldiers built their strongest entrenchments yet to appear on any battlefield of the war. Gen. Richard Ewell's Second Corps filed in on Anderson's right and built its entrenchments in the dark to conform to the elevated terrain along its front. When dawn finally arrived, Lee found that Ewell's men had created a huge salient, or bulge, in the Confederate line, pointing north in the direction of the Federals. Because of its shape, this bulge became known

as the "Muleshoe Salient." Unfortunately, salients were notoriously vulnerable to concentrated assault from both the front and sides, and the Muleshoe would prove to be a weak link in the Confederate line.

Grant probed both of Lee's flanks on May 9 and 10 without success. At Laurel Hill on May 9, Gen. John Sedgwick, commander of the Sixth Corps, was shot by a Confederate sharpshooter at a range of more than 500 yards. Sedgwick was the highest-ranking Union officer killed in the Civil War and the second-highest-ranking US officer ever killed in combat. Around 6:00 p.m. on May 10, a 24-year-old Union colonel named Emory Upton prepared an unusual assault against the Muleshoe. Six months prior to Spotsylvania, Upton had come to Grant's attention for a novel new infantry formation he had devised to capture a Confederate bridgehead at Rappahannock Station. Abandoning the standard attack—a line of men charging in a wave—he condensed his troops into a tightly packed column of men surging forward quickly with one aim: to breach the enemy's entrenchments.

Upton's tight formation burst out of the woods at 6:10 p.m. with a yell. In 60 seconds his 12 Union regiments had reached the Confederate works, driving off a startled brigade of Georgians, seizing four guns, and capturing a reserve line of works 75 yards inside the Muleshoe. But the Confederates soon recovered. Soldiers of Ewell's Second Corps counterattacked, while Southern artillery repulsed supporting units necessary to exploit the breach. Without reinforcements, Upton's men were soon outnumbered and exhausted, and the order was given to retreat. Union losses were significant—about 1,000 casualties—but they had also captured between 1,000 and 1,200 Confederate prisoners. Grant later wrote, "Upton had gained an important advantage, but a lack in others of the spirit and dash possessed by him lost it to us."

Grant was so impressed with the novel tactic that he decided to try it again two days later. This time, rather than assigning just 12 regiments, he would use two corps—four times the number of men—and arrange much better coordination. Grant ordered Gen. Winfield Hancock's Second Corps to lead the attack, this time from the north near the tip of the Muleshoe, where it was likely to be most vulnerable. Hancock's men would be supported by the Sixth Corps of Gen. Horatio Wright.

At 4:35 a.m. on the morning of May 12, 1864, 20,000 soldiers of Second Corps stormed out of the woods. They quickly smashed through the enemy entrenchments, capturing 3,000 prisoners and 20 cannon. The breach nearly cut the Army of Northern Virginia in two. But in the confined space of the Muleshoe, Hancock's units became entangled and utterly disorganized. Gen. John Gordon's reserve division frantically began counterattacking the Northerners, slowly pushing them back. At 6:00 a.m., the 15,000 men of Wright's Sixth Corps launched their supporting assault along the northwestern side of the captured Confederate trenches, where there was a slight angle in the earthworks. In a driving downpour, close-quarter fighting raged for nearly 22 hours in an area that became known as the "Bloody Angle." Union and Confederate soldiers, standing only a few feet apart, fired at each other across the works or battled one another in hand-to-hand combat. It was fighting both sides later remembered as one of the grimmest engagements of the entire war. "The

PREVIOUS SPREAD: Sunrise over the Spotsylvania Court House Battlefield.

OPPOSITE: Morning mist on the Spotsylvania Court House Battlefield.

BELOW: An 1866 photograph of Spotsylvania Court House. Three African American men are retrieving water from a pump in the foreground.

horseshoe was a boiling, bubbling and hissing cauldron of death," wrote one Union officer. "Clubbed muskets, and bayonets were the modes of fighting for those who had used up their cartridges, and frenzy seemed to possess the yelling, demonic hordes on either side."

The ghastly fighting continued past sunset and into the night. Finally around 2:00 a.m. on May 13, Lee's men fell back. The all-day fighting at the Bloody Angle had given the Confederates enough time to build new entrenchments at the base of the Muleshoe. Left behind were dead and wounded soldiers, "lying literally in heaps, hideous to look at. The writhing of the wounded and dying who lay beneath the dead bodies moved the whole mass . . ."

Over the next several days, Grant continued to probe the Southern entrenchments, searching for a weak link in the line. But additional assaults proved fruitless. On May 20 and 21, Grant again disengaged his forces and continued maneuvering south around Lee's army toward Richmond. Total Union casualties for the two weeks of fighting at Spotsylvania were 18,000 men. Lee lost about 10,000 men, but the high casualties suffered among his officers were taking a toll. On May 11, Lee lost his reliable cavalry commander, Gen. J. E. B. Stuart, during a Union cavalry raid six miles north of Richmond. Gen. James Longstreet was still out of action, recovering from his wounds suffered at the Wilderness. Even worse, Lee himself was now showing signs of strain and exhaustion brought on by the frequent fighting, dreadful casualties, and anxieties about supplies and manpower. All the while, Grant's columns were getting closer to Richmond.

BELOW: Confederate artillery position on the Muleshoe Salient.

OPPOSITE: View looking toward the Bloody Angle.

# SPOTSYLVANIA COURT HOUSE Battlefield Hikes

The Spotsylvania Battlefield History Trail circles the entire battlefield with side trails offering options for shorter hikes. Hikes are easy to moderate, with several trailside interpretive markers that describe the battle action at a particular spot. Visitors should start at the Spotsylvania Court House Exhibit Shelter off Brock Road (Virginia Route 613), where exhibits provide an overview and orientation to the site.

## Spotsylvania Battlefield History Trail
### (5.5 miles)

This hike begins at the Spotsylvania Battlefield Exhibit Shelter. The trail is marked by blazes painted on trees and by mowed paths. Footbridges are provided at points where the trail crosses Civil War trenches. Visitors can help preserve these historic battlefield features by using the walkways. The trail connects several major sites associated with the May 1864 fighting, including Upton's Road, the Bloody Angle, the east face of the Muleshoe Salient, the McCoull House site, the Harrison House site, and Laurel Hill.

## Laurel Hill Loop (1.2 miles)

To reach Laurel Hill, visitors should park at the Spotsylvania Battlefield Exhibit Shelter and follow the Spotsylvania Battlefield History Trail south across Brock Road and Hancock Road. The ground here, known as the Spindle Farm before the battle, was the last defensible position west of the strategic crossroads at Spotsylvania Court House. If the Confederates lost this ground, they would also lose Spotsylvania. The Battle of Spotsylvania Court House began here on May 8, 1864, when Union Gen. Gouverneur Warren and Gen. John Sedgwick unsuccessfully attempted to dislodge the Confederates from what became known as Laurel Hill. Gen. Richard Anderson's Confederate infantry had arrived here just in time to block the Union advance. Much of the Confederate trench works and artillery positions still survive.

## Bloody Angle Trail (1.1 miles)

This hike begins at the Bloody Angle parking area (Auto Tour Stop 3) on the Spotsylvania Battlefield driving tour. The Bloody Angle was a small bend in the Confederate earthworks within the much larger Muleshoe Salient, a huge—and vulnerable—bulge in the center of Gen. Robert E. Lee's six-mile-long defensive line. Fighting raged here for 22 hours on May 12 and 13, 1864. Soldiers from both sides engaged in grim, hand-to-hand combat at close quarters. Union troops, taking cover in the ravine in front of the earthworks, repeatedly rushed forward to attack the angle, leaving bodies piled up three, four, even five deep, forming what one veteran described as "a perfect rampart of dead." By the end of the fighting as many as 17,000 soldiers were killed, wounded, or captured in this part of the battlefield. The trail passes along the remains of the Muleshoe Salient, crosses the field where Union forces took cover, and continues to the Landram House site.

LEFT: Hiking trail along the Muleshoe Salient.

OPPOSITE: This monument marks the location of Col. Emory Upton's May 10, 1864, Union assault on the Muleshoe Salient.

# GAINES' MILL
## BATTLEFIELD

VIRGINIA  Richmond National Battlefield Park

ALMOST FROM THE FIRST SHOT OF THE CIVIL WAR, RICHMOND WAS A focal point in the conflict. The battle cry of the Northern press, "On to Richmond," resonated both for political and strategic reasons. When the Confederate government established the city as its capital in May 1861, it ensured that central Virginia would be one of the war's most important battlegrounds. Richmond also boasted a robust commercial, manufacturing, and transportation infrastructure. Tredegar Iron Works, perched on the banks of the James River, formed a prominent part of the city's industrial capability. The Richmond Armory was one of just a handful of Southern arms manufacturers. Five railroads radiated from the city like spokes on a wheel, connecting Richmond with every part of the state. The capture of the new Confederate capital would severely hurt the Rebellion, and might bring the war to a prompt close.

The Battle of First Manassas (or First Battle of Bull Run), fought on July 21, 1861, was the first attempt by Union forces to bust open the road to Richmond. When the Northerners were repulsed, President Abraham Lincoln searched for a new commander. On July 26—just five days after the Union defeat at Bull Run—Gen. George McClellan arrived in Washington from western Virginia, where he had defeated a small Confederate force at the Battle of Philippi. On August 20, McClellan took command of the newly formed Army of the Potomac. Over the next several months, the new general reorganized the army, building a powerful force of 168,000 men. He also bickered with his superiors over tactics and strategy, ultimately deciding to advance against Richmond from the southeast, using the peninsula between the James and York Rivers to facilitate his advance. The plan was a sound one, as it avoided several rivers that obstructed a direct march from Washington and Richmond: the Rappahannock, Rapidan, North Anna, Pamunkey, and Chickahominy.

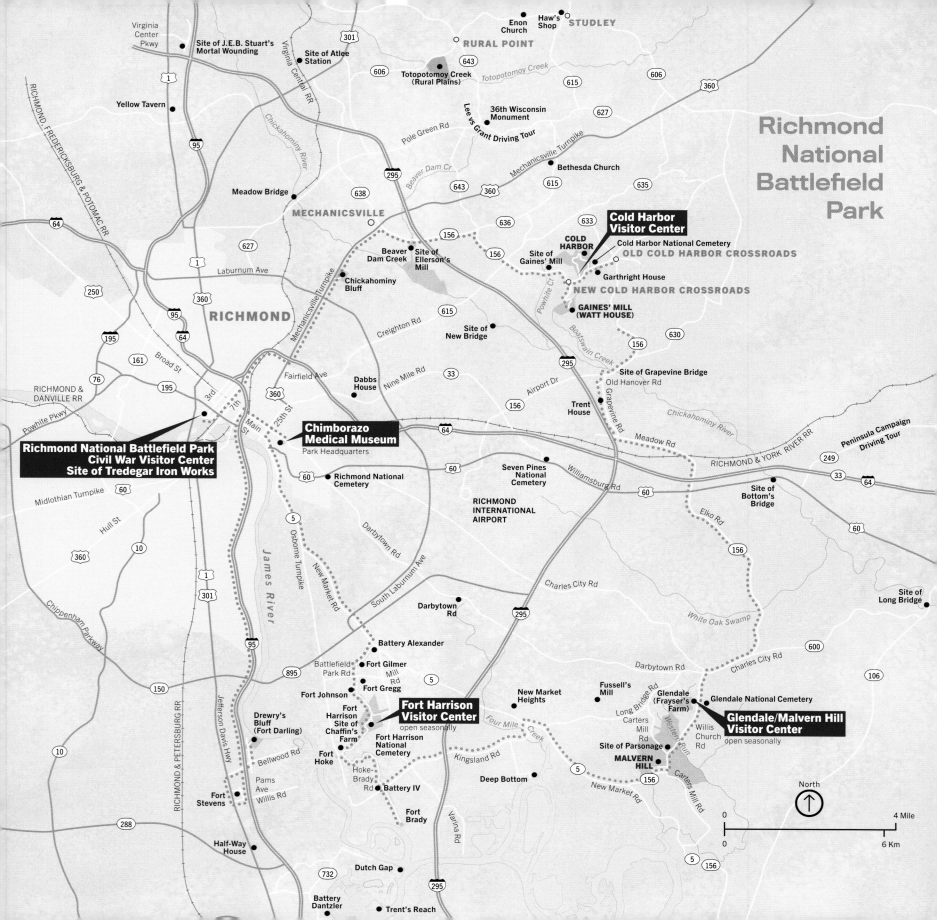

# Richmond National Battlefield Park

Virginia Center Pkwy

Site of J.E.B. Stuart's Mortal Wounding

Site of Atlee Station

Yellow Tavern

Enon Church

Haw's Shop

STUDLEY

RURAL POINT

Totopotomoy Creek (Rural Plains)

Totopotomoy Creek

36th Wisconsin Monument

Lee's and Grant Driving Tour

Pole Green Rd

Bethesda Church

Mechanicsville Turnpike

Meadow Bridge

MECHANICSVILLE

Beaver Dam Cr

Chickahominy River

Virginia Central RR

RICHMOND, FREDERICKSBURG & POTOMAC RR

Cold Harbor Visitor Center

COLD HARBOR

Cold Harbor National Cemetery

OLD COLD HARBOR CROSSROADS

Site of Gaines' Mill

Garthright House

NEW COLD HARBOR CROSSROADS

Beaver Dam Creek

Site of Ellerson's Mill

Chickahominy Bluff

Laburnum Ave

RICHMOND

GAINES' MILL (WATT HOUSE)

Boatswain Creek

Powhite Cr

Creighton Rd

Site of New Bridge

Site of Grapevine Bridge

Old Hanover Rd

RICHMOND & DANVILLE RR

Broad St

Powhite Pkwy

Fairfield Ave

Dabbs House

Nine Mile Rd

Trent House

Chickahominy River

Airport Dr

Meadow Rd

Grapevine Rd

RICHMOND & YORK RIVER RR

Peninsula Campaign Driving Tour

Richmond National Battlefield Park Civil War Visitor Center Site of Tredegar Iron Works

Chimborazo Medical Museum

Park Headquarters

Main St

Richmond National Cemetery

Seven Pines National Cemetery

Williamsburg Rd

Site of Bottom's Bridge

Midlothian Turnpike

Hull St

RICHMOND INTERNATIONAL AIRPORT

Elko Rd

James River

Osborne Turnpike

New Market Rd

Darbytown Rd

South Laburnum Ave

Chippenham Parkway

Charles City Rd

White Oak Swamp

Site of Long Bridge

Darbytown Rd

RICHMOND & PETERSBURG RR

Jefferson Davis Hwy

Battery Alexander

Battlefield Park Rd

Fort Gilmer

Mill Rd

Fort Gregg

Fort Johnson

New Market Heights

Fussell's Mill

Long Bridge Rd

Glendale (Frayser's Farm)

Glendale National Cemetery

Carters Mill Rd

Glendale/Malvern Hill Visitor Center open seasonally

Fort Harrison Visitor Center open seasonally

Fort Harrison Site of Chaffin's Farm

Fort Harrison National Cemetery

Drewry's Bluff (Fort Darling)

Fort Hoke

Bellwood Rd

Pams Ave

Willis Rd

Fort Stevens

Hoke Brady Rd

Battery IV

Kingsland Rd

Deep Bottom

Four Mile Creek

Western Run

Willis Church Rd

Site of Parsonage

MALVERN HILL

New Market Rd

Carters Mill Rd

North

Fort Brady

Varina Rd

Half-Way House

Dutch Gap

Battery Dantzler

Trent's Reach

0    4 Mile

0    6 Km

The Peninsula Campaign began in March 1862 when 121,500 men, 44 artillery batteries, 1,150 wagons, more than 15,000 horses, and tons of equipment and supplies began disembarking on the tip of Virginia's southeastern peninsula. For the next two months, McClellan slowly pushed his massive army up the peninsula toward the Confederate capital. By the end of May, Union forces had pressed the Southern army back to the outskirts of Richmond. On May 31, at the Battle of Seven Pines, Confederate Gen. Joseph Johnston launched a spoiling attack on McClellan's advance guard. Although the Southern assaults were uncoordinated and failed to break the Union line, they succeeded in halting the advance. McClellan became convinced that he was outnumbered by almost two to one—in fact his own forces outnumbered the Confederates by several thousand. The other significant outcome of the battle was the loss of Johnston, who was seriously wounded during the action. His replacement, Gen. Robert E. Lee, assumed the initiative that McClellan had conceded. Three weeks later, Lee attacked McClellan in a series of encounters known as the Seven Days' Battles. Fierce fighting forced the Federal army away from Richmond and changed the course of the war in Virginia.

On June 27, 1862, the Confederates found Gen. Fitz John Porter's Fifth Corps deployed near Gaines' Mill in a formidable position behind a marshy creek called Boatswain's Swamp. About 27,000 Union infantry were arrayed in an arc roughly a mile and a half long and supported by Federal artillery. Here the open farmland of the Watt, Adams, and McGehee families provided excellent fields of fire for about 100 cannon. Around noon, Lee's forces converged on Porter's position. The divisions of Gen. A. P. Hill and Gen. D. H. Hill launched a series of disjointed assaults and were repulsed with some of the highest casualties the war had yet seen. Additional troops under Gen. Richard Ewell and Gen. James Longstreet joined the battle, but were also unable to breach the Union line. According to Pvt. John Worsham of the 21st Virginia Infantry, "This was the strongest point I saw occupied by either army during the war."

As the afternoon drew on, however, the Confederate assaults grew in intensity. Around 7:00 p.m., Lee approached Gen. John Hood and asked, "Can you break this line?" Hood replied, "I will try." Hood's Texas Brigade pushed across Boatswain's Swamp and scaled the steep hillside, screaming the piercing rebel yell. Decimus Barziza of the 4th Texas Infantry later wrote, "Dashing up the steep bank, being within thirty yards of the enemy's works, we flew towards the breastworks, cleared them, and slaughtered the retreating devils as they scampered up the hill towards their battery."

The assault finally pierced the Federal line, and the retreat soon turned into a rout. About a mile away on the Union right, another breakthrough occurred at nearly the same time. Only darkness prevented the annihilation of Porter's corps. Union forces withdrew across the Chickahominy River, burning the bridges behind them. Combined losses on both sides totaled 15,000 men—the most casualties in any battle of the entire Peninsula Campaign.

PREVIOUS SPREAD: Union artillery position on the Gaines' Mill Battlefield.

BELOW: Watt House.

# GAINES' MILL
## Battlefield Hike

This hike starts at the Gaines' Mill Battlefield parking area. Exhibit panels at the trailhead include a map and interpretive information about the hike.

### Gaines' Mill Breakthrough Trail (1.1 miles)

This hike explores the climatic action of the Battle of Gaines' Mill, when Gen. John Hood's Confederate forces finally broke through the Union line after several hours of ferocious fighting. A soldier of the 4th Texas Infantry wrote, "Yesterday evening we was in one of the hardest fought battles ever known. I never had a clear conception of the horrors of war until last night. . . ." By early evening, Confederate forces gained the crest of the ridge here, driving back troops from New York, Pennsylvania, and Michigan commanded by Gen. Daniel Butterfield. For his determined efforts to rally the retreating Union soldiers, Butterfield was awarded the Medal of Honor. The trail descends to Boatswain's Creek, providing a clear view of the daunting terrain Southern troops had to negotiate to assault the commanding Union position.

Worm fencing marks the path of a historic road across the Gaines' Mill Battlefield.

# MALVERN HILL
## BATTLEFIELD

VIRGINIA  Richmond National Battlefield Park

FROM GAINES' MILL, GEN. ROBERT E. LEE CONTINUED HIS ASSAULTS against Gen. George McClellan's army on the peninsula. On June 29, 1862, he struck Union forces at Savage's Station. The next day, on June 30, he attacked McClellan's rear guard protecting the vital crossroads at Glendale (Frayser's Farm). A day later he found the Army of the Potomac on Malvern Hill, approximately two miles north of the James River. Here McClellan deployed 18,000 infantry and as many as 40 pieces of artillery across the hill.

Early on the morning of July 1, 1862, Lee gathered his generals near his headquarters on Willis Church Road. Frustrated by his army's failure to trap and crush McClellan's army at Glendale, Lee was anxious to resume fighting and deliver one last blow to the Federals before they could retreat to the safety of their gunboats on the James River. On the Union side, the position on Malvern Hill could not have been more formidable. The gentle slopes leading up to the ridgetop provided extensive fields of fire for their massed artillery and infantry. Steep slopes on the Union left and swampy lowlands on the right forced the Southerners to attack across the open ground.

Around 1:30 p.m. Lee issued the orders to attack. For the Confederates, almost everything went wrong. Officers failed to collect enough cannon to cover the assault. Those batteries that were brought up were either damaged or destroyed by the powerful Union guns. When the Confederate infantry attack finally went forward after 4:00 p.m., the assaults were poorly coordinated and units were engaged piecemeal. For three hours 15 Confederate brigades marched into a maelstrom of iron and lead. Charles Phillips of the 5th Massachusetts Light Artillery wrote, "As soon as they made their appearance from the woods, our artillery

opened on them with terrible effect. The air over their heads was filled with the smoke of bursting shells whose fragments plowed the ground . . ." Six cannon from one Union battery alone fired 1,392 rounds during the afternoon fighting.

Units that made it close to the Union line were blasted with canister—tin cans filled with dozens of cast-iron balls. The effect, at close range, seemed to make men disappear. As dusk approached, a few Confederate brigades persevered, closing to within 20 to 40 yards of the Federal line. On the Union left flank, Southern troops commanded by Gen. John Magruder rushed forward in hopes of silencing the deadly Federal guns. Some units engaged in bloody hand-to-hand fighting. Regiments from New York, Michigan, Massachusetts, and Pennsylvania finally repulsed the attackers with dreadful losses. By nightfall the battle had claimed 8,000 casualties—more than half of them Southerners. Confederate Gen. D. H. Hill, surveying the carnage of the battlefield, remarked that "it was not war, it was murder."

The last of the Seven Days' Battles was over. That evening, several Union generals argued in favor of a counterattack the next morning. They believed that the decisive Union victory had left Confederate forces disorganized and Richmond vulnerable to attack. But McClellan ordered a complete withdrawal from Malvern Hill to Harrison's Landing on the James River. According to historian John Keegan, McClellan's plan to avoid the river obstructions north of Richmond "by an amphibious but flanking movement to the Virginia Peninsula was strategically brilliant, and one for which he has never received correct credit." But the "withdrawal from Harrison's Landing after the Seven Days," he added, "was consonantly a serious strategic mistake. Had the landing places been kept open, Richmond would have been kept under permanent threat . . ."

## MALVERN HILL Battlefield Hike

The trail system at Malvern Hill enables visitors to see almost every corner of the battlefield. The hike starts at the Malvern Hill Battlefield parking area. Exhibit panels at the trailhead include a map and interpretive information about the hike.

### Malvern Hill Battlefield Trail (1.7 or 3.0 miles)

The white-blazed Malvern Hill Battlefield Trail is 1.7 miles long. Numerous trailside exhibits help explain the events of the battle and the surrounding historic landscape. As visitors hike back to Malvern Hill across the broad open field from the Confederate artillery battery, they are following in the footsteps of the disastrous infantry assaults into the teeth of the overpowering Union artillery. The gentle slope, combined with extensive fields of fire, allowed the Federal guns to dominate the ground. Several Confederate brigades fought to within 200 yards of the Union line, but were decimated by canister rounds. The blue-blazed Carter's Farm Trail branches off from the main loop near the Willis Church Parsonage ruins and adds about one and a half miles to the hike. This trail traverses the woods and streams where Confederate soldiers gathered to await orders to attack the Union line at Malvern Hill. It includes habitats that are ideal for bird-watching and wildlife observation.

PREVIOUS SPREAD, OPPOSITE, AND FOLLOWING SPREAD: Union artillery position on Malvern Hill.

# COLD HARBOR
## BATTLEFIELD

VIRGINIA  Richmond National Battlefield Park

ON JUNE 1, 1864, THE EASTERN ARMIES RETURNED TO THE GROUND where the Seven Days' Battles had been fought two years earlier. The objective this time was the crossroads at Cold Harbor. At Gaines' Mill, less than a mile away, the bodies of many dead soldiers from the fighting on June 27, 1862, remained unburied. During the intervening months, the two armies had fought some of the bloodiest battles in American history: Second Manassas, Antietam, Fredericksburg, Chancellorsville, Gettysburg, the Wilderness, and Spotsylvania Court House. The war in the east had become a war of attrition, with appalling casualties on both sides. Gen. Robert E. Lee still commanded the Army of Northern Virginia. But on the Northern side, Gen. George McClellan had been dismissed. Gen. Ulysses S. Grant was now in charge, and he ordered the Army of the Potomac to seize the Cold Harbor road junction. Here a network of roads spread out in all directions, and one led directly to Richmond.

Grant had spent much of May 1864 trying to outflank Lee, maneuvering inexorably toward the Confederate capital at Richmond. His army, which numbered 108,000 men, was almost double the 62,000 men under Lee's command. While the Confederates were forced to surrender territory, Lee refused to be drawn out into the open, and he fell back from one secure defensive position to another. At Cold Harbor, Grant would lose his patience and order a massive frontal assault. It was a decision he later regretted.

On May 31, 1864, Gen. Philip Sheridan's cavalry arrived at the Cold Harbor intersection. Here they ran into the Confederate cavalry of Gen. Fitzhugh Lee. A sharp contest ensued, with Confederate infantry soon joining the fight. Sheridan's horsemen, armed with Spencer repeating rifles, drove the Southerners beyond the crossroads. After dark, Lee's army began digging in, building seven miles of strong entrenchments

a half mile southwest of Cold Harbor between Totopotomoy Creek and the Chickahominy River.

The following day, Grant surveyed the situation. He reckoned Lee's army must be depleted and worn out from several weeks of incessant fighting. If a Union frontal assault broke through the Confederate defenses, it would place the Army of the Potomac between Lee and Richmond, and finally lead to a clear-cut victory. But Grant's army was also worn out from hot and dusty night marches. Gen. William "Baldy" Smith's Eighteenth Corps had marched in the wrong direction and had to retrace its route. It didn't reach Cold Harbor until late in the afternoon on June 1. The Union attack finally began at 5:00 p.m. Gen. Horatio Wright's Sixth Corps found a 50-yard gap in the Confederate line and poured through the breach. But a Southern counter-attack repulsed the Federals and closed the break. During the night, Lee's army strengthened its lines and prepared for an assault the next morning.

Grant planned another attack for 5:00 a.m. on June 2, but Gen. Winfield Hancock's Second Corps didn't arrive until 6:30 a.m. They too were exhausted after a brutal night march over narrow, dusty roads. The attack was postponed until 5:00 p.m., and then post-poned again until the following morning. The Union delays were a gift to Lee. Confederate engineers used the time to strengthen their defenses, building an inter-locking series of trenches with overlapping fields of fire. Reinforcements under Gen. John Breckinridge and Gen. A. P. Hill also arrived, strengthening the right side of the Confederate line. Lee was ready.

At 4:30 a.m. on the morning of June 3, almost 50,000 Federal troops of the Second, Sixth, and Eighteenth Corps launched a massive assault. By the end of the day, more than 6,000 of them lay dead or dying in front of the Confederate earthworks—most of them falling in the first hour of fighting. Those sol-diers who weren't killed or wounded were pinned down by the tremendous volume of Confederate fire, and they used bayonets, cups, plates, or their bare hands to dig shallow trenches for cover. The Confederates, though much better protected, suffered 1,500 casual-ties. Shortly after noon, Grant suspended the attack. In his memoir, Grant wrote, "I have always regretted that the last assault at Cold Harbor was ever made. . . . No advantage whatever was gained to compensate for the heavy loss we sustained."

The two armies remained locked in their earth-works from June 4 to June 12, exchanging artillery and sniper fire, but mostly just keeping their heads down. One veteran Virginian described the agony in the trenches: "Thousands of men cramped up in a narrow trench, unable to go out, or get up, or to stretch or to stand, without danger to life and limb . . ." On June 7, more than 100 hours after the attack, Lee and Grant finally agreed on a two-hour truce to allow the Feder-als to retrieve their wounded. By then, however, few of the wounded were found alive—thousands having died under the hot summer sun. Along just one part of the line, work parties found 244 Union dead and just three survivors. Union casualties for all 12 days of fighting totaled between 10,000 and 13,000 men.

**PREVIOUS SPREAD:** Remains of Confederate earthworks at Cold Harbor.

**OPPOSITE:** Artillery position at Cold Harbor.

**ABOVE:** Collecting the remains of dead soldiers on the Cold Harbor Battlefield at the end of the war.

# COLD HARBOR Battlefield Hike

The Union and Confederate field fortifications at Cold Harbor are some of the best examples to be found on any Civil War battlefield in the country. The trail system here provides access to almost every corner of the battlefield, covering historic ground that witnessed two weeks of intense fighting in June 1864. The Main Trail hike starts at the Cold Harbor Visitor Center.

## Cold Harbor Battlefield Trail (1.0, 1.9, or 2.3 miles)

The Main Trail is one mile long and takes visitors through the heart of the battlefield. Interpretive panels along the route explain the fighting that occurred here. Two additional trails connect with the Main Trail: the Western Trail is 0.9 miles long (for a total hike of 1.9 miles); the Extended Trail is 1.5 miles long (for a total hike of 2.3 miles). These two trails follow long stretches of original Union and Confederate entrenchments at the north end of the battlefield. Visitors can help protect the fragile earthworks by walking only on the trails.

The Battle of Cold Harbor changed the war in the east from a war of maneuver to one of siege. It demonstrated how well-selected, well-manned entrenchments, supported by artillery, were practically impregnable to frontal assaults—a lesson that influenced the strategy and tactics of future wars as well. By the summer of 1864, construction of earthen fortifications had become a refined science. Confederate engineers introduced the use of "header logs" placed on top of an earthen embankment with a narrow gap underneath, through which a soldier could fire his musket. Abatis—obstacles formed of sharpened branches laid in a row and pointing toward the enemy—slowed attacking infantrymen, making them easy targets for the riflemen behind the logs. In the coming months, earthen field fortifications would play an even larger role during the nine-month siege of Petersburg, Virginia.

Sunset on the killing fields of Cold Harbor.

# BRANDY STATION
## BATTLEFIELD

IN MID-MAY 1863, GEN. ROBERT E. LEE PREPARED TO LAUNCH HIS second invasion of the North. In preparation for his army's secret withdrawal into the Shenandoah Valley, Lee ordered his cavalry division over the Rapidan River into Culpeper County to screen and protect the impending shift of his army westward. Federal cavalry just across the Rappahannock River discovered the presence of Southern cavalry in Culpeper and concluded (erroneously) that the rebel horsemen were about to set off on a sweeping raid toward Washington, DC. Gen. Joseph Hooker—eager to avoid additional humiliation on the heels of his Chancellorsville debacle—ordered his cavalry corps to "disperse and destroy" the enemy cavalry believed to be located at Culpeper Court House.

The Battle of Brandy Station, or Fleetwood Hill as many Southerners preferred to call it, occurred on June 9, 1863. According to a Confederate staff officer, this was "the most terrible cavalry fight of the war, in fact, the greatest ever fought on the American continent." The surgeon of the 8th Illinois Cavalry concurred, writing that in "all parts of the field the severity of the fight is without precedent in cavalry warfare." What was most stunning about the battle was the sudden combat effectiveness of the Union cavalry, which had been much maligned during the first two years of the Civil War.

The Union cavalry found itself at a considerable disadvantage to its Southern opponents from the very start of the war, when more than half of the experienced US Army cavalry officers resigned their commissions to fight for the Confederacy. Early on, Union cavalry forces were often wasted by being used merely as pickets, orderlies, guards for senior officers, and messengers. At the same time, the Confederate cavalry developed considerable expertise in reconnaissance, screening operations, and combat. All that changed at Brandy

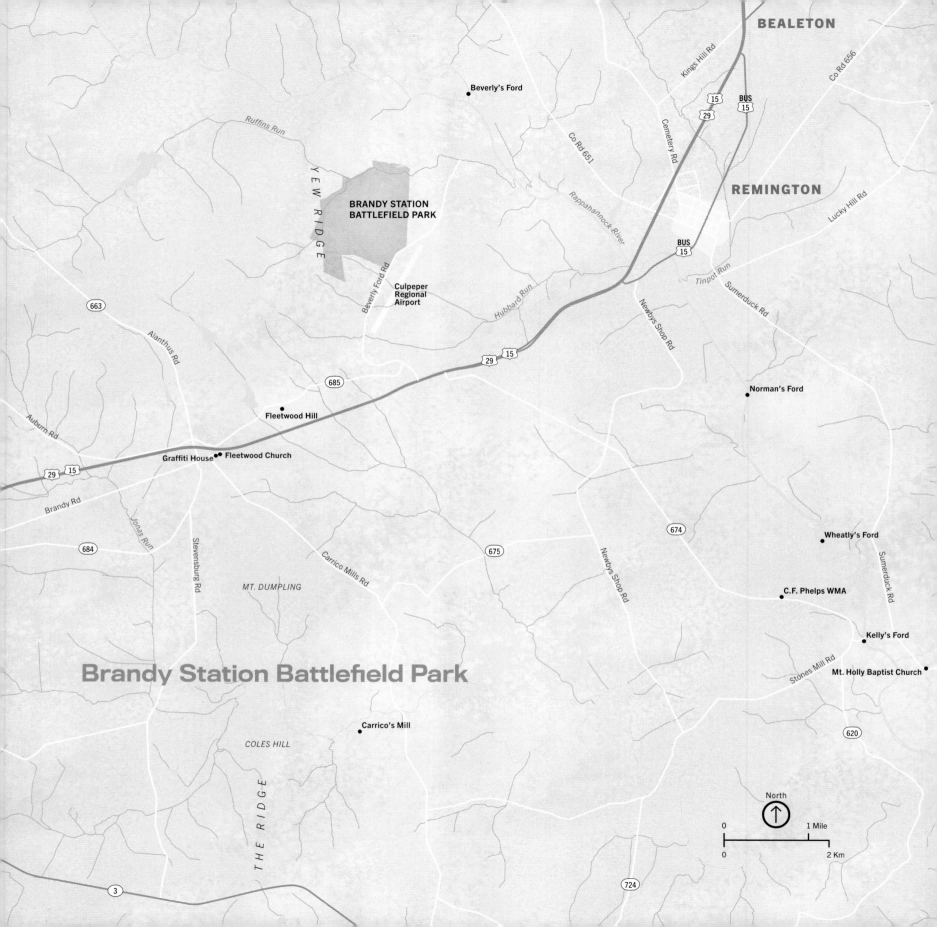

BEALETON

Beverly's Ford

REMINGTON

BRANDY STATION
BATTLEFIELD PARK

YEW RIDGE

Ruffins Run

Kings Hill Rd

Co Rd 656

15
29
BUS 15

Co Rd 651

Cemetery Rd

Rappahannock River

Lucky Hill Rd

BUS 15

Tinpot Run

Sumerduck Rd

Culpeper
Regional
Airport

Beverly Ford Rd

Hubbard Run

Newbys Shop Rd

663

Alanthus Rd

29 15

685

Norman's Ford

Fleetwood Hill

674

Auburn Rd

29 15

Graffiti House ● Fleetwood Church

Wheatly's Ford

Brandy Rd

675

Sumerduck Rd

684

Jonas Run

Stevensburg Rd

Carrico Mills Rd

Newbys Shop Rd

C.F. Phelps WMA

MT. DUMPLING

Kelly's Ford

Stones Mill Rd

Mt. Holly Baptist Church

**Brandy Station Battlefield Park**

620

Carrico's Mill

COLES HILL

North

THE RIDGE

0        1 Mile
0        2 Km

3

724

Station, a battle that—in the words of Gen. J. E. B. Stuart's own aide—"made the Federal cavalry."

Around 4:30 a.m. on the morning of June 9, Union cavalry commander Gen. Alfred Pleasonton dispatched two separate columns totaling 11,000 men across the Rappahannock River. Stuart's Confederate cavalry, concentrated around Brandy Station, totaled 9,500 men. At Beverly's Ford, four and a half miles northeast of Brandy Station, Gen. John Buford's troops scattered surprised Confederate pickets and quickly advanced along Beverly Ford Road. The Federals were also surprised; they had expected to find Stuart's men at Culpeper Court House, 10 miles from the river. Farther south, at Kelly's Ford, Gen. David Gregg led the second Union column across the river. The two columns had been instructed to meet at Brandy Station, but the presence of the Confederates altered their plans.

At St. James Church, Buford's column ran into concentrated Confederate artillery and a brigade of cavalry. The 6th Pennsylvania Cavalry, with support from the 6th US Cavalry, charged the 16 Southern fieldpieces deployed across the road. The Confederates poured canister and carbine fire into the ranks of the Union attackers. The Pennsylvanians penetrated the line of guns but were repulsed by the Virginia horsemen of Gen. William "Grumble" Jones. Halted at St. James Church, Buford redeployed his forces farther north, where he began an assault on Stuart's left flank.

Gen. William "Rooney" Lee, son of Robert E. Lee, blocked Buford's progress along Yew Ridge and at a stone wall between the Cunningham and Green Farms at the north end of the battlefield. Buford launched several mounted and dismounted charges against the wall, but blistering fire from "Rooney" Lee's brigade held the Federals back for several hours. Meanwhile, Gregg's column had also unexpectedly encountered Confederates along the road to Brandy Station. Forced to make a wide march around the enemy, he didn't reach the fighting until about 11:30 a.m. But he was now in the Confederate rear.

PREVIOUS SPREAD: Night sky over Fleetwood Hill.

BELOW: These log huts belonging to the 6th New York were erected on the Brandy Station Battlefield during the Army of the Potomac's 1863 to 1864 winter encampment.

The eruption of Union forces in the Confederate rear was the second great surprise of the day for Stuart. He quickly pulled most of his regiments from around St. James Church and sent them galloping for Fleetwood Hill, a prominent rise between the church and Brandy Station. The battle came down to a struggle for the hilltop, a contest that consumed the afternoon. Fleetwood Hill changed hands several times as the battle devolved into a giant, swirling melee. Charges and countercharges swept back and forth across the rise. By late afternoon, the Federals, exhausted from several hours of fighting, had used up all their reserves. Farther north on Yew Ridge, Confederate reinforcements finally pushed Buford back toward Beverly's Ford. Around 5:00 p.m., Pleasanton saw that further combat was fruitless and ordered his commanders back across the Rappahannock River.

In more than 10 hours of fierce fighting, Stuart lost about 500 men killed or wounded. The Federal toll was about 900 men. Stuart, who held the field at the end of the day, claimed the battle as a Confederate victory. But the Southern press was not impressed. The *Richmond Enquirer* wrote that "Gen. Stuart has suffered no little in public estimation by the late enterprises of the enemy," while the *Richmond Examiner* described Stuart's command as "puffed up cavalry." On the Union side, one trooper summed up the fight when he wrote, "This battle fully proved the Union cavalry is in no manner inferior to the rebels."

Fleetwood Hill, where some of the fiercest fighting of the battle raged.

# BRANDY STATION Battlefield Hikes

The Brandy Station Battlefield Park offers three interpretive trails across gently rolling terrain. Wayside exhibits at the trailheads and along each of the trails help explain the fighting that took place here. Visitors should start at the Graffiti House, one of the few surviving Civil War structures on the battlefield. Built in 1858, the house served as a makeshift field hospital during the battle. Because it was adjacent to the Orange and Alexandria Railroad and the turnpike between Warrenton and Culpeper, it saw frequent use by both Union and Confederate armies throughout the war. Soldiers from both sides wrote numerous notes on the walls, often adding their names and unit designations. The graffiti was rediscovered during a 1993 renovation of the house, and much of it is on display today. The house now serves as the headquarters of the nonprofit Brandy Station Foundation and a visitor center for the battlefield, and is generally only open on weekends.

## St. James Church Walking Trail (0.7 miles)

After marshaling his cavalry across Beverly's Ford, Gen. John Buford decided to test the strength of the Confederate position near St. James Church. Here he found 16 Confederate fieldpieces placed across Beverly Ford Road. The Confederates poured canister and carbine fire into the ranks of the Union cavalry. Union cavalry penetrated the line of guns but were repulsed by a brigade of Virginia horsemen. During the winter of 1863 to 1864, St. James Church was demolished for building materials when the area served as the encampment of the Army of the Potomac. The trailhead is on the north side of St. James Church Road across the street from the parking area at the intersection of St. James Church Road and Beverly Ford Road.

## Buford's Knoll Walking Trail (1.7 miles)

It was on this part of the battlefield, after being repulsed by Confederate artillery at St. James Church, that Gen. John Buford assaulted the Confederates' left flank. Gen. William "Rooney" Lee blocked Buford's progress at the stone wall between the Cunningham and Green Farms. The terrain here played a crucial role in the battle— the steep, rolling topography exhausted the mounts of Buford's cavalry. By late afternoon, Buford realized his men and their horses were

too worn out to continue the fight, and the Union troops withdrew back across Beverly's Ford. The trailhead for the Buford's Knoll Walking Trail is on Beverly Ford Road, just north of Culpeper Regional Airport.

### Fleetwood Hill Walking Trail (0.3 miles)

The high ground here, named after Henry Miller's House, Fleetwood, became the center of a series of violent cavalry charges and countercharges during the June 9, 1863, battle. Fleetwood Hill changed hands several times in the course of the fighting. At one point six Union and six Confederate regiments struggled for control of the hilltop, which was considered the most intense and prolonged combat of the battle. By late afternoon, the Union forces retired back across the Rappahannock River. The trailhead is located about a mile northeast of Brandy Station just off US Route 29.

OPPOSITE: Beverly Ford Road near the Rappahannock River.

ABOVE: Site of the 6th Pennsylvania Cavalry charge toward Yew Ridge at the north end of the Brandy Station Battlefield.

# PETERSBURG
## BATTLEFIELD

VIRGINIA  Petersburg National Battlefield

ON JUNE 13, 1864, GEN. ULYSSES S. GRANT DISENGAGED HIS UNION forces from Cold Harbor and made a swift and secret march south toward the James River. It was a move that utterly surprised Confederate Gen. Robert E. Lee. For five weeks, from May 4 to June 1, Grant had tried repeatedly to maneuver his massive army around Lee toward Richmond. By driving relentlessly south toward the Confederate capital, Grant hoped to draw the Army of Northern Virginia out into the open, where he could use his two-to-one advantage in manpower to finally defeat and destroy Lee's army. But Lee had countered each of Grant's moves brilliantly, repeatedly maneuvering his adversary onto ground where the Southerners could entrench and fight successful defensive battles.

Relentless skirmishes and major battles at the Wilderness, Spotsylvania Court House, North Anna, and Cold Harbor had taken a severe toll on both armies. The Overland Campaign, as these engagements became known, was the bloodiest in American history. In 40 days, the Army of the Potomac suffered approximately 55,000 casualties, of which 7,600 were killed. The Confederates lost 33,600 men, 4,300 of them killed. Grant, however, could count on reinforcements to replace his army's losses. Lee could not—his losses were irreplaceable.

Finally, on June 13, 1864, Grant outfoxed his adversary. The Confederates, short on cavalry, temporarily lost touch with the swift-moving Union columns as they exited their entrenchments around Cold Harbor. While Lee remained unaware of Grant's intentions, Federal army engineers constructed the longest pontoon bridge of the war. The span, an unprecedented achievement of combat engineering, stretched 2,200 feet over deep water, crossing the James River northeast of Petersburg, Virginia. On June 14 and 15, Grant deployed two Union corps opposite the entrenchments around Petersburg.

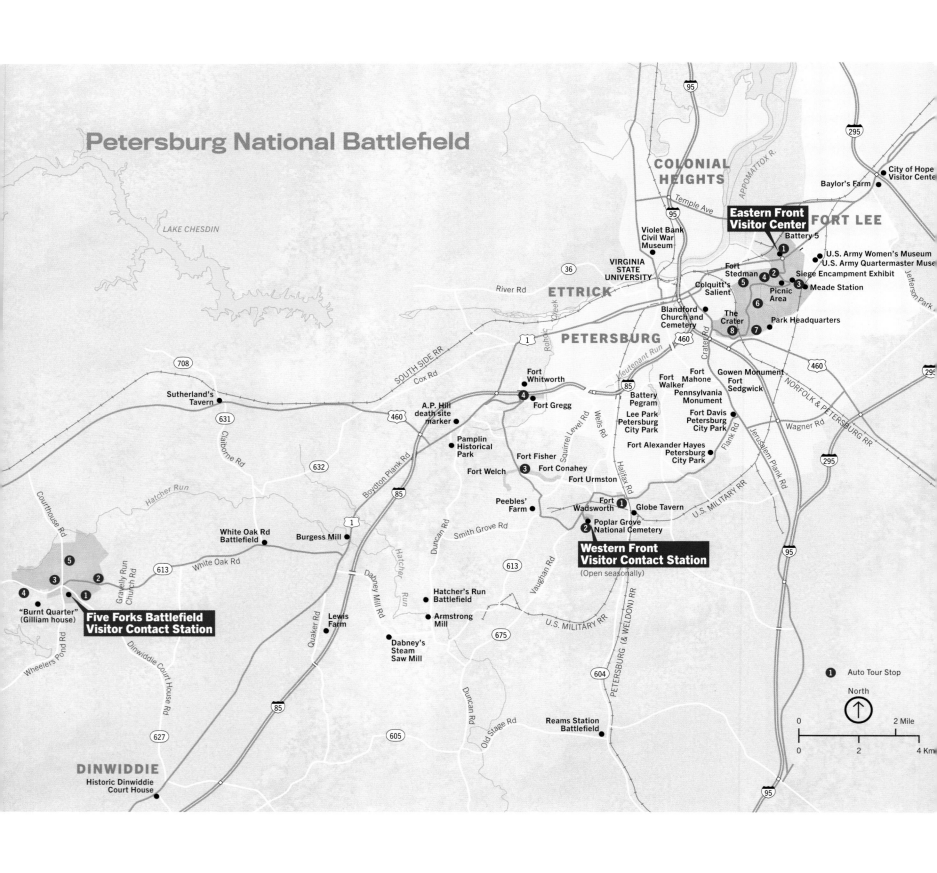

# Petersburg National Battlefield

COLONIAL HEIGHTS

FORT LEE

City of Hope Visitor Center

Baylor's Farm

LAKE CHESDIN

APPOMATTOX R.

Temple Ave

Violet Bank Civil War Museum

**Eastern Front Visitor Center**

Battery 5

① U.S. Army Women's Museum
U.S. Army Quartermaster Museum

VIRGINIA STATE UNIVERSITY

Fort Stedman ④ ②
⑤ Siege Encampment Exhibit
Colquitt's Salient ③ Meade Station

Picnic Area

River Rd

ETTRICK

Blandford Church and Cemetery

The Crater ⑥
⑧ ⑦ Park Headquarters

Jefferson Park

PETERSBURG

SOUTH SIDE RR

Cox Rd

Fort Whitworth

Fort Mahone
Fort Walker
Gowen Monument
Fort Sedgwick

NORFOLK & PETERSBURG RR

Sutherland's Tavern

A.P. Hill death site marker

Fort Gregg ④

Battery Pegram

Lee Park Petersburg City Park

Pennsylvania Monument

Fort Davis Petersburg City Park

Claiborne Rd

Pamplin Historical Park

Fort Fisher

Fort Welch
Fort Conahey ③
Fort Urmston

Fort Alexander Hayes Petersburg City Park

Wagner Rd

NORFOLK & PETERSBURG RR

White Oak Rd Battlefield

Burgess Mill

Peebles' Farm

Fort Wadsworth ①
② Poplar Grove National Cemetery

Globe Tavern

U.S. MILITARY RR

⑤
③
④ "Burnt Quarter" (Gilliam house)
① ②

**Five Forks Battlefield Visitor Contact Station**

White Oak Rd

Lewis Farm

Hatcher's Run Battlefield

Armstrong Mill

**Western Front Visitor Contact Station**
(Open seasonally)

Wheelers Pond Rd

Gravelly Run Church Rd

Dinwiddie Court House Rd

Quaker Rd

Dabney Mill Rd

Dabney's Steam Saw Mill

U.S. MILITARY RR

PETERSBURG (& WELDON) RR

Jerusalem Plank Rd

Smith Grove Rd

Vaughan Rd

DINWIDDIE

Historic Dinwiddie Court House

Reams Station Battlefield

① Auto Tour Stop

North

0   2 Mile
0   2   4 Km

## Assault on Petersburg

### June 15–18, 1864

Grant reckoned that Petersburg, 25 miles south of Richmond, was the key to capturing the Confederate capital. Five railroads and several roads converged here; its capture would cut off Richmond from supply and communication with the rest of the South and likely force Lee out onto open ground. On June 15, he was ready to launch his attack. Standing in his way was a 10-mile-long string of entrenchments and artillery redoubts known as the Dimmock Line, named for the Confederate engineer who two years earlier had designed the defenses along Petersburg's eastern perimeter. Though a formidable obstacle, the Dimmock Line lacked troops; a meager force of just 2,200 soldiers under the command of Gen. P. G. T. Beauregard blocked the eastern approach to Petersburg.

The vanguard of Grant's army was the Union Eighteenth Corps, commanded by Gen. William "Baldy" Smith. With 16,000 men, Smith cautiously approached the Dimmock Line, ever mindful of the calamity that had befallen Union forces at Cold Harbor on June 3. After delaying his attack until about 7:00 p.m., Smith's forces swept over the earthworks on a three-and-a-half-mile front, pushing the Confederates back to a weaker defensive line on Harrison's Creek. But despite this initial success and the prospect of a virtually undefended city immediately to his front, Smith decided to wait until dawn to resume his attack. It was a familiar pattern and a fateful decision. Beauregard later wrote that Petersburg "at that hour was clearly at the mercy of the Federal commander, who had all but captured it." The Confederates used the delay to fortify a new defensive line while Lee rushed reinforcements to Petersburg.

On June 16, Gen. Winfield Hancock's Second Corps captured another section of the Confederate line. On June 17, the Ninth Corps gained more ground. Union forces succeeded in severing two railroad lines and capturing several vital roads. But on June 18, when the Second, Fifth, and Eleventh Corps launched a broad assault on the Petersburg defenses, they were

**PREVIOUS SPREAD:** Sunset over Fort Stedman.

**BELOW:** Remains of Confederate earthworks at Petersburg. The Siege of Petersburg demonstrated how well-designed field fortifications were practically impregnable to frontal assaults.

repulsed with heavy casualties. At Colquitt's Salient, where the men of the 1st Maine Heavy Artillery attacked the Confederate line, they lost a staggering 632 men of the brigade's 900. Not a single man had come close to reaching the enemy's fortifications. The Confederate works were now heavily manned and the greatest opportunity to capture Petersburg without a siege was lost.

## Siege of Petersburg

### June 18, 1864–April 2, 1865

After the costly attacks of June 18, Grant ordered the Union army to dig in. The siege of Petersburg had begun. For close to 10 months, Grant's forces gradually but relentlessly isolated Petersburg and cut Lee's supply lines from the south. By April 1865, Union trenches extended more than 30 miles from the eastern outskirts of Richmond to the eastern and southwestern outskirts of Petersburg. Key objectives included the Weldon Railroad, which connected Petersburg to the South's only remaining major port at Wilmington; the South Side Railroad, which reached to Lynchburg in the west; and the Boydton Plank Road, a vital supply route from the southwest. The constant pressure severely strained Lee's manpower and resources.

For the Confederates, the siege marked months of desperately hanging on; living off diminished rations of salt pork, cornmeal, beans, and bad coffee; and hoping the people of the North would tire of the war. For soldiers of both armies it meant living in muddy trenches and log-covered hovels; enduring months of sniper fire, artillery duels, and mortar shells; and getting relief only by the tedium of drill and more drill. For the residents of Petersburg, it meant months of fear, privation, hardship, and sacrifice.

## Battle of the Crater

### July 30, 1864

As the stalemate in the trenches around Petersburg extended into the hot Virginia summer, a Union regiment from the coal-mining country of eastern Pennsylvania came up with a bold idea. Why not burrow under the Confederate entrenchments and detonate enough powder to blast open a large gap in the line? On June 24, Col. Henry Pleasants, commander of the 48th Pennsylvania, took the idea to Gen. Ambrose Burnside. The plan was approved, and Pleasants put

his miners to work near a Confederate field fortification known as Elliott's Salient. For more than a month, the Pennsylvanians carefully excavated a 510-foot tunnel beneath the Confederate line. By the end of July, Pleasants's men had packed 8,000 pounds of gunpowder into two galleries at the end of the tunnel, some 40 feet under the enemy's field fortification. On July 30, at 3:00 a.m., they ignited the fuse.

For several minutes, nothing happened. To the dismay of the Pennsylvanians, the fuse had malfunctioned. Almost two hours later, at 4:40 a.m., they lit it again. This time it worked. An enormous blast ruptured the ground, throwing dirt and fire high into the air and creating a crater 170 feet long, 80 feet wide, and 30 feet deep. According to a newspaper correspondent, "Clods of earth weighing at least a ton, and cannon, and human forms, and gun-carriages, and small arms were all distinctly seen shooting upward in that fountain of horror." Two hundred seventy-eight South Carolinians died in the blast, and two 1,700-pound cannon were hurled completely out of the works. From this momentous

OPPOSITE: The "Dictator" is an iconic image of the Siege of Petersburg. This 17,120-pound, 13-inch seacoast gun, photographed here in October 1864, could lob a 200-pound explosive shell about two and a half miles.

BELOW: Entrance to the mine tunnel beneath The Crater.

start, however, nothing else went right. Poor planning, communications, and leadership robbed the Battle of the Crater of its potentially decisive results.

First, a specially trained formation of 4,300 US Colored Troops, drilled for days on the assault, were replaced by white troops at the last moment. Gen. George Meade felt it would be "politically unwise" to place black troops in such a prominent position. Many of the replacement troops, unprepared for the scope of the blast, stopped their assault and marveled at the chaotic scene. Others advanced down through the crater instead of around the perimeter, making it difficult to proceed through the breach in the Confederate line. After being momentarily dazed by the blast, the Southerners quickly recovered and counterattacked. Many of the Union attackers took cover inside the crater, where they became trapped in a mass of disorganized men. When at last the US Colored Troops were sent in, it was too late. In a wild melee, troops on both sides engaged in close-quarter musket fire and hand-to-hand combat. The black troops suffered disproportionately as they became special targets for the Confederates, and many were killed after

they had surrendered. By midday, the horrific fighting was over. Despite the ingenious feat of the Pennsylvania coal miners, the battle that followed the explosion had accomplished absolutely nothing except the loss of nearly 3,800 Union soldiers. Grant pronounced it "the saddest affair I have witnessed in this war," and responded by relieving Burnside from command.

## Battle of Hatcher's Run
### February 5-7, 1865

From August 1864 to April 1865, most of Grant's major offensives during the Siege of Petersburg were directed against Lee's supply lines south and west of the city. The Weldon Railroad was captured on August 21, 1864. Another operation began on February 5, 1865, when Grant sent Gen. David Gregg's cavalry to intercept Confederate supply trains on the Boydton Plank Road near Dinwiddie Court House. Infantry divisions from Gen. Gouverneur Warren's Fifth Corps and Gen. Andrew Humphreys's Second Corps were deployed in support of the cavalry along Hatcher's Run.

Humphreys deployed two of his brigades near Duncan Road. Here Confederate Gen. Henry Heth found a gap in the Union line, but with the aid of timely reinforcements, the Federals repulsed three Southern assaults. Late in the day, Gen. John Gordon attempted to turn Humphreys's right flank, but was also repulsed. After three days of fighting, the Southerners succeeded in stopping the Union offensive. But the Federals extended their lines four miles closer to the South Side Railroad.

## Battle of Fort Stedman
### March 25, 1865

By the spring of 1865, the line of Confederate trenches around Richmond and Petersburg extended over a 37-mile front. Only two supply routes into Petersburg were still open—the Boydton Plank Road and the South Side Railroad. Gen. Robert E. Lee's army was weakened by desertion, disease, and a shortage of supplies, and outnumbered by Grant's army about 125,000 to 50,000. Clearly desperate, Lee sought the counsel of Gen. John Gordon. Lee's only choices, as Gordon saw it, were surrender, retreat, or attack. Lee chose the last option.

In his last offensive action of the Civil War, Lee amassed nearly half of his army in an attempt to break through Grant's Petersburg defenses and threaten his

PREVIOUS SPREAD: Elliott's Salient, where coal miners from the 48th Pennsylvania detonated 8,000 pounds of gunpowder, creating a crater 170 feet long, 80 feet wide, and 30 feet deep.

BELOW: Hatcher's Run Battlefield, southwest of Petersburg, Virginia.

supply depot at City Point. On March 25, 1865, Gordon launched a predawn assault across the narrow plateau in front of Colquitt's Salient toward the Union line. His bold attack quickly overpowered the garrisons of Fort Stedman and nearby Batteries X, XI, and XII, opening a gap nearly 1,000 feet wide in the Union line. But the Confederates soon came under a killing cross fire, and the attack began to founder. Counterattacks from the Union Ninth Corps contained, cut off, and captured more than 1,900 of Gordon's men.

Artillery fire from Fort Haskell immediately south of Fort Stedman also took a horrific toll. When a Confederate assault attempted to advance across the ravine between the two forts, a Federal trooper recalled that the fort's "cannon belched forth grape and our muskets were discharged upon the hapless band. It was an awful surprise for the surprisers, and fifty mangled bodies lay there in the abatis." Gordon later wrote that the failure to take Fort Haskell had doomed the entire Confederate attack.

## Battle of Five Forks

### April 1, 1865

The Confederate defeat at Fort Stedman severely weakened Lee's army. He knew that it was only a matter of time before Grant would again attempt to sever Petersburg's last two supply lines: the South Side Railroad and the Boydton Plank Road. In late March 1865, Grant ordered Gen. Philip Sheridan and his cavalry to advance upon the South Side Railroad, using the crossroads several miles southwest of Petersburg known as Five Forks. Lee recognized his peril, and ordered Gen. George Pickett's infantry and the cavalry of Gen. Fitzhugh Lee to hold the vital crossroads "at all hazards." After discovering that Pickett's forces were entrenched at Five Forks, Sheridan secured infantry support from Gen. Gouverneur Warren's Fifth Corps.

Late on the afternoon of April 1, Sheridan hit the front and right flank of the Confederate line with the cavalry troopers of Gen. Thomas Devin and Gen. George Armstrong Custer. Small-arms fire from the mostly dismounted horsemen pinned down the Confederates while the massed infantry of Fifth Corps prepared to assault Pickett's left flank. Pickett, meanwhile, was attending a shad bake on the north bank of Hatcher's Run, one and a half miles from the battlefield, when the fighting broke out. He had

wrongly assumed that Sheridan would be unlikely to attack so late in the day, and even worse, had placed no one in command during his absence. When he was finally alerted to the Union attack, it was too late.

Warren's assault finally commenced about 4:15 p.m., crushing the Confederate left flank and taking scores of prisoners. Although Fifth Corps had performed well, Sheridan was nevertheless dissatisfied with Warren's performance, and he relieved him of command. In his after-action report, Sheridan cited what he perceived to be Warren's lack of effort in getting his troops ready for the attack. Warren's men were stunned by the action. Many of his soldiers wrote strongly worded defenses of their general, blaming the dismissal on Sheridan's jealousy of Warren's role in the victory. Eighteen years later, in 1883, the Warren Court of Inquiry ruled that Sheridan's removal of Warren had indeed been unjustified.

None of this changed the outcome of the battle on April 1, 1865. The resounding Union triumph at Five Forks ensured the capture of the South Side Railroad, broke the right flank of the Petersburg line, and heralded the end of the nine-month stalemate.

South Side Railroad trestle across Indian Town Creek west of Petersburg, Virginia.

## Petersburg Breakthrough
### April 2, 1865

April 2, 1865, proved to be the day of reckoning at Petersburg. The thinly held Confederate lines had been stretched to the breaking point by months of Union attacks and maneuvering to the south and west. Lee's army, reduced by desertions and casualties from recent battles, no longer had the manpower to maintain its 37 miles of entrenchments. With Lee's right flank unmasked by Pickett's defeat at Five Forks, Grant ordered a full-scale assault against the entire Confederate line.

Success would finally come west of Petersburg's main entrenchments, not far from Union Fort Fisher. Here Gen. Horatio Wright, commander of Sixth Corps, deployed his 14,000 attackers in a wedge-shaped formation across a battlefront one mile wide. About 2,800 Confederates under the command of Gen. A. P. Hill waited in their trenches. At the point of the wedge were 2,200 men of the 5th Vermont Infantry Regiment. At 4:40 a.m., the Vermonters stepped out to lead the assault. As they pushed closer to the Confederate fortifications, they encountered multiple rows of obstructions and endured a brutal fire from small arms and artillery.

"With a cheer we went on getting through the abatis the best way we could," recalled Lt. Robert Pratt of the 5th Vermont. The line surged forward, and soon the Vermonters ascended Hill's earthworks and engaged the enemy in desperate hand-to-hand fighting. The rest of Wright's Sixth Corps soldiers followed, and the superior Union numbers quickly held sway. Most of the North Carolinians and Georgians in this section of the line surrendered, while many more were killed or wounded. A North Carolina officer later wrote, "We fought desperately, but our thin line was pushed back by sheer force of numbers until it was broken in pieces." By 5:15 a.m., the US flag flew above the Confederate works.

The Sixth Corps Breakthrough proved to be the decisive battle of the Petersburg Campaign. When Lee got word of the breach, he immediately wired Richmond that he could "hold his position no longer," and intended to evacuate Petersburg and Richmond that night. Lee also learned of another devastating loss—Gen. A. P. Hill was shot and killed while riding toward the site of the Sixth Corps Breakthrough.

PREVIOUS SPREAD: Union Napoleon guns at Fort Stedman.

OPPOSITE: Breakthrough Trail, Pamplin Historical Park.

# PETERSBURG Battlefield Hikes

The Petersburg Battlefield is composed of several sites connected by a 33-mile-long automobile route. Many of the sites, including Hatcher's Run Battlefield, Pamplin Historical Park, and units within Petersburg National Battlefield, offer excellent hiking trails. The Eastern Front unit of Petersburg National Battlefield is crisscrossed by 19.5 miles of superbly maintained hiking trails. The battlefield terrain ranges from easy to moderate, with a few ridges and steep ravines around preserved field fortifications. Obtain hiking information, a free park map, and an Eastern Front trail map at the visitor center.

## Confederate Battery 5 Trail (0.7 miles)

This hike starts at the Eastern Front Visitor Center. The trail covers ground where the first major attacks against Petersburg occurred on June 15, 1864. Highlights include Battery 5 of the Confederate Dimmock Line, and the position of the famous Union mortar, the "Dictator," a 13-inch seacoast gun that could lob a 200-pound explosive shell about two and a half miles.

## Battle of Fort Stedman Trail (2.8 miles)

This hike begins at the Fort Stedman parking area (Auto Tour Stop 5) on the Eastern Front Driving Tour. The trail, described in the *Battle of Fort Stedman Trail Guide* available at the visitor center, features 10 points of interest across the area where Gen. Robert E. Lee launched his last major assault of the Civil War. The attack on Fort Stedman was a desperate attempt by Confederate troops to break the Union siege on Petersburg. The trail follows the initial Confederate breakout from Colquitt's Salient, explores remnants of original Civil War fortifications, and crosses Harrison's Creek, where a Union counterattack by the 200th Pennsylvania Infantry stopped the Confederate advance. The hike continues to Fort Haskell, where several Confederate assaults were repulsed, ultimately forcing the rebels to retreat. The hike's final stop is at Fort Stedman, which Union troops recaptured after fierce hand-to-

hand fighting. A soldier later wrote that the fort "was the first place I saw footprints of men in puddles of blood. . . . It was hell!"

## The Crater Trail (0.6 miles)

This hike starts at the Crater parking area (Auto Tour Stop 8) on the Eastern Front Driving Tour. It was here, at 4:40 a.m. on the morning of July 30, 1864, that Pennsylvania troops exploded a mine under Elliott's Salient, blowing an 80-foot-wide hole in the Confederate line. The follow-up attack by the Union Ninth Corps to exploit the gap failed miserably. In a brutal melee that lasted several hours, Virginia troops finally repulsed the Federals. By the time the fighting was over, about 3,800 Federals were killed, wounded, or captured. The Confederates lost fewer than 1,200 men, including those killed by the explosion. Interpretive markers along the trail tell the grim story.

## Hatcher's Run Battlefield Trail (1.7 miles)

Fighting here during the three-day engagement known as the Battle of Hatcher's Run took place on February 5, 1865. This trail covers ground where elements of Gen. Andrew Humphreys's Second Corps and Gen. David Gregg's cavalry advanced against the Confederates in one of several attempts to capture the Boydton Plank Road—a vital supply route for Petersburg and Richmond. The trail follows a long stretch

of pristine Confederate field fortifications constructed in September and October 1864. The trail and battlefield site, owned by the Civil War Trust, are about three-quarters of a mile north of Armstrong Mill on Duncan Road. Exhibit panels at the trailhead include a map and interpretive information about the hike.

## Five Forks Battlefield Trails (8.5 miles)

The battle at this star-shaped intersection would become known as the "Waterloo of the Confederacy." Today, eight and a half miles of trails crisscross the Five Forks Battlefield, a unit of Petersburg National Battlefield. For an interesting half-mile hike (one way), visitors can follow the Devin Trail from the visitor center to the Five Forks intersection. This trail covers the ground where Union cavalrymen under Gen. Thomas Devin advanced toward Five Forks on the morning of April 1, 1865. Their orders were to test the strength of the Confederate defenses along White Oak Road. Repulsed by intense Confederate musket and cannon fire, they pulled back and waited for Union infantry. At 4:15 p.m., the cavalrymen dismounted and advanced again, using these trees for cover. "We again moved forward," wrote E. M. Johnson of the 2nd New York Cavalry, "firing slowly from behind the trees." By early evening, Union forces had overrun Five Forks and the Confederate line melted away.

## The Breakthrough Trail (2.1 miles)

The nine-month-long siege of Petersburg ended on April 2, 1865. In the predawn darkness of that spring morning, 14,000 Union soldiers attacked the Confederate fortifications that are preserved in the woods here. The Breakthrough Trail takes visitors to the Confederate picket line, through the valley of Arthur's Swamp, past remnants of a rare military dam, and follows the route of the 5th Vermont Infantry, which spearheaded the assault of Gen. Horatio Wright's Union Sixth Corps. A series of interpretive signs help explain the dramatic events that led to the Union breakthrough. The terrain is gently rolling, and the trail is well maintained for easy walking. Visitors should start at the National Museum of the Civil War Soldier in Pamplin Historical Park, where trail maps and guides are available. There is an entrance fee for the park. From the museum to the trailhead is 0.3 miles one way. There are three options for the Breakthrough Trail: the Main Loop is 1.5 miles long; the Intermediate Loop is 0.7 miles long; and the Short Loop is 0.3 miles long. Visitors can extend their hike by following the Petersburg Battlefields Trail, which connects the Confederate works in Pamplin Historical Park to the Union works around Fort Welch and Fort Fisher in Petersburg National Battlefield. This trail connects to the Main Loop of the Breakthrough Trail, covers approximately two miles round trip, and takes about 90 minutes to walk.

South Carolina Monument at The Crater.

# APPOMATTOX COURT HOUSE
## BATTLEFIELD

VIRGINIA  Appomattox Court House National Historical Park

ON THE EVENING OF APRIL 2, 1865, AFTER THE UNION BREAKTHROUGH at Petersburg, Virginia, Gen. Robert E. Lee ordered his army to retreat. The Confederates succeeded in extricating themselves from their entrenchments, and by midnight were marching westward in two columns along the course of the Appomattox River. Lee hoped to link up with Gen. Joseph Johnston's Army of Tennessee, which was battling the forces of Gen. William Tecumseh Sherman in North Carolina. But first his troops were in desperate need of food and supplies. Lee's men arrived at Amelia Court House on April 4, but there were no provisions. Wagons were dispatched to the surrounding country to forage, but the delay cost the Confederates a day's worth of marching.

Meanwhile, two Union columns pursued the retreating Confederates. Gen. George Meade led the Army of the Potomac, while Gen. Edward Ord, commander of the Army of the James, followed along a parallel route to the south. Lee now pushed his army toward Appomattox Station, where a supply train awaited him. But the Confederate delay at Amelia Court House had allowed Federal forces to close in on Lee's army. As the retreating Southern columns became more ragged, gaps developed in their line of march. At Sailor's Creek, a few miles east of Farmville, Gen. Philip Sheridan's cavalry cut off two Confederate corps—one fourth of Lee's army— under Gen. Richard Anderson and Gen. Richard Ewell. On April 6, in a severe fight with the Union Sixth Corps, the trapped Southerners were soundly defeated. Most of the 7,700 Confederates were either killed, captured, or wounded. Watching the debacle from a nearby hill, Lee exclaimed, "My God! Has the army been dissolved?"

As Grant's forces closed in around Lee on April 7, the Union commander sent his adversary a letter calling on him to accept the inevitable outcome:

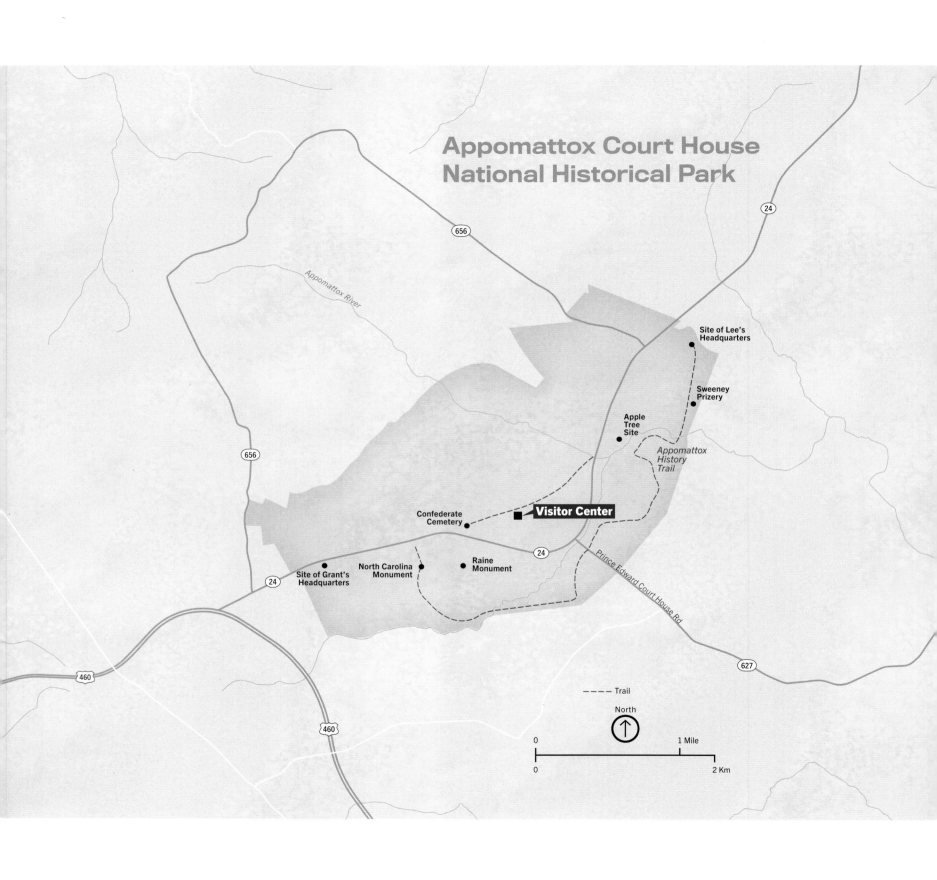

# Appomattox Court House National Historical Park

656

24

Appomattox River

656

Site of Lee's Headquarters

Sweeney Prizery

Apple Tree Site

Appomattox History Trail

Confederate Cemetery

**Visitor Center**

24

Prince Edward Court House Rd

Site of Grant's Headquarters

North Carolina Monument

Raine Monument

24

24

627

460

460

– – – Trail

North
↑

0                   1 Mile

0                   2 Km

*The result of last week must convince you of the hopelessness of further resistance . . . in the struggle. I feel that it is so and regard it as my duty to shift from myself the responsibility for any further effusion of blood by asking you to surrender that portion of the C. S. Army known as the Army of Northern Virginia.*

Lee refused the request, and pressed on toward Appomattox Station. On April 8, Union cavalry under Gen. George Armstrong Custer captured and burned three supply trains waiting for Lee's army at Appomattox Station. Both the Army of the Potomac and the Army of the James were now converging on Appomattox. When the remnants of Lee's army arrived at Appomattox Station late on the afternoon of April 8, they found Union cavalry blocking their path. Three divisions of Sheridan's cavalry and infantry from the Union Fifth and Twenty-Fourth Corps blocked the way south and west. Lee consulted with his generals and determined that one more attempt should be made to reach the railroad and escape. At dawn on April 9, Gen. John Gordon's corps attacked the Union cavalry blocking the stage road, but after an initial success, Union infantry stopped the Confederate advance.

Around 8:30 a.m., Gordon sent a note to Lee, stating ". . . my command has been fought to a frazzle, and unless Longstreet can unite in the movement, or prevent these forces from coming upon my rear, I cannot long go forward." Receiving the message, Lee replied, "There is nothing left for me to do but to go and see General Grant, and I would rather die a thousand deaths."

At around 2:00 p.m. on the afternoon of April 9, 1865, Lee and Grant met at the McLean House in the village of Appomattox Court House with a group of officers. The terms for surrender were as generous as Lee could have hoped for: his men would not be imprisoned or prosecuted for treason; officers were allowed to keep their sidearms; and the defeated men would be allowed to take home their horses and mules to carry out the spring planting. Grant even supplied food to the rebels, who were desperately low on rations. Lee said the terms would have a very happy effect among the men and do much toward reconciling the country.

As Lee left the McLean House and rode away, Grant's men began cheering in celebration, but Grant ordered an immediate stop. "I at once sent word, however, to have it stopped," he later wrote. "The Confederates were now our countrymen, and we did not want to exult over their downfall."

**PREVIOUS SPREAD:** Worm fencing along the historic Richmond-Lynchburg Stage Road.

**BELOW, LEFT:** The McLean House at Appomattox Court House, April 1865.

**BELOW, RIGHT:** Union troops at Appomattox Court House after the war.

OPPOSITE: Old road through Appomattox Court House National Historical Park.

RIGHT, TOP: Field at Appomattox Court House National Historical Park.

RIGHT, BOTTOM: Historic Richmond-Lynchburg Stage Road.

FOLLOWING SPREAD: Battlefield illumination along the historic Richmond-Lynchburg Stage Road in front of the McLean House.

# APPOMATTOX COURT HOUSE Battlefield Hikes

Appomattox Court House National Historical Park has five miles of trails. Visitors should start at the visitor center, where trail maps and information are available.

**Appomattox History Trail** (4.0 miles one way)
This hike starts either at the Lee's Headquarters parking area or North Carolina Monument parking area along Virginia Route 24. This white-blazed trail crosses the entire park, connecting the North Carolina Monument parking area to the Lee's Headquarters parking area. Most of the trail is wide with gentle changes in elevation, but some sections are steep, rocky, and uneven. After periods of heavy rain, some sections of the trail along the Appomattox River and Plain Run may be muddy and temporarily flooded. Good birding opportunities can be found along this trail as it weaves through hardwood forests, pine stands, and open fields. Points of interest include the site of Lee's Headquarters, where the Confederate commander held his last council of war on the evening of April 8, 1865. Sweeney Prizery was a tobacco-packing house where local farmers brought their crops to be packed in hogsheads, or large barrels, for shipment to market. Many Confederate soldiers camped in this vicinity during the night of April 8 and during the days following the surrender. On the morning of April 9, before the surrender, Union Gen. George Armstrong Custer's cavalry fought with Confederate forces around the Prince Edward Court House Road intersection near the top of the ridge. The trail passes the site where the first Confederate flag of truce was carried into the Union lines about midmorning on April 9. The bearer, Confederate Capt. Robert Sims of Gen. James Longstreet's staff, was seeking a cessation of the fighting until Lee and Grant could meet to discuss surrender terms. Sims was first received near the top of the hill by Custer. The North Carolina Monument was placed by the State of North Carolina to commemorate actions by its troops during the final battle fought by Lee's army.

**Nature Trail Spur** (0.4 miles)
This orange-blazed spur trail connects with the Appomattox History Trail near the Lee's Headquarters parking area. The American Society of Foresters maintains trail markers that identify trees and provide information on how the forest changes. Some sections of this trail are uneven and rocky.

**Sears Lane Trail Spur** (0.6 miles)
This blue-blazed trail connects with the Appomattox History Trail at the North Carolina Monument parking area and follows the historic Sears Lane just east of the Raine Cemetery. Grant traveled on this lane to bypass Confederate troops as he rode to Appomattox Court House to discuss surrender terms with Lee. Now covered with hardwood forest, this lane once passed through open fields of tobacco, grains, and other crops. During periods of heavy rain, sections of the trail may be temporarily flooded.

LEFT: Site of the last skirmish at Appomattox Court House.

OPPOSITE: Overton Hillsman House at Sailor's Creek Battlefield, Virginia.

WESTERN

VIRGINIA
SHENANDOAH VALLEY

# McDOWELL
# BATTLEFIELD

IN THE SPRING OF 1862, SOUTHERN MORALE HAD REACHED A LOW POINT. Following the successful summer of 1861, particularly at the Battle of First Manassas (First Battle of Bull Run), prospects for the Confederacy had quickly declined. Union armies in the Western Theater, particularly those under Gen. Ulysses S. Grant, won significant battles at Fort Donelson and Shiloh, taking control of Kentucky and much of west Tennessee. In Virginia, Gen. George McClellan's massive Army of the Potomac was approaching Richmond from the southeast, while Gen. Irvin McDowell was poised to hit Richmond from the north with another large corps. In western Virginia, Gen. Nathaniel Banks was threatening the Shenandoah Valley, one of the Confederacy's most valuable and strategic regions.

Known as "the breadbasket of the Confederacy," the Shenandoah Valley was both agriculturally rich and strategically important. As recently as 1860, the area produced 2.5 million bushels of wheat—accounting for about 19 percent of Virginia's entire crop. The valley was also rich in livestock, crucial for provisioning the Confederate armies operating in the state. Union control would not only deny these irreplaceable resources to the Confederacy, but also further squeeze Southern forces defending Richmond. According to Gen. Thomas "Stonewall" Jackson, "If this Valley is lost, Virginia is lost."

In early May 1862, Jackson's immediate concern was a Union force threatening the upper Shenandoah Valley. About 6,000 men under Gen. Robert Milroy—the leading elements of Gen. John Frémont's army—were advancing through the Allegheny Mountains east toward Staunton, Virginia. If Federal forces captured Staunton, they could cut off the vital Virginia and Tennessee Railroad. Even more ominous, if Frémont and Banks were allowed to combine their armies, Jackson's forces could be overwhelmed.

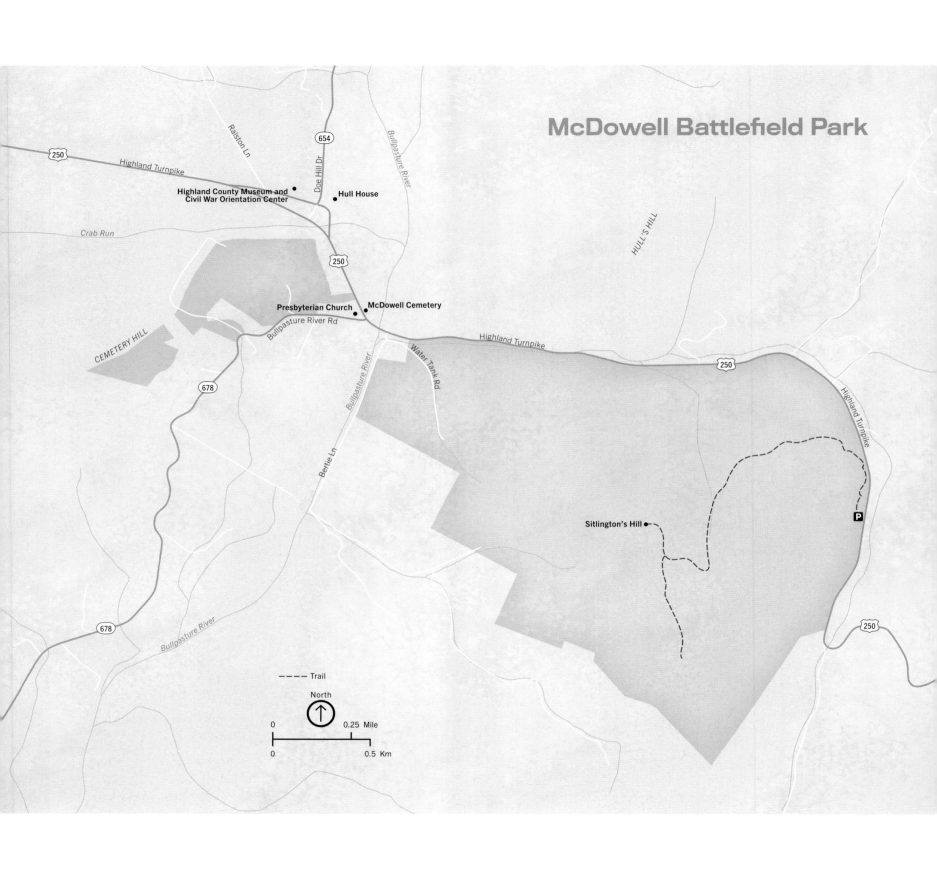

# McDowell Battlefield Park

250 Highland Turnpike

654

Ralston Ln

Doe Hill Dr

Bullpasture River

**Highland County Museum and Civil War Orientation Center**

**Hull House**

HULL'S HILL

Crab Run

250

**Presbyterian Church**  **McDowell Cemetery**

Bullpasture River Rd

Highland Turnpike

CEMETERY HILL

678

Bullpasture River

Water Tank Rd

Bertie Ln

250

Highland Turnpike

**Sitlington's Hill**

P

678

Bullpasture River

250

- - - - Trail

North
↑

0              0.25  Mile

0              0.5  Km

After more than a month of skirmishing with Banks's army, Jackson skillfully concealed his own army's intentions and slipped west out of the Shenandoah Valley into the Allegheny Mountains. On May 8, 1862, he advanced along the Parkersburg Turnpike west of Staunton toward McDowell, Virginia, where he met up with 2,800 men under Gen. Edward "Allegheny" Johnson. The Confederates, who now numbered 10,000 men, began deploying across the long, sinuous crest of Sitlington's Hill east of McDowell.

Milroy's force, which was camped in McDowell on the west side of the Bullpasture River, was reinforced around 10:00 a.m. by additional infantry under Gen. Robert Schenck. Milroy recommended a preemptive assault on Sitlington's Hill before Confederate artillery could be deployed on the high ground. Schenck, who was Milroy's superior, approved. At about 4:30 p.m., 2,300 Federal troops crossed the river and advanced up the hill. Their initial assault almost broke Johnson's right flank, but Jackson sent up reinforcements and the Federals were repulsed. A second assault targeted a salient in the Confederate center that was exposed to fire from two sides. Here the 12th Georgia Infantry—the only non-Virginians on the Southern side—took heavy casualties. Of its 540 men, the regiment suffered 180 casualties. Still, the Georgians stood their ground. "We did not come all this way to Virginia," exclaimed a Georgian private, "to run before Yankees." Jackson brought up additional reinforcements, and fierce fighting continued until about 10:00 p.m., when the Union troops finally withdrew.

Union casualties totaled 259 men, while the Confederates lost 420—one of the rare cases in the Civil War where attacking forces lost fewer men than the defenders. Jackson attempted to pursue the retreating Federals, but by the time his men started, Milroy and Schenck were already 13 miles away. The battle was the first victory of Jackson's famous Valley Campaign. Employing speed, audacity, and deception, Jackson's 17,000 men marched 646 miles in 48 days. They won several battles as they successfully engaged three separate Union armies totaling 52,000 men, and prevented any Federal forces from reinforcing McClellan's offensive against Richmond.

PREVIOUS SPREAD: Fort Edward Johnson, a network of Confederate earthworks on Shenandoah Mountain about five miles east of McDowell, Virginia. Gen. Edward "Allegheny" Johnson abandoned the position when the Confederates advanced west against Union forces at McDowell.

ABOVE: Union forces withdrew west from Sitlington's Hill through this hollow.

# MCDOWELL Battlefield Hike

This trail starts at the McDowell Battlefield parking area on the south side of US Route 250, approximately one mile west of the top of Bullpasture Mountain and two miles east of the village of McDowell.

### McDowell Battlefield Trail (1.4 miles one way)

This trail climbs 400 feet through steep ravines to the top of Sitlington's Hill and the core of the McDowell Battlefield. A good place to visit before starting the hike is the McDowell Battlefield Civil War Orientation Center at the Highland County Museum (behind Obaugh Funeral Home).

ABOVE: Wooded landscape along the McDowell Battlefield Trail up to Sitlington's Hill.
OPPOSITE: Bullpasture River through the McDowell Battlefield.

# THIRD WINCHESTER
## BATTLEFIELD

VIRGINIA  Third Winchester Battlefield Park

FOR MUCH OF THE CIVIL WAR, UNION GENERALS MET WITH HUMILIATION in Virginia's Shenandoah Valley. Because the valley is oriented from southwest to northeast between steep ridges of the Blue Ridge and Allegheny Mountains, it formed a natural avenue for Confederate invasion into the North. Harpers Ferry, where the waters of the Shenandoah River converge with the Potomac, was just 60 miles from Washington, DC.

In a six-week span during the spring of 1862, Gen. Thomas "Stonewall" Jackson outfoxed and outfought three Union generals in five separate battles, even though Federal forces possessed a considerable advantage in manpower. In September 1862, Jackson managed to surround Harpers Ferry and force its surrender. He captured almost 12,700 men—the largest single capture of Union troops during the entire war. During the 1863 Gettysburg Campaign, Gen. Robert E. Lee used the valley to advance virtually unseen into Maryland and Pennsylvania. Gen. Jubal Early enjoyed similar success in July 1864, when he marched down the valley with virtually no resistance, raiding the nation's capital and throwing a frightful scare into the Union high command.

In August 1864, Gen. Ulysses S. Grant had seen enough. On August 5, he convened a meeting of his generals at the Thomas House on the Monocacy Battlefield near Frederick, Maryland, where just a month before Early had defeated a small Union army. Here Grant devised a plan to drive Early from the Shenandoah Valley once and for all, and to systematically lay waste to "the breadbasket of the Confederacy."

Grant chose Gen. Philip Sheridan for the job. Sheridan was instructed not only to defeat Early's army and drive the Confederates out of the valley, but also to prevent the valley's abundance of wheat, corn, meat, and especially draft animals from aiding the Southern war effort any longer. On August 6, Grant told his

# Third Winchester Battlefield Park

Trail - - - -

North

↑

0        0.25  Mile

0              0.5  Km

Visitor Center

Trailhead

Confederate Flank Trail

Huntsberry Farm Trail

Huntsberry Farm

Cannon

Fence

ARTILLERY KNOLL

Huntsberry Farm Trail

Hackwood

Redbud Run

Battle Trail

Battle Trail

Middle Field Trail

MIDDLE FIELD

Fence

Middle Field Trail

SECOND WOODS

Union Trail

Redbud Run

Battle Trail

Union Trail

FIRST WOODS

Union Trail

Regency Lakes Dr

Trailhead

West Woods Trail

Regency Lakes Dr

Lake Wisdom Dr

Ash Hollow Run

First Woods Dr

Morgan Mill Rd

Trailhead

TownePlace Suites

Winchester Gateway

Regency Lakes Dr

WINCHESTER

Amoco Ln

Redbud Rd

Park Centre Dr

Redbud Run

Baker Ln

Baker Ln

Redbud Rd

Marquis Ct

Lick Run

Redbud Rd

Redbud Run

11

81

661

662

661

661

7

81

81

new general, "Give the enemy no rest ... do all the damage to railroads and crops you can. Carry off stock of all descriptions, and negroes, so as to prevent further planting. If the war is to last another year, we want the Shenandoah Valley to remain a barren waste."

One day later, on August 7, 1864, Sheridan took command of the Army of the Shenandoah at Harpers Ferry. Soon the town bulged with almost 50,000 troops. Quartermaster, commissary, and ordnance supplies were piled high in the old armory buildings, creating so much activity that Union Corp. Charlie Moulton wrote, "There was nothing but a perfect jam all day and night in the streets ..."

Still, Sheridan got off to a slow start. He spent much of August and early September probing Early's positions, skirmishing almost daily along a line generally running north-south along Opequon Creek. Union forces were deployed along the east side of the creek near Berryville, Summit Point, and Charles Town, West Virginia; the Confederates held positions just west of the creek between Winchester, Stephenson, and Brucetown, Virginia, using the Valley Pike as a crucial artery for moving troops, maintaining military supply, and managing communications. By mid-September, Grant had grown restless. The two generals conferred on September 17 in Charles Town, and agreed that Sheridan would begin his attacks within four days.

Early mistook Sheridan's lack of aggressiveness to mean he was reluctant to fight. He knew only too well that the Shenandoah had been the "valley of humiliation" for several Union commanders. As a consequence, he didn't hesitate to send his two largest infantry divisions, two brigades of cavalry, and an artillery battalion—totaling about 7,500 men—north to Martinsburg, West Virginia, on September 17. As it happened, this was the very same day Grant and Sheridan were meeting in Charles Town. Early's orders were to further disrupt operations along the Baltimore and Ohio Railroad.

Sheridan soon learned of the deployment, and decided it was a perfect opportunity to strike Early's divided army. Sheridan held a substantial advantage in manpower. His Army of the Shenandoah was composed of three infantry corps and three cavalry divisions totaling 39,000 men. Early's Army of the Valley totaled just 14,000 men—more than half of whom were now marching toward Martinsburg.

Before dawn on September 19, 1864, two Union corps advanced across Opequon Creek and through Berryville Canyon. Their target was the lone Confederate division of Gen. Stephen Ramseur, deployed across the Berryville Pike east of Winchester. Early immediately recognized the threat, and recalled his forces from Martinsburg. Meanwhile, Ramseur's troops succeeded in slowing the passage of the Union troops through the narrow canyon, which had quickly become clogged with soldiers, artillery caissons, and wagon trains.

It was midday before the Union Sixth and Nineteenth Corps were finally formed up for their attack. By then, the Confederate divisions of Gen. Robert Rodes and Gen. John Gordon had returned from Martinsburg and rejoined Ramseur's men. At 11:40 a.m., the two Federal corps advanced out of the woods and across a broad field toward the Confederate lines east of Winchester. Due to a bend in the Berryville Pike and the rough terrain, the Union columns became separated. Still, the attackers pressed on, succeeding in pushing the Confederate lines back through a second line of woods toward the Valley Pike. Rodes was killed

PREVIOUS SPREAD: Position of Maj. James Breathed's Confederate artillery battery on Third Winchester Battlefield.

ABOVE: Hackwood Lane through Third Winchester Battlefield.

FOLLOWING SPREAD: Smithfield Crossing on Opequon Creek, north of Winchester, Virginia. Confederate infantry clashed with Union cavalry here on August 29, 1864, in a prelude to the Third Battle of Winchester.

by an exploding shell. Some of Gordon's Georgians broke and fell back—the first time they had ever done so without orders. But a swift Southern counterattack exploited the gap in the Union line and drove the Federals back. The Second Division of Nineteenth Corps alone suffered 1,500 casualties in less than an hour.

Union reserve divisions blunted the Confederate counterattack, and for two hours the armies fired away at one another in a bloody stalemate. Sheridan finally called up his reserves, and around 3:00 p.m., Gen. George Crook's Army of West Virginia joined the fight with two fresh divisions. The division of Col. Isaac Duval advanced north of Redbud Run toward the Confederate left flank. Col. Rutherford B. Hayes, future president of the United States, led the assault across Redbud Run toward the Hackwood House. Hayes later wrote, "To stop was death. To go on was probably the same; but on we started again. . . . The rear and front lines and different regiments of the same line mingled together and reached the rebel side of the creek with lines and organizations broken; but all seemed inspired by the right spirit, and charged the rebel works pell-mell in the most determined manner."

Crook's First Division advanced along the south side of Redbud Run, supported by elements of the bloodied Sixth and Nineteenth Corps. The combined assaults were too much for the outnumbered Confederates. "For thirty minutes the battle that ensued was perfectly terrific," recalled one Union participant, "but then the forces in our front gave way, and in an instant we were over their works, and after them with yells and shouts of victory." Early reformed his lines closer to Winchester around Fort Collier, but a massed Union cavalry charge up the Valley Pike overwhelmed the Confederate left flank. A New York veteran later wrote, "The cavalry poured upon and rushed through a great herd of stampeding rebels." Early's line collapsed, and his army fled in disarray south through Winchester.

The Third Battle of Winchester was the bloodiest battle ever fought in the Shenandoah Valley. It resulted in more casualties than from Jackson's entire 1862 Valley Campaign. By the end of September 17, Sheridan had lost about 5,000 men. Early's army suffered about 3,600 casualties—fewer men, but still about 25 percent of his army. Winchester, which had changed hands some 72 times during the Civil War, changed hands for the last time.

OPPOSITE: Redbud Run. Col. Rutherford B. Hayes, future president of the United States, led a Union assault across the creek near here.

FOLLOWING SPREAD: Position of Maj. James Breathed's Confederate artillery battery on the Huntsberry Farm.

# THIRD WINCHESTER Battlefield Hikes

More than six miles of interconnected trails crisscross Third Winchester Battlefield. The terrain is predominantly flat except for short, steep climbs on either side of Redbud Run. A loop hike around the entire battlefield on portions of all three trails described below is about 5.8 miles long. Wayside exhibits at the trailhead and along each of the trails help explain the fighting that took place here. Visitors should park across the street from the Third Winchester Battlefield Visitor Center.

## Confederate Flank Trail
**(0.9 miles one way)**
This trail begins across Redbud Road from the visitor center at the Third Winchester Battlefield parking area, and ends on the south bank of Redbud Run, where it connects with the Battle Trail. The trail covers ground used by one of Gen. George Crook's divisions as it made a flanking march around the north end of the Confederate line and across Redbud Run during the afternoon of September 19, 1864. A side trail leads to the position of Confederate Maj. James Breathed's six-gun horse artillery battalion on the Huntsberry Farm.

## Battle Trail (2.2 miles)
This trail, which connects with the Confederate Flank Trail at Redbud Run, loops across the principal areas of combat during the battle, including the Middle Field, Second Woods, and West Woods. The Hackwood House, which sits on private property just west of the trail, was the sight of fierce fighting as Union forces turned the Confederate left flank. It was on this part of the battlefield where Col. George Patton Sr.—grandfather to US World War II Gen. George Patton Jr.—was fatally wounded.

## Union and Middle Field Trail (2.3 miles)
These trails connect with the Battle Trail at the western edge of the Middle Field. The trails pass through wooded terrain—now known as the First Woods—where Union commanders of the Sixth and Nineteenth Corps formed up their columns for the late-morning assault against the Confederates. The Middle Field Trail travels along a bluff above Redbud Run, revealing the difficult terrain facing Union troops who were separated along either side of the creek.

LEFT: A wooden footbridge carries the Confederate Flank Trail across Redbud Run.

OPPOSITE: Confederate Flank Trail through Third Winchester Battlefield.

# FISHER'S HILL
# BATTLEFIELD

VIRGINIA  Fisher's Hill Battlefield Park

FOLLOWING HIS DEFEAT AT THE THIRD BATTLE OF WINCHESTER, GEN. Jubal Early's Army of the Valley fell back from Winchester, Virginia, to Fisher's Hill, five miles south of Strasburg. Here a range of hills stretched across the Shenandoah Valley between Signal Knob and Little North Mountain, straddling the Valley Pike. "This was the only position in the whole Valley," wrote Early, "where a defensive line could be taken . . ." Early's army had been reduced to just 9,500 men, barely enough to hold the four-mile-long ridge. He hoped the natural strength of Fisher's Hill would discourage a Union attack. But Gen. Philip Sheridan would not be deterred, ever mindful of his orders from Gen. Ulysses S. Grant to "put himself south of the enemy, and follow him to the death."

Sheridan arrived at the base of Fisher's Hill on the evening of September 20, 1864. His forces marched with high spirits following their decisive victory at the Third Battle of Winchester just three days earlier. Union Lt. John Gould wrote, "I marched down that road with a grand consciousness that for once the Shenandoah had not been the 'Valley of Humiliation' . . . I began to feel that my days of retreating before a victorious enemy have ended." The Confederates, in contrast, despaired. Cavalryman John Opie wrote, "What was left of our army had now lost all confidence in General Early as a leader . . ."

Sheridan, recognizing that a frontal assault would "entail unnecessary destruction of life," met with his corps commanders to develop an alternative plan. Gen. George Crook, commander of the Army of West Virginia, recommended a flanking maneuver against the Confederate left, similar to the attack he had successfully executed at the Third Battle of Winchester. Sheridan approved the plan, and 5,500 men of Crook's Eighth Corps began their march on the evening of September 21.

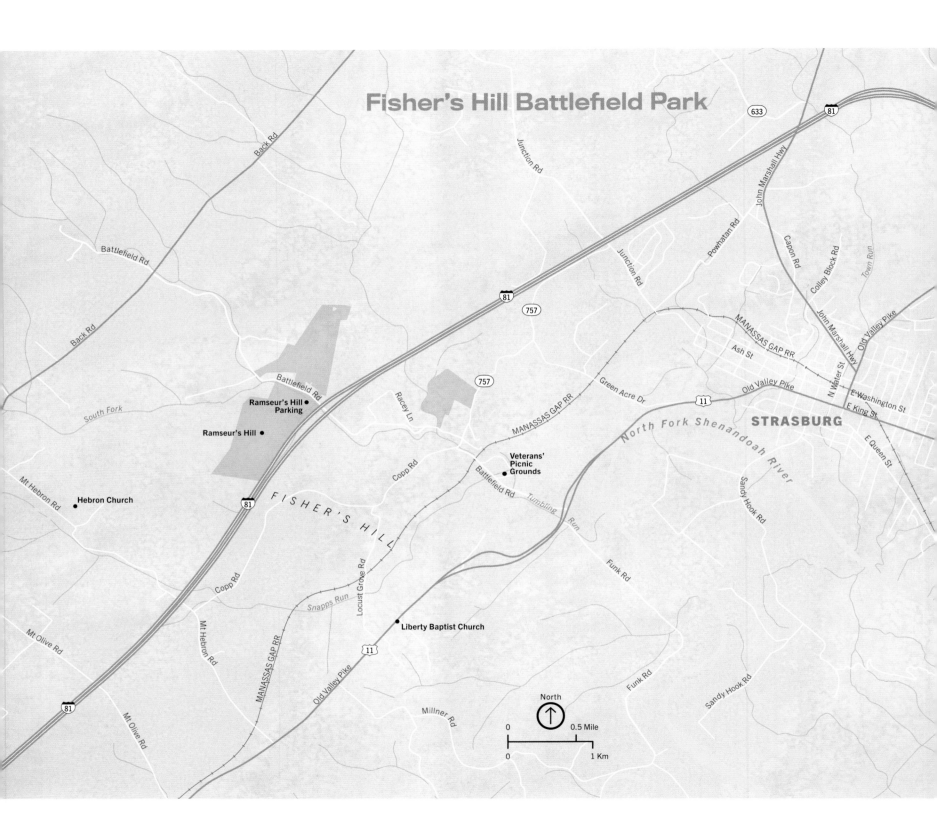

# Fisher's Hill Battlefield Park

633

81

Back Rd

Junction Rd

John Marshall Hwy

Battlefield Rd

Junction Rd

Powhatan Rd

Cabon Rd

Colley Block Rd

Town Run

81

757

Back Rd

MANASSAS GAP RR

Old Valley Pike

John Marshall Hwy

Ash St

N Water St

South Fork

Battlefield Rd

757

Racey Ln

Green Acre Dr

Old Valley Pike

E Washington St

Ramseur's Hill
Parking

MANASSAS GAP RR

**STRASBURG**

Ramseur's Hill

North Fork Shenandoah River

E King St

Copp Rd

Veterans'
Picnic
Grounds

Sandy Hook Rd

E Queen St

Mt Hebron Rd

Hebron Church

81

F I S H E R ' S   H I L L

Battlefield Rd

Tumbling Run

Copp Rd

Locust Grove Rd

Funk Rd

Mt Hebron Rd

MANASSAS GAP RR

Snapps Run

Liberty Baptist Church

Funk Rd

Mt Olive Rd

11

Old Valley Pike

Sandy Hook Rd

81

Mt Olive Rd

11

Millner Rd

North

0        0.5 Mile

0              1 Km

While the two divisions of Crook's corps marched, hidden by darkness and the woods of Little North Mountain, the Union Sixth and Nineteenth Corps massed north of Fisher's Hill, diverting attention from the flanking maneuver. At approximately 4:00 p.m. on September 22, 1864, Crook's men advanced down the wooded slopes of Little North Mountain directly into the Confederate left flank, "sweeping down their works like a western cyclone . . ."

Gen. Stephen Ramseur's division manned this part of Fisher's Hill, with only a thin line of cavalry covering the extreme left flank. Ramseur quickly reformed a brigade of Alabama infantry to face the assault, and they briefly stymied the Union attackers. But soon Crook's men turned the Alabama brigade's left flank. Col. Rutherford B. Hayes, future president of the United States, wrote, "They seemed to give up all hope of holding their works and fled in confusion toward the turnpike . . ."

In short order Ramseur's entire division gave way under the weight of the Federal attack. Early ordered the next division in line—Gen. John Pegram's—to stem the Union assault. But Pegram's regiments also gave way, and the remaining Confederate divisions on Fisher's Hill fell like dominoes from west to east. Early quickly ordered a withdrawal. As darkness fell his army was in full retreat southward on the Valley Pike. Confederate casualties totaled 1,235, while Sheridan lost just 528 men.

By September 25, Early's army had retreated all the way to Brown's Gap in the Blue Ridge Mountains, several miles southeast of Harrisonburg. With most of the Shenandoah Valley now cleared of Confederates,

PREVIOUS SPREAD: Ramseur's Hill.

BELOW: View looking across Ramseur's Hill.

# FISHER'S HILL Battlefield Hike

This trail starts at the Ramseur's Hill Trail parking area. Wayside exhibits at the trailhead and along the trail explain much of the fighting that took place here.

**Ramseur's Hill Trail** (1.4 miles)

The left flank of Gen. Jubal Early's infantry line was deployed across the top of this hill. Visitors can follow the battlefield trail to explore the Confederate position, which was the scene of the decisive fighting at the battle. The trail climbs approximately 170 feet to the top of the hill and provides excellent views of Signal Knob, the Blue Ridge Mountains, and the Shenandoah Valley.

Sheridan began the punitive operations of his mission, to "eat out Virginia clear and clean . . . so that crows flying over it for the balance of this season will have to carry their provender with them." In an action commonly referred to as "the Burning," Federal forces destroyed farms and crops, confiscated Negroes and livestock, and left behind "a barren waste."

On October 7, 1864, Sheridan reported to Grant, "I have destroyed over 2,000 barns filled with wheat, hay, and farming implements; over 70 mills, filled with flour and wheat; have driven in front of the army over 4,000 head of stock, and have killed and issued to the troops not less than 3,000 sheep." According to historian Gary Gallagher, Sheridan's siege of the valley "constituted the first large-scale demonstration that the strategy of exhaustion could accomplish the psychological and logistical damage envisioned by Grant." The destruction presaged the scorched-earth tactics of Gen. William Tecumseh Sherman's March to the Sea through Georgia. Instead of following the traditional strategy of merely cutting off military supply lines, Grant had turned his attention to the whole population of the Confederacy and its sustaining resources. The South would suffer these harsh tactics for the remainder of the war.

View looking west toward Little North Mountain from Ramseur's Hill.

WEST VIRGINIA
MARYLAND
PENNSYLVANIA

# HARPERS FERRY
## BATTLEFIELD

O N  S EPTEMBER  4 ,  1862 ,  ADVANCE  ELEMENTS  OF  THE  A RMY  OF  N ORTHERN Virginia crossed the Potomac River into Maryland at White's Ford, just 39 miles upstream from Washington, DC. Confederate Gen. Robert E. Lee was intent on carrying the war to the North. Invading Maryland would take the war out of Virginia, obtain much-needed supplies, damage Northern morale in advance of the November elections, and potentially liberate Maryland, a slave-holding state that stayed with the Union but was divided in its sympathies.

The main body of Lee's army, some 40,000 strong, encamped around Frederick, Maryland. Lee expected the Union garrison at Harpers Ferry—now cut off from the nation's capital and Gen. George McClellan's Army of the Potomac—to retreat northward, clearing the way for him to establish communications through the Shenandoah Valley. But Union commanders had other ideas.

Harpers Ferry was garrisoned by the Railroad Brigade, comprising some 14,000 Union troops entrusted with guarding the Baltimore and Ohio Railroad. The garrison was commanded by Col. Dixon Miles, a 59-year-old veteran of the Mexican War, where he was brevetted three times for gallant and distinguished service. Unfortunately, his reputation was ruined at the Battle of First Manassas, where he was accused of drunkenness while commanding the Union's reserve division. Although cleared of the charges, the damage was done, and Miles's career was irreparably tarnished.

On September 5, 1862, Miles received a clear directive from Gen. John Wool in Baltimore: "Be energetic and active, and defend all places to the last extremity. There must be no abandonment of a post, and shoot the first man that thinks of it . . ." Two days later Gen. Henry Halleck, President Lincoln's general in chief, reiterated

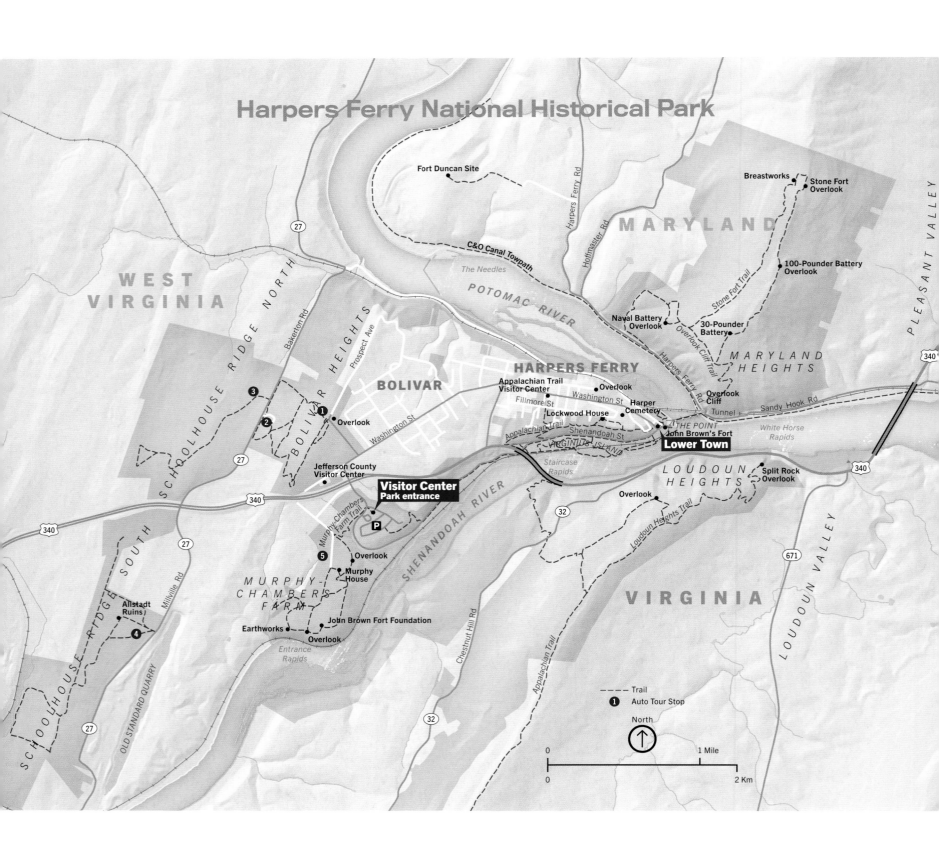

# Harpers Ferry National Historical Park

Fort Duncan Site

Breastworks  Stone Fort Overlook

Harpers Ferry Rd

Hoffmaster Rd

MARYLAND

C&O Canal Towpath

The Needles

100-Pounder Battery Overlook

Stone Fort Trail

27

WEST VIRGINIA

POTOMAC RIVER

Naval Battery Overlook

30-Pounder Battery

MARYLAND HEIGHTS

Bakerton Rd

SCHOOLHOUSE RIDGE NORTH

BOLIVAR HEIGHTS

Prospect Ave

Overlook Cliff Trail

HARPERS FERRY

Appalachian Trail Visitor Center

Overlook

Washington St

Harpers Ferry Rd

Overlook Cliff

340

BOLIVAR

Fillmore St

Lockwood House

Harper Cemetery

Tunnel

Sandy Hook Rd

3

Appalachian Trail

Shenandoah St

THE POINT

White Horse Rapids

1

Overlook

Washington St

VIRGINIUS ISLAND

John Brown's Fort

**Lower Town**

2

27

Jefferson County Visitor Center

Staircase Rapids

LOUDOUN HEIGHTS

Split Rock Overlook

340

**Visitor Center**
Park entrance

Overlook

340

P

32

671

Murphy-Chambers Farm Trail

SHENANDOAH RIVER

27

5

Overlook

Murphy House

MURPHY-CHAMBERS FARM

VIRGINIA

SCHOOLHOUSE RIDGE SOUTH

Millville Rd

Allstadt Ruins

John Brown Fort Foundation

Appalachian Trail

LOUDOUN VALLEY

4

Earthworks

Overlook

Entrance Rapids

Chestnut Hill Rd

OLD STANDARD QUARRY

27

32

- - - Trail

1 Auto Tour Stop

North
↑

0 _____ 1 Mile

0 _____ 2 Km

the order: "Our army in motion. It is important that Harper's Ferry be held to the latest moment. The Government has the utmost confidence in you, and is ready to give you full credit for the defense it expects you to make."

Harpers Ferry, situated at the foot of the Shenandoah Valley where the Potomac and Shenandoah Rivers converge, had already paid dearly for its strategic location. It served as a railroad junction, river crossing, and, from 1799 to 1861, home to a federal armory and arsenal—the same site John Brown had raided in 1859. The day after Virginia seceded from the Union, on April 18, 1861, Federal forces set fire to the armory and arsenal buildings as 360 Virginia troops advanced on the town. By the time the militiamen entered Harpers Ferry, the Large Arsenal, Small Arsenal, and some 15,000 arms were consumed by fire. Just two months later, Confederate troops blew up the Baltimore and Ohio Railroad bridge and completed the destruction of the abandoned armory buildings. In four years of war, the town changed hands no fewer than eight times. On June 20, 1863, Harpers Ferry even changed states, becoming part of West Virginia when Virginia's western counties seceded and rejoined the Union.

To deal with the threat posed by Harpers Ferry to his routes of supply and communication, Lee issued Special Orders, No. 191. His instructions boldly divided the Army of Northern Virginia into four parts. One part, under the command of Gen. James Longstreet, was instructed to advance toward Hagerstown, Maryland. Gen. Thomas "Stonewall" Jackson, placed in overall command of the three remaining columns, was directed to capture Harpers Ferry. Jackson was perfect for the mission; he had served almost two months as commander of the Virginia troops at Harpers Ferry when the war began. His knowledge of the terrain was invaluable and helped mitigate the extraordinary risk of dividing his columns into three separate wings.

One column, commanded by Gen. John Walker, crossed the Potomac River near Point of Rocks 10 miles downstream from Harpers Ferry and proceeded to Loudoun Heights. Gen. Lafayette McLaws's column was ordered to take Maryland Heights, which at 1,448 feet was the tallest of the ridges surrounding Harpers Ferry. McLaws understood the topography well: "So long as Maryland Heights was occupied by the enemy," he wrote, "Harper's Ferry could never be occupied by

us. If we gained possession of the heights, the town was no longer tenable to them."

Jackson led the third column, marching west from Frederick to Boonsboro, Maryland, crossing the Potomac River at Williamsport, and forcing Federal troops to evacuate Martinsburg, Virginia. Around noon on September 13, Jackson's troops took up positions along Schoolhouse Ridge immediately west of Harpers Ferry. At the same time two of McLaws's infantry brigades advanced south along the crest of Elk Ridge—the northern extension of Maryland Heights. Rebel yells echoed up the steep slopes as Confederate troops made their way through rugged ravines and tangled vegetation. The untested 126th New York, in the army fewer than two weeks, faced its first fire standing beside the veteran 39th New York and 32nd Ohio. The Union troops put up "a most obstinate and determined resistance." But chaos and confusion swept the line after Col. Eliakim Sherrill of the 126th New York was wounded. Col. Thomas Ford, Union commander on Maryland Heights, requested reinforcements, but none arrived. Inexplicably, the order was given for the troops to fall back. After nine hours of fierce fighting,

PREVIOUS SPREAD: View of Harpers Ferry and the confluence of the Shenandoah (left) and Potomac Rivers from Split Rock Overlook on Loudoun Heights.

BELOW: Company A, 22nd New York State Militia, in column formation on Camp Hill in 1862. A Union camp is visible in the distance on Bolivar Heights.

Union troops fled down the mountain, handing the high ground to McLaws.

By 10:00 a.m. on September 14, Walker accomplished what Miles had considered impossible—positioning artillery along the undefended crest of Loudoun Heights. Miles had failed to post a single unit here, assuming Union artillery on Maryland Heights would command the 1,200-foot ridge that towered above the Shenandoah River. At about 1:00 p.m. Walker's guns opened fire on Harpers Ferry. McLaws's guns on Maryland Heights and Jackson's artillery along Schoolhouse Ridge joined the bombardment.

The intensity of the barrage severely shook the spirit of the Federal troops. Col. William Trimble of the 60th Ohio wrote that there was "not a place where you could lay the palm of your hand and say it was safe." Capt. Samuel Armstrong of the 125th New York painted an even grimmer picture: "I tell you it is dreadful to be a mark for artillery. Bad enough for any but especially for raw troops; it demoralizes them—it rouses one's courage to be able to fight in return, but to sit still and calmly be cut in two is too much to ask."

Still, the Union garrison held out. Jackson, pressed to finish the job and rejoin Lee in Maryland, had one more move up his sleeve. On the evening of September 14 he launched a night assault against Federal skirmishers on Bolivar Heights—the only ridge at Harpers Ferry still in Union hands. This feigned attack was successful in diverting attention from the surreptitious movements of Gen. A. P. Hill. Throughout the night, Hill's men dragged five batteries up steep ravines along the Shenandoah River to the plateau at the Chambers Farm, planting his artillery 1,000 yards from the exposed Union left flank. Hill later wrote that "the fate of Harpers Ferry was sealed."

The Union garrison, surrounded by 23,000 Confederates and out of long-range shells to answer the artillery barrage, surrendered on the morning of September 15. At around 9:00 a.m. white flags were raised all along Bolivar Heights. Minutes later, a stray Confederate shell exploded directly behind Miles, mortally wounding the ill-fated Union commander. Jackson captured almost 12,700 men at Harpers Ferry—the largest single capture of Union troops during the entire war. The Confederates also seized 73 cannon, 200 wagons, and about 13,000 small arms. Jackson was finally free to rejoin Lee at the pivotal Battle of Antietam just 17 miles away in Sharpsburg, Maryland.

BELOW, LEFT: Stone Fort ruins at the summit of Maryland Heights.

BELOW, RIGHT: John Brown's Fort.

OPPOSITE: Union soldier from Company A, 22nd New York State Militia, poses for a photograph on Camp Hill in 1862.

OPPOSITE: Union artillery position on Bolivar Heights.

RIGHT, TOP: View of St. Peter's Church and the Potomac River from Jefferson Rock.

RIGHT, BOTTOM: Bridge pier ruins in the Shenandoah River.

# HARPERS FERRY Battlefield Hikes

Several trails crisscross the riverbanks and heights that surround Harpers Ferry, West Virginia. Hikes are moderate to strenuous, with the most challenging trails on Loudoun Heights and Maryland Heights. Visitors should start at the national park visitor center on Cavalier Heights, where detailed trail maps are available.

## Bolivar Heights-Skirmish Line Trail
### (0.3 to 2.4 miles)

This trail starts at the Bolivar Heights parking area (Auto Tour Stop 1). Bolivar Heights was the last position Union forces held before surrendering to Gen. Thomas "Stonewall" Jackson on September 15, 1862. The easiest walk is the 0.3-mile Crest Loop on top of Bolivar Heights. The Upper Loop (1.3 miles) continues along the crest of the ridge, passing infantry trenches and an artillery redoubt, and provides excellent views of Maryland Heights, Loudoun Heights, and the gap between them where the Potomac River flows to the east. The hike continues down a wooded trail to a lovely view of Schoolhouse Ridge. Visitors can extend their hike through the field by following the Union Skirmish Line Loop, for a total of 2.4 miles.

## Camp Hill-Virginius Island-Hall's Island Trail (2.0 to 3.0 miles)

This trail passes the Commanding Officers Quarters on Camp Hill, where President Abraham Lincoln spent the night after conferring with Union Gen. George McClellan following the Battle of Antietam. Several abandoned armory residences served as officer's quarters and housed troops throughout the war. Hikers can explore the industrial ruins of Hall's Rifle Works and Virginius Island along the Shenandoah River shoreline and follow a section of the Appalachian Trail up to Jefferson Rock. Here Thomas Jefferson stood on October 25, 1783, describing the scene in his *Notes on the State of Virginia*: "The passage of the Patowmac through the Blue Ridge is perhaps one of the most stupendous scenes in Nature."

## Loudoun Heights Trail (7.5 miles)

This path follows the Appalachian Trail across the Shenandoah River to a steep climb up Loudoun Heights. Visitors can hike through an old government timberland where trees were cut for charcoal—essential fuel for the armory forges in the 19th century; see ruins of a Union blockhouse; and enjoy one of the best views of Harpers Ferry and the Potomac River from Split Rock.

## Maryland Heights Trail (4.5 or 6.5 miles)

This trail starts at John Brown's Fort in the Lower Town Historic District. Visitors can hike across the Potomac River and along the old Chesapeake and Ohio Canal before ascending the steep slopes of Maryland Heights. The trail to the spectacular overlook cliffs passes Civil War powder magazines and an artillery battery. For a longer hike (6.5 miles), visitors can continue up the mountain to the 1,448-foot summit. So steep is the terrain here that Lt. Charles Morse, who guided President Abraham Lincoln up these same slopes on October 2, 1862, later wrote, "I showed the way until we got to a path where it was right straight up, when Abraham backed out." The trail to the summit skirts the remains of infantry trenches, artillery redoubts, a military camp, and an unfinished stone fort.

## Murphy-Chambers Farm Trail
### (1.5 or 2.7 miles)

This hike starts either at the Murphy-Chambers Farm parking area (Auto Tour Stop 5) or at the Cavalier Heights Visitor Center. For almost 15 years, from 1895 to 1909, John Brown's Fort stood on this farm. Visitors can follow this trail to learn about the fort's curious travels, and to see the positions Gen. A. P. Hill's artillery batteries took when they sealed the fate of the Union garrison on September 15, 1862. The farm also affords an excellent view of the Shenandoah River upstream from Harpers Ferry.

## Schoolhouse Ridge South Trail
### (1.2 or 2.5 miles)

This hike starts at the Schoolhouse Ridge South parking area on Millville Road (Auto Tour Stop 4). Visitors can hike across the south end of Schoolhouse Ridge, which includes Courtney's Battery Trail (1.2 miles) and the Allstadt Farm Trail (2.5 miles).

## Schoolhouse Ridge North Trail
### (1.75 miles)

This hike starts at the Schoolhouse Ridge North parking area just off Bakerton Road (Auto Tour Stop 3). Visitors can hike across the north end of Schoolhouse Ridge on the Moler Farm Trail, where Confederate forces completed the encirclement of the Union garrison at Harpers Ferry on September 13, 1862.

Armorer's house, circa 1834, on Camp Hill. Several Union soldiers from Company A, 22nd New York State Militia, were photographed in front of this house in 1862.

# ANTIETAM
## BATTLEFIELD

MARYLAND  Antietam National Battlefield

MISSED OPPORTUNITIES AND BAD LUCK HAD PLAGUED BOTH THE UNION and Confederate armies as they prepared to square off in Sharpsburg, a quiet rural farming community in western Maryland. Gen. Robert E. Lee had invaded Maryland to press the offensive against the North. But the delay in securing the surrender of Harpers Ferry, and news that Gen. George McClellan was uncharacteristically pressing the attack against the gaps in South Mountain, forced him to play defense. McClellan, on the other hand, had uncovered the entire Confederate battle plan when Lee's "Lost Orders" fell into his hands, but he failed to press his advantage and catch the divided Confederates. If the "Lost Orders" had never been found, or if Harpers Ferry had held out for just one more day, the course of the campaign—and maybe the entire war—might have changed.

Lee's bold plan to divide his army into four columns was conceived and executed at Frederick on September 9, 1862. Special Orders, No. 191, as Lee's written instructions to his commanders were called, spelled out the deployment of Confederate forces in considerable detail. How fortuitous it was that just four days later, as McClellan's Army of the Potomac settled into its camps around Frederick on the heels of Lee's army, a Union soldier found a copy of the document. About noon on September 13, Corp. Barton Mitchell of the 27th Indiana Volunteers discovered an envelope with three cigars wrapped in a piece of paper lying on the ground. The "Lost Orders" were taken to McClellan, who quickly realized the importance of the find. "Now I know what to do!" he confided to a subordinate. "Here is a paper with which, if I cannot whip Bobby Lee, I will be willing to go home."

Just one day later, on September 14, 1862, Union soldiers advanced against Confederate forces guarding the gaps on South Mountain. Hotly contested engagements at Crampton's Gap, Fox's Gap, and Turner's Gap

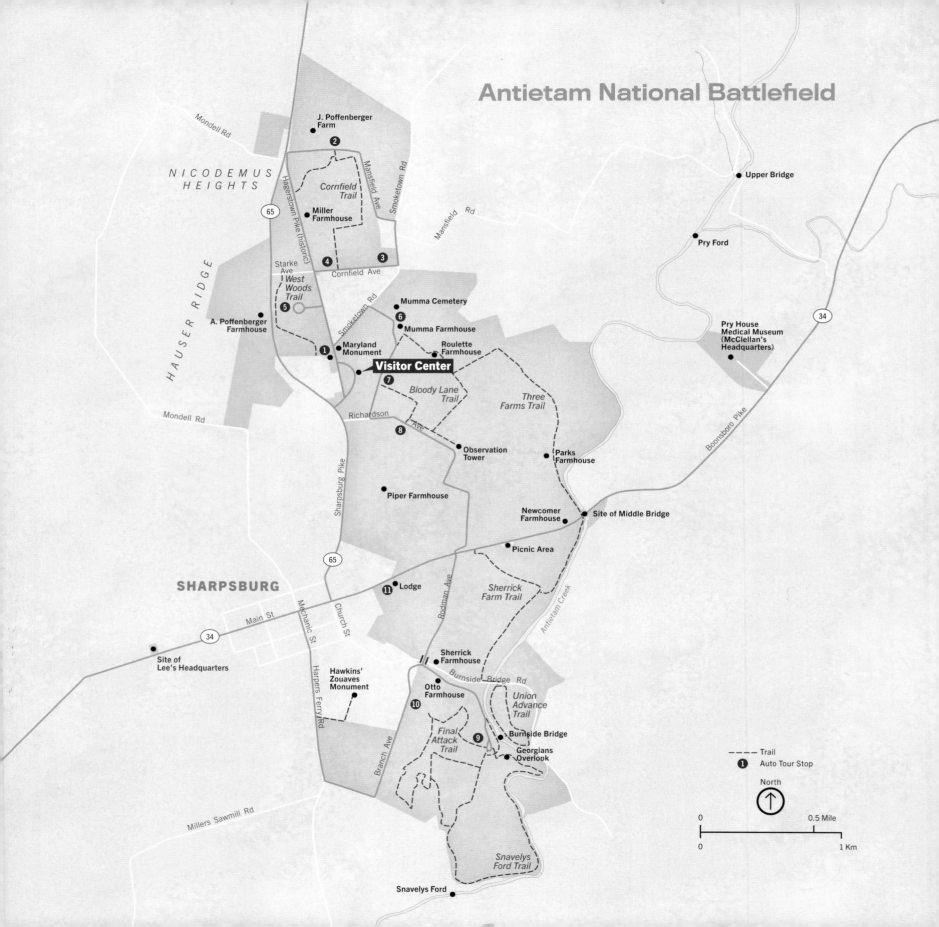

# Antietam National Battlefield

Mondell Rd

J. Poffenberger Farm
**2**

Upper Bridge

*NICODEMUS HEIGHTS*

Mansfield Rd

Pry Ford

*Cornfield Trail*

Smoketown Rd

65

Hagerstown Pike (historic)

Miller Farmhouse

Pry House Medical Museum (McClellan's Headquarters)

34

*HAUSER RIDGE*

Starke Ave

**4**          **3**

Cornfield Ave

*West Woods Trail*

A. Poffenberger Farmhouse

**5**

Mumma Cemetery

Smoketown Rd

**6**

Mumma Farmhouse

Roulette Farmhouse

**1**   Maryland Monument

**Visitor Center**

Mondell Rd

**7**

*Bloody Lane Trail*

*Three Farms Trail*

Richardson

Ave

**8**

Observation Tower

Parks Farmhouse

Sharpsburg Pike

Piper Farmhouse

Newcomer Farmhouse

Site of Middle Bridge

Boonsboro Pike

65

Picnic Area

**SHARPSBURG**

**11**  Lodge

Rodman Ave

*Sherrick Farm Trail*

Antietam Creek

Main St

Mechanic St

Church St

34

Site of Lee's Headquarters

Sherrick Farmhouse

Burnside Bridge Rd

Harpers Ferry Rd

Hawkins' Zouaves Monument

Otto Farmhouse

*Union Advance Trail*

**10**

Branch Ave

*Final Attack Trail*

**9**   Burnside Bridge

Georgians Overlook

Millers Sawmill Rd

*Snavelys Ford Trail*

Snavelys Ford

- - - - Trail

**1**  Auto Tour Stop

North

↑

0                    0.5 Mile

0                         1 Km

forced the Confederates to retreat. But not quickly enough. Their stubborn resistance, and the timely surrender of the Union garrison at Harpers Ferry, gave Lee just enough time to reassemble his forces on the low ridge between Antietam Creek and the Potomac River around the town of Sharpsburg.

The Confederate forces occupied a formidable defensive position along the high ground west of Antietam Creek. Gen. James Longstreet's command held the center and right of the Confederate line, while Gen. Thomas "Stonewall" Jackson's men, recently arrived from their capture of Harpers Ferry, held the left. Lee's position was strengthened with the mobility afforded by the Hagerstown Turnpike that ran north and south along the ridge.

Over the next two days, September 15 and 16, McClellan deployed his forces east of the creek. The Army of the Potomac held a numerical advantage—approximately 75,500 men to the Army of Northern Virginia's 40,000. But the uneven ground east of Antietam Creek made maneuvering such a large army more difficult, requiring careful coordination of troop dispositions and movements. McClellan's plan was to attack Lee's left and when "matters looked favorably" attack the Confederate right. Succeeding in either assault, McClellan would then strike at Lee's center. Any failure to coordinate these attacks across the Union front would severely hinder the battle plan.

At dawn on September 17, 1862, three separate Union attacks, advancing from north to south, struck hard at the Confederate left. Gen. Joseph Hooker's First Corps made the initial assault, followed by Gen. Joseph Mansfield's Twelfth Corps. Part of Gen. Edwin Sumner's Second Corps made the final assault. But already McClellan's battle plan began to break down into a series of uncoordinated attacks. Nearly three hours of savage, unprecedented fighting raged across the Cornfield, East Woods, and West Woods. Repeated Union attacks and equally vicious Confederate counterattacks swept back and forth across the battlefield. A storm of cannonballs, canister, and musket balls took a terrible toll on attackers and defenders alike. Despite the Union army's numerical advantage, Jackson's forces near the Dunker Church held their ground.

The horrific clash on the Confederate left caused nearly 8,550 combined casualties. Hooker described the scene in a letter that still resonates today: "In the time I am writing, every stalk of corn in the northern and greater part of the field was cut as closely as could have been done with a knife, and the slain lay in rows precisely as they had stood in their ranks a few moments before. It was never my fortune to witness a more bloody, dismal battlefield."

The battle now shifted to the Confederate center, where the Sunken Road became the next killing ground. The late-morning Union advance here was met by two brigades of Confederate defenders deployed along the old country lane. For about three hours 2,200 Confederates, later reinforced by additional troops, held off the attacks of Gen. William French's division and Gen. Israel Richardson's division, totaling nearly 10,000 men. The Sunken Road provided a perfect breastwork for the Confederate defenders, and each Union assault was repulsed with murderous fire. Finally, after a considerable loss of life, Richardson's troops managed to turn the right flank and fire down into the sunken lane. The Confederate line crumbled, but the Union attackers had suffered too many

PREVIOUS SPREAD: Union artillery piece in a barley field on the Miller Farm.

BELOW: Dead soldiers lying in front of the Dunker Church on Antietam Battlefield.

casualties to press their advantage. Seeing the dead in the Sunken Road, an observer wrote, "They were lying in rows like the ties of a railroad, in heaps like cordwood mingled with the splintered and shattered fence rails. Words are inadequate to portray the scene." The old country road became known from that day forward as the "Bloody Lane."

Throughout the morning, as threats emerged across different parts of the battlefield, Lee was able to shift his men to withstand each of the uncoordinated Union thrusts. The next threat emerged a mile and a half south of the Sunken Road on the Confederate right. Here Antietam Creek separated the two armies, and Gen. Ambrose Burnside needed to push his men across the stone bridge that would later bear his name. Burnside commanded 50 guns and four divisions totaling some 12,500 troops. Opposing him on the steep ridge across the creek were two artillery batteries and

about 400 men of the 2nd and 20th Georgia Regiments. Two attempts to storm the bridge directly were repulsed. A third attempt launched just after noon finally succeeded, but only after Gen. Isaac Rodman's division was able to cross Antietam Creek at Snavelys Ford two miles downstream and threaten the Georgians' flank. The Confederates had succeeded in delaying Burnside's advance for three hours.

The Union delays continued. After taking the stone bridge at 1:00 p.m., Burnside spent two more hours reorganizing his forces before advancing across the arduous terrain between Antietam Creek and the village of Sharpsburg. The delay proved critical. Just as the Union advance began to push into Lee's right flank, Gen. A. P. Hill's reinforcements, arriving in late afternoon after a forced march of 17 miles from Harpers Ferry, stopped him. The battle ended at about 6:00 p.m. In 12 hours of ferocious fighting, the lines of battle

**OPPOSITE:** Union signal station on Elk Mountain, Maryland, overlooking Antietam Battlefield in October 1862.

**ABOVE:** View looking across Antietam Battlefield.

had not shifted significantly. Of the nearly 100,000 soldiers engaged in the battle, about 23,000 were killed, wounded, or missing. More Americans died in battle on September 17, 1862, than on any other day in the nation's military history.

The next day, September 18, the opposing armies gathered their wounded and buried their dead. Later that night the Confederates withdrew back across the Potomac River to Virginia, ending Lee's first invasion into the North. Although the battle ended in a draw, Lee's retreat gave President Abraham Lincoln the "victory" he needed to issue the Emancipation Proclamation. This document reshaped the Civil War, giving the conflict two goals: to preserve the Union and end slavery.

The battle also brought a pioneering nurse into the spotlight. Seeing the bandages, lanterns, and food Clara Barton brought to wounded soldiers in his Antietam hospital, surgeon Charles Dunn christened her the "Angel of the Battlefield." Barton went on to found the American Red Cross in 1881.

BELOW: Maryland Monument.

OPPOSITE: Burnside Bridge and Antietam Creek.

LEFT, TOP: Bloody Lane, showing the 132nd Pennsylvania Infantry Monument and observation tower.

LEFT, BOTTOM: Private Soldier Monument, Antietam National Cemetery.

OPPOSITE: Winter view of Bloody Lane. During the annual Battlefield Illumination, 23,000 candles are placed on the battlefield to show the number of casualties that occurred here in a single day.

FOLLOWING SPREAD: Bloody Lane Trail through Antietam Battlefield.

# ANTIETAM Battlefield Hikes

Antietam National Battlefield has almost 13 miles of trails. Hikes are generally easier across the northern part of the battlefield and become more strenuous in the steeper terrain around Burnside Bridge in the park's southern section. Hikers should start at the visitor center north of Sharpsburg, Maryland, where detailed trail maps are available.

### Cornfield Trail (1.5 miles)

This trail starts and ends at the North Woods parking area (Auto Tour Stop 2). The path covers most of the area where the early morning fighting took place. Lt. Matthew Graham, Company H, 9th New York Volunteers, later described the carnage: "I was lying on my back, supported on my elbows, watching the shells explode overhead and speculating as to how long I could hold up my finger before it would be shot off, for the very air seemed full of bullets . . ." There were more casualties in and around the Cornfield than anywhere else on the battlefield.

### Bloody Lane Trail (1.6 miles)

This hike starts at the Sunken Road parking area (Auto Tour Stop 8). The trail winds through the historic Mumma and Roulette Farms, following in the footsteps of Union soldiers as they advanced against murderous Confederate fire from the Sunken Road. Visitors can climb the battlefield's only observation tower for a panoramic view of the entire area, or walk through the Sunken Road and survey the Confederate position in what has since become known as the Bloody Lane.

### West Woods Trail (1.5 miles)

This hike begins at the West Woods parking area (Auto Tour Stop 5). Throughout the morning of the battle, the Union army launched numerous attacks in and around this woodlot, attempting to drive the Confederates from the field. Gen. John Sedgwick's Union division lost more than 2,000 killed and wounded during one of these attacks in the West Woods.

### Sherrick Farm Trail (1.3 miles)

This trail starts at the intersection of the park tour road and State Route 34. It meanders through farm fields and woodlots typical of Antietam. The trail ends at the famous Burnside Bridge. Visitors should use extra caution when crossing the modern Burnside Bridge Road.

### Three Farms Trail (1.6 miles)

This trail connects to the Bloody Lane Trail in the north and the Sherrick Farm Trail in the south. It also takes hikers to some of the quietest and most beautiful areas of the park. For groups or others with more than one vehicle, a great option is to park one car at the visitor center and a second car at Burnside Bridge, and walk from one end of the battlefield to the other.

### Union Advance Trail (1.0 mile)

This hike begins at the Burnside Bridge parking area (Auto Tour Stop 9) and explores both sides of Antietam Creek at Burnside Bridge. Visitors can see where two Confederate regiments totaling just 400 men on the west side of the creek held off four Union divisions for almost three hours, and then cross over Burnside Bridge to positions on the east side of the creek where the Union Ninth Corps made its assaults to capture the bridge. Here visitors can judge for themselves whether Henry Kyd Douglas, a member of Gen. Thomas "Stonewall" Jackson's staff, was observant or sarcastic when he wrote about Burnside Bridge after the battle: "Go and look at it, and tell me if you don't think Burnside and his corps might have executed a hop, skip, and jump and landed on the other side. One thing is certain, they might have waded it that day without getting their waist belts wet in any place."

### Final Attack Trail (1.7 miles)

This hike starts at the Burnside Bridge parking area (Auto Tour Stop 9). After capturing Burnside Bridge, more than 8,000 Union soldiers crossed Antietam Creek. They marched across the fields where the trail is located for the final assault to drive the Confederates from Maryland, only to be turned back by Gen. A. P. Hill's timely arrival. The steep, rugged terrain across this part of the battlefield helps explain why it took Burnside two hours to organize his columns before advancing.

### Snavelys Ford Trail (1.8 miles)

This hike begins at the Burnside Bridge parking area (Auto Tour Stop 9). The Snavelys Ford Trail follows Antietam Creek for much of its length. The hike is mostly flat and shady except for one uphill climb at the end of the trail.

### Crampton Gap, Fox Gap, and Turners Gap Trail (6.5 miles one way)

These three gaps along South Mountain—about nine miles east of Sharpsburg—saw fierce fighting on September 14, 1862, as Gen. George McClellan's Union forces pursued Gen. Robert E.

Lee's divided army. About 12,000 Confederate defenders held off advance units of the Army of the Potomac, withdrawing after dark in the face of overwhelming numbers. Today the Appalachian Trail connects all three battlefields. Visitors can base their hike at Crampton Gap, site of Gathland State Park and the War Correspondents Memorial, dedicated to 157 war reporters, artists, and photographers who documented the Civil War.

OPPOSITE: Roulette Farm.

ABOVE: Pry House, which served as Gen. George McClellan's headquarters.

# GETTYSBURG
## BATTLEFIELD

PENNSYLVANIA  Gettysburg National Military Park

ACCORDING TO NATIONAL PARK SERVICE STATISTICS, MORE THAN ONE million people visit Gettysburg every year. The popularity of the battlefield is nothing new: in 1899, 9,000 vehicles carrying 36,000 people traveled the roads through the battlefield in just one month. Today visitors can tour the battlefield by automobile, bicycle, tour bus, scooter, Segway, horse-drawn carriage, on horseback, and yes, even on foot. Perhaps more than any other battlefield, Gettysburg defines the Civil War not only for most Americans, but also for foreign visitors. For many, it is the only Civil War battlefield they ever visit.

President Abraham Lincoln, in his second inaugural address, said that on "the progress of our arms . . . all else chiefly depends." Gettysburg was no exception. The battle turned back Confederate Gen. Robert E. Lee's most ambitious invasion of the North, defined the "high water mark of the Confederacy," and gave us the Gettysburg Address—Lincoln's poignant speech that proclaimed the Civil War as a struggle for the preservation of the Union, with "a new birth of freedom" that would bring true equality to all of its citizens. Gettysburg also marked the bloodiest three days of combat during the entire Civil War.

Following his drubbing of Gen. Joseph Hooker—the Army of the Potomac's third commander in two years—at Chancellorsville, Lee again took the initiative against his Union adversary. It was time to shift the fighting away from war-torn Virginia, where Lee was unable to provide sufficient food for his army or forage for his horses. An invasion of Pennsylvania would provide access to rich farmlands. Victory would also bolster the Northern Peace Democrats, who favored a negotiated end to the war. And the morale of his soldiers had never been higher: "The troops of Lee were now at the zenith of their perfection and glory," wrote Lt. D. Augustus Dickert of South Carolina. According to Col. Edward Alexander, "Nothing gave me much concern as long as

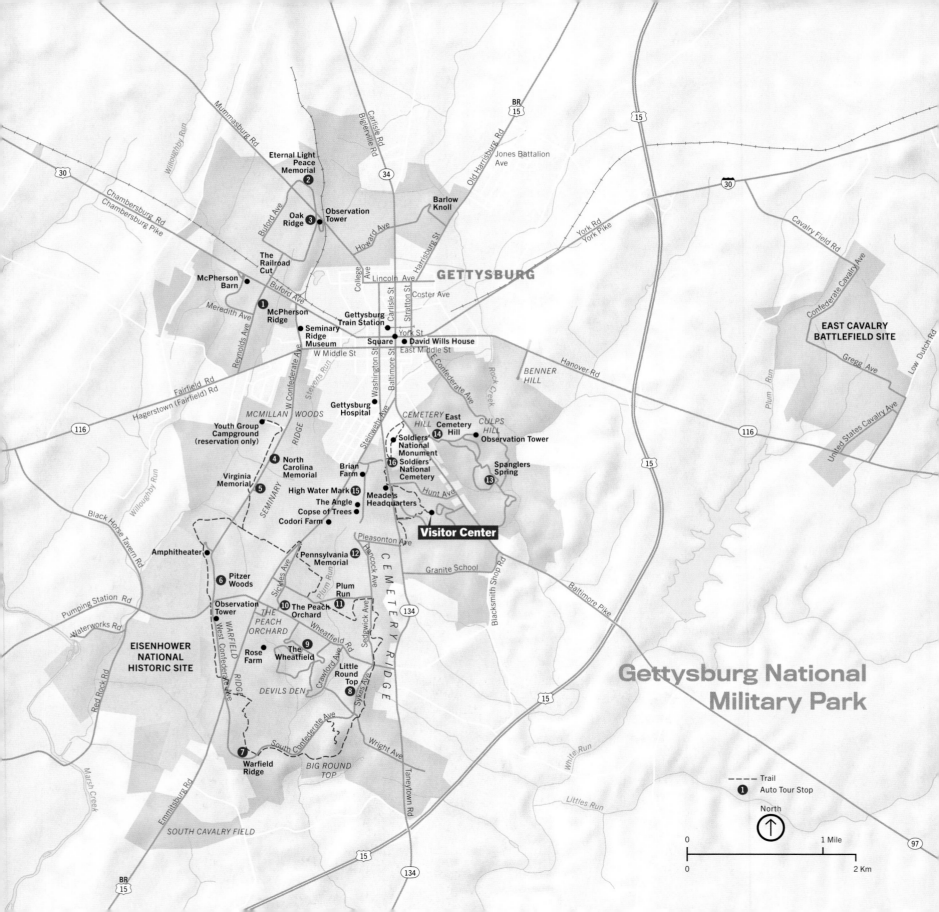

**Gettysburg National Military Park**

Mummasburg Rd

BR 15

30

Willoughby Run

Chambersburg Rd
Chambersburg Pike

Carlisle Rd

Biglerville Rd

34

Old Harrisburg Rd

Jones Battalion Ave

15

30

Eternal Light Peace Memorial **2**

Oak Ridge **3**   Observation Tower

Barlow Knoll

Buford Ave

Howard Ave

Harrisburg St

Cavalry Field Rd

Confederate Cavalry Ave

The Railroad Cut

McPherson Barn

Meredith Ave

Buford Ave

McPherson Ridge **1**

Seminary Ridge Museum

College Ave

Lincoln Ave

Carlisle St

Stratton St

Coster Ave

**GETTYSBURG**

**EAST CAVALRY BATTLEFIELD SITE**

Reynolds Ave

Gettysburg Train Station

York St

Square   David Wills House

York Rd
York Pike

Hanover Rd

Fairfield Rd

Hagerstown (Fairfield) Rd

W Middle St

E Middle St

Washington St

Baltimore St

E Confederate Ave

Stevens Run

Rock Creek

**BENNER HILL**

Gregg Ave

Low Dutch Rd

116

116

MCMILLAN WOODS

Gettysburg Hospital

Youth Group Campground (reservation only)

*SEMINARY RIDGE*

Steinwehr Ave

**CEMETERY HILL**   East Cemetery Hill **14**

*CULPS HILL*   Observation Tower

Plum Run

United States Cavalry Ave

North Carolina Memorial **4**

Virginia Memorial **5**

Brian Farm

Soldiers' National Monument

Soldiers' National Cemetery **16**

Spanglers Spring

High Water Mark **15**

The Angle

Copse of Trees

Codori Farm

Meade's Headquarters

**13**

Black Horse Tavern Rd

Willoughby Run

Hunt Ave

Amphitheater

Pennsylvania Memorial **12**

Pleasonton Ave

**Visitor Center**

Pitzer Woods **6**

Plum Run

Plum Run **11**

Granite School

Blacksmith Shop Rd

Baltimore Pike

Pumping Station Rd

Waterworks Rd

Observation Tower

*THE PEACH ORCHARD*

Sickles Ave

The Peach Orchard **10**

Wheatfield Rd

Hancock Ave

Sedgwick Ave

134

15

*WARFIELD RIDGE*

West Confederate Ave

Rose Farm

The Wheatfield **9**

Crawford Ave

Little Round Top

Sykes Ave

**CEMETERY RIDGE**

Taneytown Rd

Red Rock Rd

Emmitsburg Rd

**7**

Warfield Ridge

*DEVILS DEN*

**8**

South Confederate Ave

Wright Ave

*BIG ROUND TOP*

Marsh Creek

*SOUTH CAVALRY FIELD*

White Run

15

Littles Run

97

BR 15

134

15

- - - Trail

**1** Auto Tour Stop

North ↑

0 ———— 1 Mile

0 ———— 2 Km

I knew that General Lee was in command. . . . We looked forward to victory under him as confidently as to successive sunrises."

In late June 1863, the Army of Northern Virginia—reorganized into three corps under Gen. Richard Ewell, Gen. A. P. Hill, and Gen. James Longstreet—marched across the Blue Ridge Mountains into the Shenandoah Valley and crossed the Potomac River near Williamsport, Maryland. On June 28, with the Army of the Potomac again on his heels, Lee gathered his forces around Cashtown, Pennsylvania, 25 miles east of Chambersburg and about eight miles northwest of Gettysburg. On that same day Lincoln replaced Hooker with Gen. George Meade, commander of the Union Fifth Corps. One of Meade's first acts was to dispatch Gen. John Buford's cavalry division of 2,700 men to locate the Confederate columns.

Buford's troops rode into Gettysburg on June 30, where they encountered a Confederate brigade reconnoitering the town. Twelve roads converged at Gettysburg, radiating in all directions like the spokes of a wagon wheel. Buford immediately recognized the strategic importance of the place. He deployed his men along McPherson Ridge to the north and west of town and sent word to Gen. John Reynolds, commander of First Corps, to hurry up with his infantry. Another great battle was looming.

About 8:00 a.m. on July 1, 1863, fighting began in earnest along the Chambersburg Pike. Combat spread north and south along McPherson Ridge as additional forces from both sides arrived. Gen. Henry Heth's division engaged Buford's cavalry, which was stretched precariously thin along the ridge. Around 9:00 a.m. the first infantry brigades of First Corps arrived, relieving Buford's cavalry and bolstering the Union defenders. Heth's attack was repulsed, but as Reynolds urged his men into action, a bullet struck him in the back of the head, and the general fell dead from his horse.

Gen. Oliver Howard's Eleventh Corps was next to arrive on the battlefield, deploying north of Gettysburg. Around 1:00 p.m., Gen. Robert Rode's division pressed the attack against Union positions on Oak Ridge and McPherson Ridge. The First Corps troops fended off the attacks, but when Confederate assaults struck the Union left flank around 3:30 p.m., the First Corps line began to crumble. At about the same time, Gen. Jubal Early's division smashed Howard's Eleventh Corps

north of town on Barlow Knoll. By 4:30 p.m. both Union corps were in full retreat.

As units fell back into Gettysburg, the retreat turned into a rout. A Wisconsin volunteer wrote: "On every side our troops were madly rushing to the rear. My heart sank within me. I lost all hope." Union troops fell back onto Cemetery Hill and Culps Hill south of town. The day was saved when Gen. Winfield Hancock, commander of Second Corps, brought order to the battlefield and helped avert disaster. Lee's army had carried the day, but more Union troops were still on the road. The impending arrival of Second, Third, Fifth, and Twelfth Corps portended renewed fighting the next day.

On the morning of July 2, Meade's army occupied the high ground south of Gettysburg. His right flank was anchored on the wooded slopes of Culps Hill. Resembling a fishhook, his lines extended around Cemetery Hill, then south along the low crest of Cemetery Ridge. Gen. Daniel Sickles's Third Corps, comprising about 10,000 men, anchored the left flank of the Union line. Meade had ordered Sickles

PREVIOUS SPREAD: Gen. George Gordon Meade Monument on Cemetery Ridge.

ABOVE: Cannon in The Wheatfield.

to occupy the southern end of Cemetery Ridge as far as the slopes of Little Round Top. But Sickles defied Meade's orders, pushing his line forward to what he determined was more favorable ground along the Emmitsburg Road. The far end of his line angled southeast on a low ridge between a peach orchard and a boulder-strewn area called Devils Den. Lee would soon exploit this exposed angle and thinly manned line.

Lee ordered Longstreet to attack this Union position, committing the brigades of Gen. John Hood and Gen. Lafayette McLaws in a sequential series of attacks against Sickles's exposed flank. Lee also ordered Ewell to launch an attack against Culps Hill on the Union right to prevent Meade from shifting troops and reinforcing Sickles. Longstreet objected to the plan, arguing it would be wiser to face Meade's forces on ground more suitable to the Confederates. But Lee was determined to attack. Longstreet took several hours to maneuver his divisions, delaying the assault until late afternoon.

At 4:00 p.m. on July 2, Hood's and McLaws's divisions struck hard against Sickles's Third Corps,

engaging in some of the bloodiest fighting of the war. Hood's troops led the assault, overrunning Federal infantry and three guns of the 4th New York Battery at Devils Den. Confederate forces then threatened to take the rocky crest of Little Round Top, which was undefended. Possession of this high ground would give the Confederates a clear line of fire down the entire length of the Union line on Cemetery Ridge.

Gen. Gouverneur Warren, Meade's chief engineer, alerted Union commanders of the threat. Col. Strong Vincent's brigade arrived minutes before the 15th and 47th Alabama Regiments approached Little Round Top, repulsing repeated assaults across the boulder-strewn woods. Gen. Stephen Weed's brigade joined the fight, and with the Parrott guns of Battery D, 5th US Artillery, it repulsed the 4th and 5th Texas. On the left flank, a dramatic downhill bayonet charge by Col. Joshua Chamberlain's 20th Maine drove the 15th Alabama back down the ridge, capturing dozens of prisoners and sending the Confederates scurrying for cover. Union forces had secured Little Round Top.

To the west of Little Round Top, Confederate assaults continued against Sickles's line. A wheat field on the farm of Joseph Sherfy changed hands six times with charge followed by countercharge. At 6:30 p.m., four Mississippi regiments in McLaws's command crushed the Federal line at the peach orchard salient, forcing the Third Corps troops to retreat back to Cemetery Ridge. Veterans called this part of the battlefield a "whirlpool of death." Sherfy's wheat field became known as The Wheatfield and his peach orchard became known as The Peach Orchard.

On Culps Hill at the other end of the Union line, Ewell's troops didn't launch their attack until around 7:00 p.m.—too late to provide the diversion that Lee was hoping for. Troops from the Union Twelfth Corps, deployed behind formidable log breastworks along the crest of the hill, repelled the Confederate attack. Lee's army had bent but not broken the Union line. Convinced that heavy Federal losses at the southern end of Cemetery Ridge had considerably weakened Meade's army, Lee was certain a massed assault against the Union center on the following day would breach the line and drive the Army of the Potomac from the field.

Longstreet again had grave doubts about a head-on charge against the center of the Union line, expressing his concern that such an assault would

BELOW: Union artillery position above Devils Den.

OPPOSITE: July 1863 photograph of dead Confederate soldier at Devils Den.

risk unacceptable losses with little chance of success. Lee again overruled him, and Longstreet spent the rest of the morning maneuvering the divisions of Gen. George Pickett, Gen. Johnston Pettigrew, and Gen. Isaac Trimble for the attack. At 1:00 p.m. on July 3, 170 Confederate cannon launched a bombardment of the Union positions on Cemetery Ridge. Union artillery returned fire, and for two hours the greatest artillery barrage of the Civil War raged.

Around 3:00 p.m. the divisions of Pickett and Pettigrew and two brigades of Trimble—some 12,000 men in all—launched their attack across the expanse between Seminary Ridge and Cemetery Ridge. As the Confederate soldiers moved forward, Federal artillery roared back to life, tearing great gaps in the advancing lines. Formations broke up into clusters of men sprinting toward the stone wall and copse of trees that marked the line of Hancock's Second Corps defenders.

Capt. Edward Bowen of the 114th Pennsylvania described the ghastly scene: "The enemy rapidly crossed the intervening space. Our batteries, loaded with grape and canister, were trained upon them at point-blank range and opened again upon them with deadly effect. Still they closed up the gaps and pressed on. Our men reserved their fire and allowed them to come so far as in their judgment was far enough, and then blazed upon them such a withering musketry fire as literally mowed them down."

Led by Gen. Lewis Armistead, soldiers of Pickett's division concentrated their charge toward a projecting angle in the low stone wall. Here Armistead and some 200 attackers managed to climb over the wall. Federal reinforcements charged into the melee to plug the breach, and Armistead was mortally wounded. "Pickett's Charge," as the assault became known, was repulsed with devastating losses. Pickett's division suffered 2,655 casualties; Pettigrew lost about 2,700 men. The area around The Angle became known as the "high water mark of the Confederacy."

PREVIOUS SPREAD: View looking east across the battlefield toward Little Round Top (left) and Big Round Top.

LEFT: McPherson Ridge from Oak Ridge northwest of Gettysburg.

The bloodiest three days of fighting during the entire Civil War had finally come to a close. Total casualties for the Battle of Gettysburg were 51,000 men—23,000 for the Union army and as many as 28,000 for the Confederates. Decimated by its losses, Lee's Army of Northern Virginia began its slow retreat back to Virginia on July 4.

## Soldiers' National Cemetery

In the aftermath of the fighting, most of the dead lay in hastily dug and inadequate graves across the battlefield. The situation so distressed Pennsylvania Gov. Andrew Curtin that he commissioned David Wills, a local Gettysburg attorney, to acquire land for a proper burial ground for the Union dead. In August 1863, the state acquired 17 acres for a cemetery. Eventually some 3,512 Union soldiers from 17 states were reinterred in Soldiers' National Cemetery. Following the war, the remains of 3,320 Confederate soldiers were removed from the battlefield to cemeteries across the South.

Soldiers' National Cemetery was dedicated on November 19, 1863. The principal speaker was Edward Everett, who delivered a well-received two-hour oration rich in historical detail and classical allusion. He was followed by President Abraham Lincoln, who had been asked to make "a few appropriate remarks." Lincoln's speech contained 272 words and took about two minutes to deliver. The Gettysburg Address transformed the battlefield from a scene of carnage into a symbol, giving meaning to the sacrifice of the dead and inspiration to the living:

*Four score and seven years ago our fathers brought forth on this continent a new nation, conceived in liberty, and dedicated to the proposition that all men are created equal.*

*Now we are engaged in a great civil war, testing whether that nation, or any nation so conceived and so dedicated, can long endure. We are met on a great battlefield of that war. We have come to dedicate a portion of that field, as a final resting place for those who here gave their lives that that nation might live. It is altogether fitting and proper that we should do this.*

*But, in a larger sense, we can not dedicate, we can not consecrate, we can not hallow this ground. The brave men, living and dead, who struggled here, have consecrated it, far above our poor power to add or detract. The world will little note, nor long remember what we say here, but it can never forget what they did here. It is for us the living, rather, to be dedicated here to the unfinished work which they who fought here have thus far so nobly advanced. It is rather for us to be here dedicated to the great task remaining before us—that from these honored dead we take increased devotion to that cause for which they gave the last full measure of devotion—that we here highly resolve that these dead shall not have died in vain—that this nation, under God, shall have a new birth of freedom—and that government of the people, by the people, for the people, shall not perish from the earth.*

BELOW: Gravesite markers of unknown soldiers in the Soldiers' National Cemetery.

OPPOSITE: View from Little Round Top showing the monument of Union Gen. Gouverneur Warren.

PREVIOUS SPREAD: View looking west across Cemetery Ridge. The Vermont Monument (left), dedicated on October 9, 1889, was the first large state monument erected on the battlefield.

LEFT, TOP: Union artillery piece in front of the Ohio Monument on East Cemetery Hill.

LEFT, BOTTOM: View looking toward the Codori Farm from Cemetery Ridge. Pickett's Charge took place across this ground.

OPPOSITE: Equestrian statue of Confederate Gen. James Longstreet.

FOLLOWING SPREAD: View of Devils Den (center) from Union artillery position on Little Round Top.

# GETTYSBURG Battlefield Hikes

Several miles of trails crisscross the Gettysburg Battlefield. A few hikes are described in detailed guidebooks that may be purchased at the Gettysburg Museum Store in the park visitor center. For other trails, visitors can consult the official park map and guide, which is available at no charge. During their hikes, visitors can help preserve and protect the battlefield by not climbing or sitting on monuments, markers, wayside exhibits, stone walls, cannon, or limbers. Hikers should start at the National Park Service information desk at the far end of the visitor center, just off Baltimore Pike southeast of Gettysburg.

### Cemetery Ridge Trail (1.0 mile one way)

This trail begins at the visitor center and covers ground along Cemetery Ridge defended by Union soldiers against Pickett's Charge on the third day of the battle. The trail includes Meade's Headquarters at the Leister Farm, the High Water Mark Monument and Copse of Trees, several state battlefield monuments, and The Angle, where about 200 Confederates followed Gen. Lewis Armistead over the wall. Troops of the 71st and 72nd Pennsylvania Infantry Regiments

repulsed the attack, mortally wounding Armistead. For more information, visitors may purchase the *Cemetery Ridge Trail Walking Tour* booklet at the Gettysburg Museum Store.

### Devils Den Trail (1.1 miles)

This trail begins at the Devils Den parking area on Crawford Avenue near Little Round Top. The path passes over Devils Den and continues along Houck's Ridge—ground first held by Union infantry and artillery on July 2, 1863. The trail

circles back along the bed of an old trolley line operated by the Gettysburg Electric Railway Company from 1893 to 1917. This part of the hike covers ground where the Confederate 1st Texas Infantry and 20th Georgia Infantry assaulted the Union line on the afternoon of July 2, driving the Federal forces back onto Little Round Top. For more information, visitors may purchase the *Devils Den Trail Walking Tour* booklet at the Gettysburg Museum Store.

### Soldiers' National Cemetery Trail
(0.5 or 2.0 miles)

This trail begins at the Soldiers' National Cemetery parking area on Taneytown Road. The hike traverses the cemetery grounds where Union soldiers from the battle are interred, and where President Abraham Lincoln delivered the Gettysburg Address. Points of interest include the Lincoln Speech Memorial, Soldiers' National Monument, and the graves of more than 3,500 Union soldiers. Visitors may also start this hike at the visitor center, for a total round trip of two miles. For more information, visitors may purchase the *Soldiers' National Cemetery Trail Walking Tour* booklet at the Gettysburg Museum Store.

### Pickett's Charge Trail (1.0 mile one way)

Hikers can follow in the footsteps of two Confederate divisions—12,000 soldiers of the Army of Northern Virginia—as they advanced against the center of the Union line on Cemetery

Ridge. The trail starts near the Virginia Memorial on Seminary Ridge (Auto Tour Stop 5) and continues across a mile of open field, across the Emmitsburg Road, and on to The Angle, where the assault finally collapsed. It was here that the ground became forever known as the "high water mark of the Confederacy."

### Billy Yank Trail (10.0 miles)
This way-finding route was set up by a local Boy Scouts of America Council and is meant to be a historical experience through the eyes of Union troops. The trail visits Meade's Headquarters, Cemetery Ridge, The Peach Orchard, The Wheatfield, Little Round Top, Big Round Top, the Confederate battle line along Seminary Ridge,

and finally The Angle, where Pickett's Charge was repulsed by Federal forces. For more information, visitors may purchase the *Gettysburg Heritage Trail Guide* at the Gettysburg Museum Store. The booklet contains historic information, directions, and contemporary color photographs of the battlefield.

### Johnny Reb Trail (4.0 miles)
This way-finding route was also set up by a local Boy Scouts of America Council and is meant to be a historical experience through the eyes of Confederate troops. The trail explores Cemetery Hill, Culps Hill, Spanglers Spring, and several battlefield monuments. For more information, visitors may purchase the *Gettysburg Heritage Trail Guide* at the Gettysburg Museum Store.

OPPOSITE: 17th Pennsylvania Cavalry Monument on McPherson Ridge.

ABOVE: Double rainbow above Cemetery Ridge.

# MONOCACY
## BATTLEFIELD

MARYLAND  Monocacy National Battlefield

In June 1864, the Confederate capital at Richmond, Virginia, was being squeezed hard by Union forces. To the east, Gen. Ulysses S. Grant's Army of the Potomac was digging in for a siege, extending its formidable lines from Richmond south around Petersburg. To the west, Gen. David Hunter had driven a small Confederate army out of the Shenandoah Valley and was marching on Lynchburg, a key railroad junction and supply base. If left unchecked, both threats could sever Richmond's supply lines and doom the Confederate defenders. Gen. Robert E. Lee, commander of the Army of Northern Virginia, had to act.

In a bold move, Lee dispatched his Second Corps under Gen. Jubal Early to counter the threat posed by Hunter. With 15,000 men—one quarter of Lee's entire army—Early was ordered to protect Lynchburg, sweep Hunter's forces from the Shenandoah Valley, invade Maryland, and threaten Washington, DC. Lee's aim was to compel Grant to divert forces to defend the nation's capital, relieving pressure on his beleaguered troops at Richmond and Petersburg. He also hoped that another invasion would further erode public support for the war in the North. It was a risky plan, but Lee's options—and those of the Confederacy—were becoming increasingly limited.

On June 17 and 18, 1864, Early engaged the Union forces near Lynchburg, chasing Hunter back across the Blue Ridge Mountains and Shenandoah Valley all the way to West Virginia. Lynchburg was safe, and the valley, a natural route of invasion into Maryland, now lay completely open. On June 23, Early commenced the last major Southern invasion into Union territory. Averaging almost 20 miles a day, his Second Corps traveled quickly down the Shenandoah Valley, approaching Harpers Ferry on July 4. The Union defenders cautiously retreated across the Potomac River, retiring to their now formidable defense works on Maryland

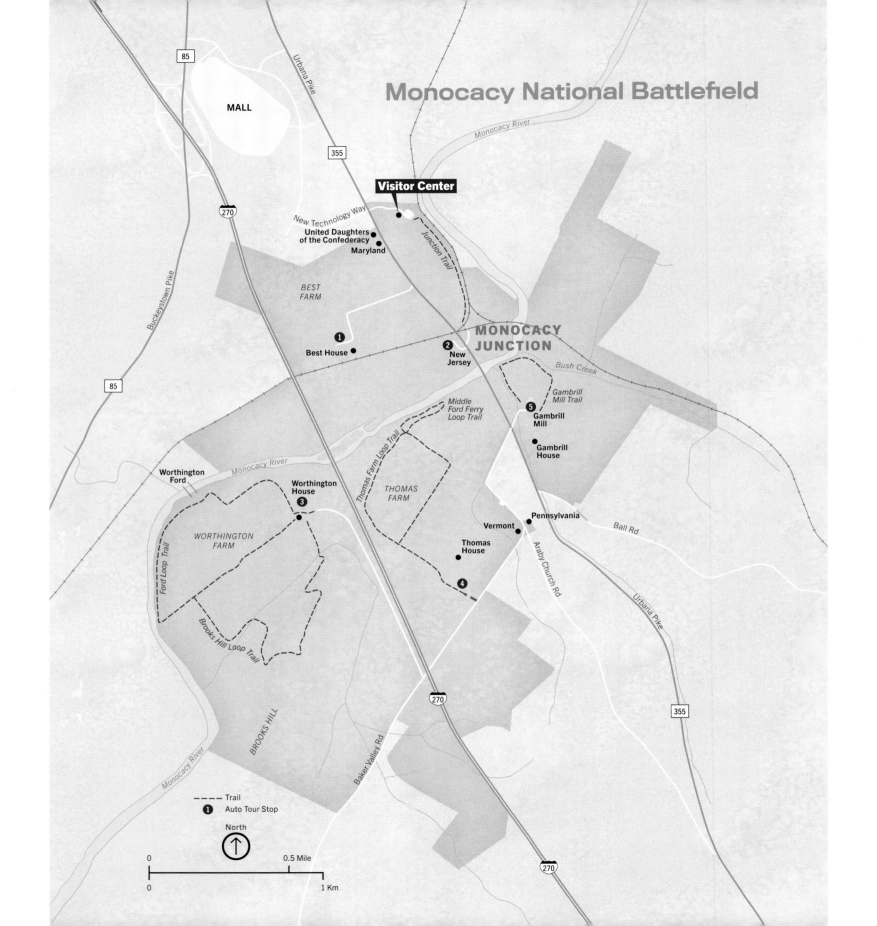

# Monocacy National Battlefield

MALL

Visitor Center

United Daughters
of the Confederacy

Maryland

*BEST
FARM*

New Technology Way

Junction Trail

❶

Best House

❷ New Jersey

**MONOCACY
JUNCTION**

Bush Creek

*Gambrill
Mill Trail*

❺

Gambrill
Mill

*Middle
Ford Ferry
Loop Trail*

Gambrill
House

Thomas Farm Loop Trail

Monocacy River

Worthington
Ford

Worthington
House

❸

*THOMAS
FARM*

Pennsylvania

Vermont

Ball Rd

*WORTHINGTON
FARM*

Thomas
House

❹

Araby Church Rd

Ford Loop Trail

Urbana Pike

Brooks Hill Loop Trail

Baker Valley Rd

*BROOKS HILL*

Monocacy River

- - - Trail
❶ Auto Tour Stop

North
⬆

0 ————— 0.5 Mile
0 ————— 1 Km

85

Urbana Pike

355

270

85

270

355

Heights. The next morning, the Union signal station on Maryland Heights spied Early's columns crossing the river about eight miles upstream at Pack Horse Ford. The Confederates attempted to "compel the evacuation of Maryland Heights," but the Union forces stood firm. Early was forced to bypass the fortress, and he continued his advance toward Frederick, Maryland.

Meanwhile in Baltimore, John Garrett, president of the Baltimore and Ohio Railroad, was receiving telegraph reports of widespread depredations against his line in western Maryland and West Virginia. He urgently passed these reports on to Washington, but the Union authorities did not take them seriously. Surely these Confederate forces were simply partisans or cavalry raiders. Garrett then appealed directly to Gen. Lew Wallace, commander of the Middle Department headquartered in Baltimore.

Wallace decided to take action, and on July 5, he dispatched troops to Monocacy Junction, where a spur line from Frederick met the Baltimore and Ohio

Railroad mainline. Here, adjacent to the iron railroad bridge, a covered wagon bridge conveyed the Georgetown Pike across the Monocacy River. Wallace began collecting any and all troops he could muster. By July 7 he had gathered only 3,200 men, mostly unseasoned "100 days" men—troops who had only enlisted for 100 days of service. He also counted just seven pieces of artillery. Fortunately, Grant finally recognized the threat and dispatched two brigades—about 3,400 men—from Sixth Corps under Gen. James Ricketts from the Petersburg, Virginia, area.

On the evening of July 8, Wallace received word that Confederate infantry was approaching Monocacy Junction from the west. It was now apparent that Early's target was Washington. With the arrival of Ricketts's veteran brigades from Petersburg, the Union forces now totaled about 6,600 men—still fewer than half of Early's total command. The Confederates also possessed 36 pieces of artillery to Wallace's seven. Undaunted, Wallace deployed his small force along a

**PREVIOUS SPREAD**: Monocacy River through Monocacy Battlefield.

**BELOW**: View looking across the Thomas Farm.

three-mile line southeast of the Monocacy River. A small force of about 275 men was posted just west of the river at the junction to protect the iron railroad bridge and covered wagon bridge.

On the morning of July 9, 1864, Confederate skirmishers from Gen. Stephen Ramseur's division advanced down the Georgetown Pike toward Monocacy Junction. The skirmishers were supported by Confederate artillery firing from the Best Farm just a short distance west of the river. Coincidentally, it was on the Best Farm two years earlier where Union skirmishers discovered Lee's "Lost Orders" at the outset of the Antietam Campaign. Lt. George Davis of the 10th Vermont Volunteers described the action at the junction: "When the enemy advanced, about 8:30 a.m. along the pike from Frederick . . . I brought up my 10th Vermonters to this point, and after a severe fight for about an hour, the enemy retired. . . . About 11 a.m. a second, a more severe attack was made upon our right and rear by which they intended to cut us out and take us prisoner."

Davis's men repelled this second attack, but Wallace, fearing the Confederates might capture the covered wagon bridge, ordered it burned. Still, the Union defenders held fast, and were only driven off by a third and final attack around 3:30 p.m. Davis wrote that he "was pursued so closely by the enemy that five of my own company were seized forcibly by the enemy grabbing the coat collar, so close to me that if one more man had to be taken it would have been me." By the end of the day, only 75 men remained under Davis's command. Davis was later awarded the Medal of Honor for his valiant defense of Monocacy Junction.

While the opposing forces clashed at Monocacy Junction, Early decided to redirect his attack downstream rather than risk a direct frontal assault against the strong Federal position. Early's cavalry commander, Gen. John McCausland, found Worthington Ford, crossed the Monocacy River, and around 10:30 a.m. deployed his 1,200 men across the Worthington Farm astride the Union left flank. McCausland was convinced he was facing "100 days" men, and ordered his cavalry to dismount and attack the Union position. Instead, the veterans of Ricketts's Sixth Corps were waiting behind a fence line dividing the Worthington and Thomas Farms. In unison, the Federals rose and unleashed a withering volley into the Confederate ranks, forcing them to fall back in confusion.

Thomas Farm on Monocacy Battlefield.

Around 2:30 p.m., the Confederate cavalry was reorganized for a second assault. Bypassing the Union skirmish line by deploying near Brooks Hill, McCausland's men struck directly at the Thomas House. They succeeded in dislodging the Union defenders, but Ricketts's men quickly counterattacked and drove the Confederates back to the Worthington Farm.

Early now ordered his infantry into the battle. About 3,600 veterans commanded by Gen. John Gordon forded the river and deployed across the Worthington Farm. Three of Gordon's brigades advanced, moving in a sequential series of attacks that struck the Union lines hard: Georgians assaulted the left flank at 3:30 p.m., Louisianans struck the center at 3:45 p.m., and Virginians pressed the right flank at 4:00 p.m.

The Union line was pushed back to the Georgetown Pike, but still managed to stall the three-pronged attack. Finally, around 4:30 p.m., amid a continuous Confederate artillery bombardment from the Best Farm across the Monocacy River, Ricketts's right flank was pushed back, allowing Confederate fire to enfilade the Union line. Wallace could hold his position no longer. The entire line crumbled and Union forces retreated, falling back past Gambrill Mill toward Monrovia, Maryland. Gordon later wrote that "the battle of Monocacy was one of the severest ever fought by my troops."

Wallace's fierce defense at the Monocacy River cost him 1,294 casualties. But the Confederate victory came at a high cost as well: they suffered an estimated 900 casualties, and the delay gave Grant's reinforcements just enough time to bolster the defenses around Washington. Two days later, on July 11, Early's army reached Fort Stevens on the outskirts of Washington. The Confederates declined to test the city's strong fortifications, and withdrew back across the Potomac River near Leesburg, Virginia. Early took small consolation when he told one of his officers, "Major, we haven't taken Washington, but we scared Abe Lincoln like hell."

BELOW: 14th New Jersey Infantry Regiment Monument.

OPPOSITE: Outbuildings on the Best Farm, originally a 748-acre plantation known as L'Hermitage.

# MONOCACY Battlefield Hikes

Monocacy National Battlefield has more than seven miles of hiking trails. Most trails traverse the battlefield over level to gently rolling terrain. Only the Brooks Hill Loop has a short steep climb where caution is advised. Some fields on the battlefield are under agricultural lease, so visitors should be aware that some of the fences are electrified to keep in cattle. Hikers should start at the visitor center off Maryland Route 355 southeast of Frederick, where detailed trail maps are available.

## Junction Trail (0.5 miles one way)

This trail begins at the visitor center and provides scenic views of the historic railroad junction with interpretive wayside exhibits along the way. It was on this part of the battlefield that Lt. George Davis and his 10th Vermont Volunteers held off multiple assaults by Confederate skirmishers for much of the day.

## Ford Loop Trail (2.1 miles)

This hike begins at the Worthington Farm parking area (Auto Tour Stop 3). It crosses the Worthington Farm and follows along the Monocacy River to the site of Worthington Ford. Here, on July 9, 1864, Gen. John McCausland's cavalry and Gen. John Gordon's infantry crossed the river and deployed for battle. As the battle raged throughout the day, the Worthington family took refuge in the cellar of their nearby house. Six-year-old Glenn Worthington observed the action through the slats of the boarded-up windows. In 1932, he published the first book detailing the battle, *Fighting for Time*, and was instrumental in the area's designation as a national battlefield.

## Brooks Hill Loop Trail (1.9 miles)

This hike begins at the Worthington Farm parking area (Auto Tour Stop 3). It encompasses a section of the battlefield adjacent to the Worthington Farm where Confederate Gen. John Gordon deployed his infantry regiments for an attack against Union positions on the Thomas Farm. The trail also highlights many significant natural resources, and from a vantage point on top of Brooks Hill, hikers can see much of the battlefield.

## Thomas Farm Loop Trail
### (2.2 or 2.7 miles)

This hike begins at the Thomas Farm parking area (Auto Tour Stop 4). Caught between the two armies, the Thomas Farm became the focal point of the battle. Confederate artillery pummeled the Thomas House, striking the structure several times while the Thomas and Gambrill families took refuge in the cellar. Confederate cavalry and infantry staged three separate assaults against Union forces deployed across the farm, finally pushing the defenders off the field with a three-

pronged attack between 3:30 and 4:30 p.m. The Middle Ford Ferry Loop connects to the Thomas Farm Loop Trail, adding an optional half-mile hike along the Monocacy River.

### Gambrill Mill Trail (0.7 miles)
This hike starts at the Gambrill Mill parking area (Auto Tour Stop 5). This short handicap-accessible trail provides views of the Monocacy River, railroad bridge, and highway bridge at Monocacy Junction. It was through this part of the battlefield that Union forces retreated after being dislodged from the Georgetown Pike by Gen. John Gordon's infantry regiments. Gambrill Mill, known historically as Araby Mill, was originally a three-story stone gristmill built in 1830. During the battle the structure served as a field hospital.

OPPOSITE: Gambrill Mill.

ABOVE: Worthington House, where the Worthington family took refuge in the cellar during the battle.

WEST TENNESSEE
MISSISSIPPI
LOUISIANA

# FORT DONELSON
## BATTLEFIELD

THE GEOGRAPHY OF THE CIVIL WAR'S WESTERN THEATER DIFFERED significantly from that in the East. While the landscape north of Richmond, Virginia, was perforated by streams and rivers flowing west to east from the Blue Ridge to the Chesapeake Bay—causing fits for Union armies trying to advance on the Confederate capital—in the West several major rivers provided direct avenues for attack. The Mississippi, Tennessee, and Cumberland Rivers all led deep into Southern territory, giving Union commanders several options for invading the Confederacy. In February 1862, an obscure and largely unproven brigadier general, Ulysses S. Grant, took advantage of this geography to launch an invasion into Tennessee.

With the support of a Union gunboat fleet commanded by Flag Officer Andrew Foote, Grant moved his army south along the Tennessee River. His first objective was Fort Henry, a Confederate stronghold defending the river just south of the Kentucky border. As it turned out, the cannon of Fort Henry could not match the firepower of Foote's gunboats. Effective naval gunfire and the appearance of two Union divisions that Grant had landed from riverboats just north of the fort threatened to overwhelm Fort Henry's defenses. The Confederate commander sent the bulk of his garrison—about 2,500 men—to Fort Donelson, and on February 6, Fort Henry surrendered.

Grant followed up his victory by marching his army 12 miles overland to Fort Donelson. At Donelson the Confederates held a much stronger position. Two river batteries, mounting 12 heavy guns, defended the Cumberland River. An outer line of defense works stretched along the high ground from Hickman Creek to the north to the village of Dover to the south. Fort Donelson was the last obstacle protecting the approaches to Nashville, Tennessee—the state capital and one of the South's few manufacturing centers. On February 11, Gen. John Floyd took command of the fort. His 17,000 Confederate soldiers, combined with strong artillery

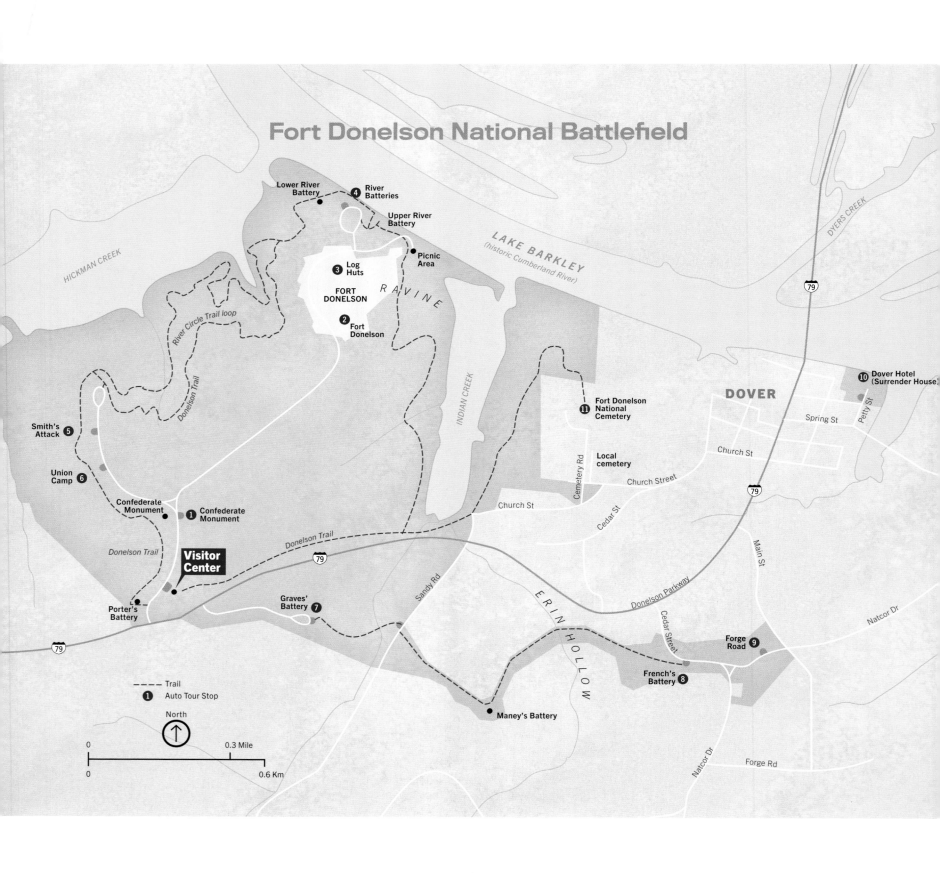

# Fort Donelson National Battlefield

Lower River Battery

River Batteries **4**

Upper River Battery

LAKE BARKLEY
(historic Cumberland River)

DYERS CREEK

HICKMAN CREEK

Picnic Area

Log Huts **3**

FORT DONELSON

**2** Fort Donelson

R A V I N E

River Circle Trail loop

Donelson Trail

INDIAN CREEK

Smith's Attack **5**

Union Camp **6**

Confederate Monument

**1** Confederate Monument

Donelson Trail

Donelson Trail

**Visitor Center**

Porter's Battery

Graves' Battery **7**

Sandy Rd

Fort Donelson National Cemetery **11**

Local cemetery

Church St

Church Street

Church St

Cemetery Rd

Cedar St

DOVER

Spring St

Church St

**10** Dover Hotel (Surrender House)

Petty St

Main St

Donelson Parkway

Natcor Dr

E R I N   H O L L O W

Cedar Street

French's Battery **8**

Forge Road **9**

Natcor Dr

Forge Rd

Maney's Battery

- - - Trail

**1** Auto Tour Stop

North

↑

0 ——— 0.3 Mile

0 ——— 0.6 Km

positions and earthworks, convinced Floyd that a hasty retreat was unnecessary. By February 13 some 15,000 Union troops nearly encircled the outer works of the fort. Several inches of snowfall and a cold winter wind sent shivers through both armies.

On the afternoon of February 14, the cold, quiet landscape was shattered by artillery fire from Union gunboats. Foote's fleet, consisting of the ironclads *St. Louis*, *Pittsburg*, *Louisville*, and *Carondelet*, and the timberclads *Conestoga* and *Tyler*, advanced up the Cumberland River and exchanged "iron valentines" with the 12 big guns of the Confederate river batteries. During the 90-minute duel, Southern shells wounded Foote and inflicted such extensive damage upon the Union fleet that it was forced to retreat. Grant's soldiers could hear the Confederate cheers as the Union gunboats withdrew.

The Confederate commanders also rejoiced at the repulse of the gunboats, but they soon recognized another danger. Grant was receiving reinforcements daily and had almost completely encircled Fort Donelson. If the Confederates did not move quickly, they would be surrounded and starved into submission. Gen. Gideon Pillow was designated to lead a breakout attempt, evacuate the fort, and march to Nashville. Massing his troops against the Union right flank just south of the fort, the Confederates attacked Grant's infantry at dawn on February 15. Fierce fighting raged throughout the morning, forcing the Union troops to give ground. Disaster loomed for Grant's army.

But in what would become one of the oddest and most improbable acts on any Civil War battlefield, just as the escape route to Nashville appeared open, Pillow ordered the attacking troops back to their earthworks. Over the strong objections of Floyd and Gen. Simon Buckner, Pillow argued that his men needed to regroup and resupply before evacuating the fort. Grant immediately launched a vigorous counterattack, retaking most of the lost ground and again sealing the Confederates inside the fort. Reasoning that the breakout attempt must have also weakened the fort's defenses somewhere else, Grant ordered Gen. Charles Smith to attack the right flank of the outer defense works. Smith exhorted his volunteers from Iowa, Indiana, and Missouri, shouting, "You volunteered to be killed for love of country and now you can be." The attackers drove off the thin line of Confederate defenders and seized the outer entrench-

ments just before nightfall. Union forces were now poised to seize Fort Donelson the following morning.

During the night, the Confederate commanders discussed their options. They determined that surrender was the only viable choice. The following morning, on February 16, Floyd and Pillow turned over command of Fort Donelson to Buckner and slipped away to Nashville. Floyd, who was a wanted man in the North for alleged graft and secessionist activities when he was secretary of war in the Buchanan administration, feared capture. Pillow also feared Northern reprisals. Disgusted at the show of cowardice, a furious Col. Nathan Bedford Forrest announced, "I did not come here to surrender my command." Under cover of darkness, the Confederate cavalry commander led his 700 horsemen out of Fort Donelson through the shallow, icy waters of Lick Creek.

On the morning of February 16, Buckner sent a note to Grant requesting a truce and asking for terms of surrender. He was hoping for generous terms from his old West Point friend, but was dismayed by Grant's

**PREVIOUS SPREAD**: Lower River Battery overlooking Lake Barkley (historic Cumberland River).

**ABOVE**: Battery B, 1st Regiment, Illinois Light Artillery, commanded by Capt. Ezra Taylor at Fort Donelson, Tennessee.

# FORT DONELSON
## Battlefield Hikes

Trails at Fort Donelson provide opportunities to explore the beautiful natural scenery along Lake Barkley (the historic Cumberland River), as well as the rugged topography that shaped much of the February 1862 fighting. Hiking is moderate to difficult, and insect repellant is highly recommended during the warmer months of the year. Hikers can obtain trail information and a park map at the visitor center.

### Donelson Trail (3.4 miles)

This loop trail begins and ends at the visitor center. Highlights include the site of Union Gen. Charles Smith's successful assault against the right wing of the outer Confederate defenses, the Lower River Battery, the Upper River Battery, and Fort Donelson. The River Circle Trail intersects with the Donelson Trail in two places: near the site of Smith's Attack at the right end of the Confederate outer defenses (Auto Tour Stop 5) and near the Lower River Battery, creating a shorter loop trail. A 0.75-mile spur trail also leads to Fort Donelson National Cemetery (Auto Tour Stop 11).

### Maney's Battery Trail (0.9 miles one way)

This strenuous hike begins at Graves' Battery (Auto Tour Stop 7), proceeds across the steep terrain where the Confederates placed their outer defense artillery at Maney's Battery, and ends at the left wing of the outer defenses at French's Battery (Auto Tour Stop 8).

answer: "No terms except an unconditional and immediate surrender can be accepted. I propose to move immediately upon your works." Buckner, who considered his old friend's demand "ungenerous and unchivalrous," accepted the terms. The surrender was a personal humiliation for Buckner and a strategic defeat for the Confederacy. The South lost approximately 13,000 men, 48 pieces of artillery, and control of the Cumberland River, which led to the evacuation of Nashville. The North had not only won its first great victory of the war, but also gained a new hero—Ulysses "Unconditional Surrender" Grant.

Confederate artillery position and earthworks on the outer defenses of Fort Donelson.

# SHILOH
# BATTLEFIELD

TENNESSEE  Shiloh National Military Park

THE CAPTURE OF FORTS HENRY AND DONELSON IN FEBRUARY 1862 forced Confederate Gen. Albert Sidney Johnston to abandon Kentucky and Middle Tennessee. To prevent a Union advance against the strategic railroad hub at Corinth, Mississippi, Johnston had assembled 44,000 troops. If Corinth fell into Union hands, Confederate communications along the vital Memphis and Charleston and Mobile and Ohio Railroads would be severed. In mid-March 1862, Grant's Army of the Tennessee, totaling about 45,000 men, steamed up the Tennessee River and disembarked at Pittsburg Landing—22 miles north of Corinth. Here Grant was ordered to await the arrival of Gen. Don Carlos Buell's Army of the Ohio with another 18,000 men. Buell's command was marching overland from Nashville, Tennessee. Once united, the combined armies would march on Corinth.

While the Union commanders were unsure of Johnston's location, Confederate cavalry knew well the disposition of Union troops. Johnston learned that Grant's army was encamped around Pittsburg Landing and that Buell's reinforcements had not yet arrived. Grant did not choose to fortify his position; rather, he set about drilling his men—many of whom were raw recruits. The Confederate commander saw an opportunity to seize the initiative and attack. Johnston's plan was to surprise Grant's men at Pittsburg Landing, and once engaged, drive directly toward the landing, turn the Union left flank, and cut them off from their best route of escape. By trapping the Federals between his own army and the dense undergrowth and swampland west of the Tennessee River, he hoped to destroy Grant's entire force.

The battle that erupted at dawn on April 6, 1862, developed into the fiercest combat yet seen in the Civil War. Johnston's men stormed out of the woods and assailed the forward Federal camps around Shiloh Church.

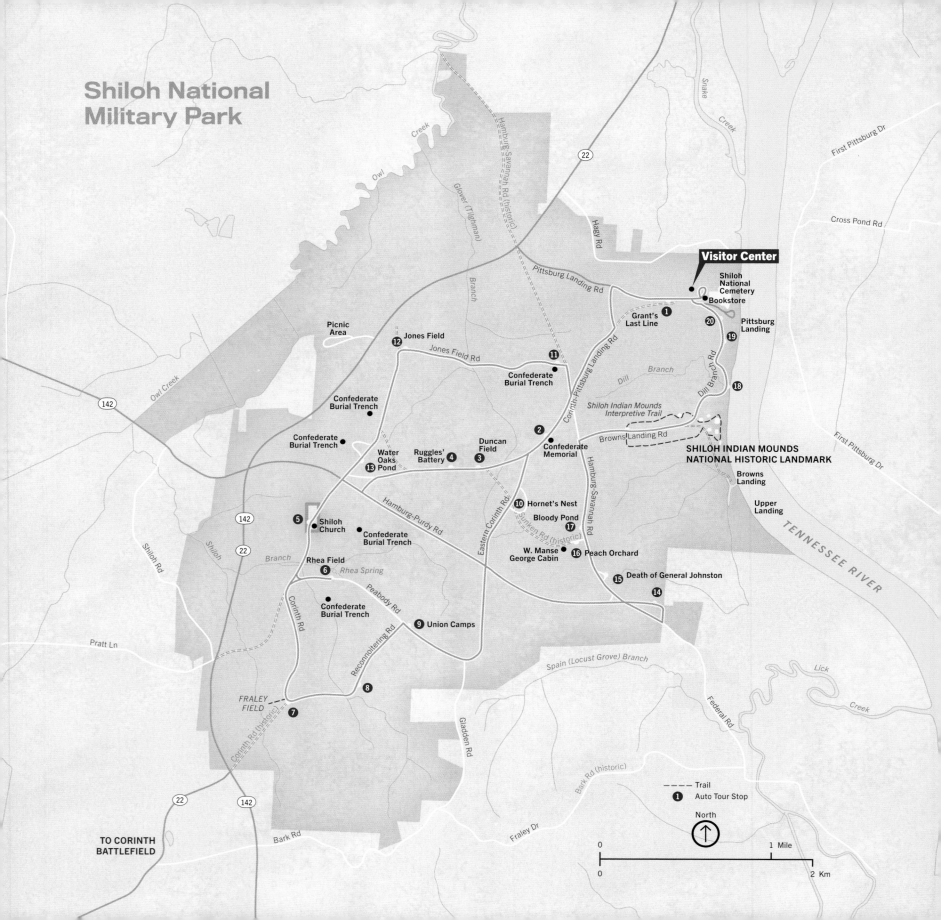

# Shiloh National Military Park

Picnic Area

Jones Field

Owl Creek

Glover (Tilghman)

Branch

Hamburg-Savannah Rd (historic)

Pittsburg Landing Rd

Hagy Rd

Snake Creek

Cross Pond Rd

First Pittsburg Dr

**Visitor Center**

Shiloh National Cemetery
Bookstore

Grant's Last Line

Pittsburg Landing

Jones Field Rd

Confederate Burial Trench

Dill Branch

Dill Branch Rd

Confederate Burial Trench

Confederate Burial Trench

Water Oaks Pond

Ruggles' Battery

Duncan Field

Confederate Memorial

Shiloh Indian Mounds Interpretive Trail

Browns Landing Rd

**SHILOH INDIAN MOUNDS NATIONAL HISTORIC LANDMARK**

Browns Landing

Upper Landing

Hamburg-Purdy Rd

Eastern Corinth Rd

Hornet's Nest

Bloody Pond

Corinth-Pittsburg Landing Rd

Hamburg-Savannah Rd

TENNESSEE RIVER

Shiloh Church

Confederate Burial Trench

Sunken Rd (historic)

W. Manse George Cabin

Peach Orchard

Shiloh Branch

Rhea Field

Rhea Spring

Confederate Burial Trench

Peabody Rd

Death of General Johnston

Corinth Rd

Shiloh Rd

Union Camps

Reconnoitering Rd

Spain (Locust Grove) Branch

Gladen Rd

Lick Creek

Pratt Ln

FRALEY FIELD

Corinth Rd (historic)

Federal Rd

Bark Rd (historic)

Fraley Dr

Bark Rd

- - - Trail

① Auto Tour Stop

**North**

0        1 Mile
0        2 Km

**TO CORINTH BATTLEFIELD**

Grant's army was taken by complete surprise. Soon desperate fighting engulfed the Union camps. Grant's men stubbornly contested the onslaught, but the determined Confederate advance pushed them back almost two miles toward Pittsburg Landing. As the Confederate battle lines advanced across ground covered by scrubby woodland and broken forest, however, units became intermixed and disoriented. Johnston, rallying his disorganized troops to press the assault on the Union left flank, didn't realize he'd been hit in a furious storm of musket fire. A musket ball tore through his leg, slicing an artery. Within minutes, the Confederate commander bled to death.

Still, the Confederate advance pressed forward. Only at the center of Grant's ragged three-mile battlefront did the Federal line hold firm. Here a wooden rail fence and sunken road—little more than a farm lane through an impenetrable oak forest—offered a small measure of protection. About 6,000 Union troops here fought off as many as 14 Confederate attacks. Col. James Fagan of the 1st Arkansas Infantry later wrote, "Here we engaged the enemy three different times, and braved a perfect rain of bullets, shot, and shell. Exposed, facing great odds, with the enemy in front and on the flank, the regiment endured a murderous fire until endurance ceased to be a virtue."

Soldiers called this place the Hornet's Nest, from the sound of musket balls clipping and shredding the leaves and branches above their heads. Frustrated by their mounting losses, the Confederates assembled 11 batteries—a total of 62 cannon—all trained on the half-mile stretch of Union ground. At about 4:30 p.m., a barrage of artillery fire decimated the stubborn Northern infantrymen. The beleaguered defenders, now isolated far out in front of the hard-pressed Union line and hopelessly outnumbered, were finally ordered to retreat. More than 2,000 Federals were captured in the dense thicket.

As the day wore on, the Southern attack continued to lose coordination as corps, divisions, and brigades became severely entangled. Fighting finally ended at nightfall. Grant's battered divisions retired to a strong position extending west from Pittsburg Landing, where massed artillery and rugged ravines protected their front and flanks. Some of Grant's subordinates urged retreat given the appalling losses the Union army had suffered. Grant, who was known for commenting, "I will take no backward step," refused.

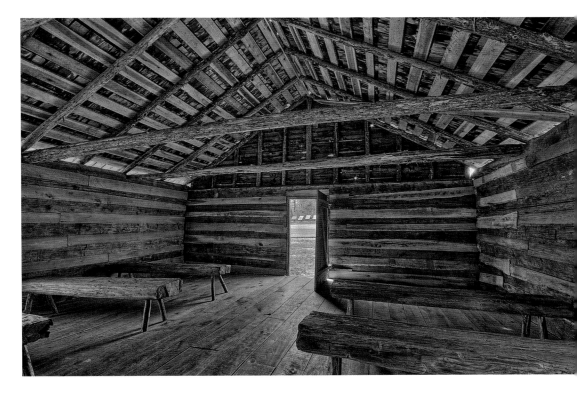

Overnight, reinforcements from Buell's army reached Pittsburg Landing. The division of Gen. Lew Wallace, which had been camped several miles away, also arrived on the battlefield. Gen. P. G. T. Beauregard, now in command of the Confederates, planned to finish the destruction of Grant's army the next day. At dawn on April 7, however, it was Grant who attacked. For six hours, the combined Union armies, now numbering more than 54,500 men, hammered Beauregard's depleted ranks, which had been reduced to as few as 34,000 troops. Despite mounting desperate counterattacks, the exhausted Confederates could not stem the increasingly stronger Federal tide. Forced back to Shiloh Church, Beauregard skillfully withdrew his outnumbered command and retreated to Corinth.

The Federals, also severely battered in the two days of fighting, did not press the pursuit. The Battle of Shiloh, or Pittsburg Landing, was over. It had cost both sides a combined total of 23,746 men killed, wounded, or missing—the largest loss of men so far in the Civil War. In the face of such appalling casualties, Grant faced a chorus of critics. In response, President Abraham Lincoln said, "I can't spare this man, he fights."

**PREVIOUS SPREAD:** Tennessee Monument near Water Oaks Pond.

**ABOVE:** Interior of Shiloh Church.

PREVIOUS SPREAD: Pittsburg
Landing on the Tennessee River.

LEFT: Artillery position on Jones
Field. Union forces rallied here
around noon on April 6,
1862, mounting a counterattack
that briefly checked the
Confederate offensive.

OPPOSITE: Capt. Marshall Polk's Tennessee Battery on Rhea Field. On April 6, 1862, the Confederates sustained devastating losses in repeated assaults against Union positions across Shiloh Branch.

RIGHT, TOP: Monuments in the Hornet's Nest.

RIGHT, BOTTOM: J. D. Putnam Monument. Putnam, a member of Company F, 14th Wisconsin Volunteer Infantry, was killed on April 7, 1862, during a charge against a Confederate battery.

FOLLOWING SPREAD: View from the Sunken Road.

# SHILOH Battlefield Hikes

Established on December 27, 1894, Shiloh National Military Park is one of the oldest and best-preserved Civil War battle-fields in the country. But the wooded landscape can be as confusing and impenetrable today as it was to soldiers during the battle. With the lone exception of the half-mile-long Sunken Road, the battlefield lacks a dominant physical feature to help orient the visitor. There is no major historic road bisecting it, no open high ground, and no perceptible creek or stream across which fighting took place. To get their bearings, hikers should start at the visitor center. The park does not have established battlefield trails with accompanying directions and interpretive literature, so it recommends that visitors make use of the Shiloh Military Trails website, established by a Boy Scouts of America Council from Memphis, Tennessee. The website describes Shiloh Battlefield hikes ranging from two miles (Battlefield Trek) to 14 miles (Shiloh Military Trail). The park bookshop also sells battlefield maps that show more detailed trail information than what is available on the official park map. Hiking is generally easy to moderate, with some steep terrain along the eastern end of the park near the Tennessee River. Visitors should pack ample drinking water, and insect repellant is recommended for the warmer months of the year.

## Sunken Road Trail (0.75 miles one way)

This historic trace follows the center of the Union line on the first day of fighting, passing along the edge of Duncan Field and the Hornet's Nest, past the W. Manse George cabin, and ending between The Peach Orchard and Bloody Pond. Union troops were shoulder to shoulder along the length of the Sunken Road, where rail fencing and the rutted roadway offered some protection to the hard-pressed soldiers. The Union line here was finally shattered by concentrated artillery fire from 11 Confederate batteries deployed along the south edge of Duncan Field. To hike along the entire Sunken Road, visitors should start at the Duncan Field parking area (Auto Tour Stop 3). The Battlefield Trek described on the Shiloh Military Trails website is a two-mile version of this hike that includes Illinois Battery F at Wicker Field and Ruggles' Battery on the south edge of Duncan Field.

## Confederate Advance Trail
### (0.5 miles one way)

Hikers can follow the path of the Confederate advance onto Shiloh Battlefield along the old

Corinth Road. The trail starts and ends at Ed Shaw's Restaurant at the intersection of Tennessee Routes 22 and 142, southeast of the battlefield. The Historical Trail described on the Shiloh Military Trails website begins along this same historic trace. Traveling in a northeasterly direction, the trail passes Wood's Field and Fraley Field—the two open areas adjoined at their corners. It was at this junction of the two fields where Union soldiers faced the surprise onslaught of Gen. Albert Sidney Johnston's Confederates at 4:55 a.m. on the morning of April 6, 1862. The old Corinth Road trace ends at the Fraley Field parking area (Auto Tour Stop 7) on Reconnoitering Road.

## Shiloh Indian Mounds Interpretive Trail
### (1.3 miles)

The Shiloh Indian Mounds are the remains of a prehistoric town that was occupied about 800 years ago. The loop trail has 13 interpretive wayside exhibits that explain the unique site. The hike is easy to moderate. The trail cuts through the complex, which sits between two steep ravines enclosed by the remains of a palisade—a 20-foot defensive structure made of wood and mud. The Tennessee River runs along the site's eastern boundary. Visitors should use caution when hiking along the eastern section of the trail, which has the steepest elevation change.

OPPOSITE: Bloody Pond.

ABOVE: Ruggles' Battery. Here the Confederates assembled 11 batteries—a total of 62 cannon—to dislodge Union forces from the Hornet's Nest.

# VICKSBURG
## BATTLEFIELD

MISSISSIPPI  Vicksburg National Military Park

FROM THE START OF THE CIVIL WAR, CONTROL OF THE MISSISSIPPI RIVER south of Cairo, Illinois, was vitally important to the North. The river was crucial to the transport of troops and supplies, and isolating Texas, Arkansas, and Louisiana from the rest of the Confederacy would considerably weaken the South. "The Mississippi is the backbone of the Rebellion," contended President Abraham Lincoln, "it is the key to the whole situation."

By late summer of 1862, only Vicksburg, Mississippi, and Port Hudson, Louisiana, blocked Union control of the river. Vicksburg sat atop a high bluff overlooking a bend in the Mississippi River, surrounded by almost impenetrable ridges and ravines. The place was a natural fortress. Artillery batteries protected the riverfront; a maze of swamps and bayous made approach from the north or south almost impossible; and a ring of forts with 172 guns guarded all the land approaches. So important was Vicksburg that Union forces would hammer away at it for more than a year. The Confederates tried just as desperately to hold it, deftly countering every Union threat. It wasn't until spring of 1863 that Gen. Ulysses S. Grant formulated a plan that would lead to Vicksburg's fall. It proved to be one of the more remarkable campaigns of the Civil War.

Grant decided to march his 45,000-man army down the west side of the Mississippi, where the ground was better suited for his long columns. He would cross the river well below Vicksburg, advance against the state capital in Jackson, and then wheel around and attack Vicksburg from the east. On March 31, 1863, the Union army left its encampments at Milliken's Bend, 20 miles northwest of Vicksburg.

Union gunboats and transports met the army at Bruinsburg, south of Vicksburg, on April 30, ferrying the troops across the Mississippi River. Grant then struck east, living off the land instead of waiting for supply

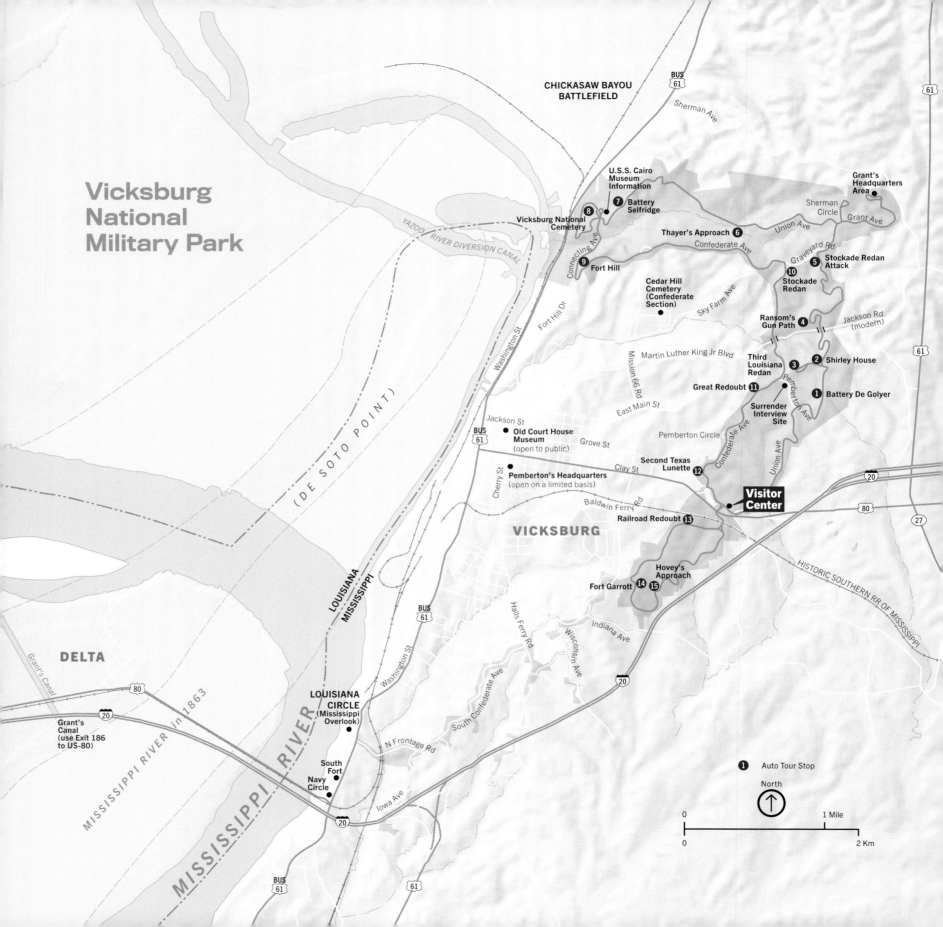

# Vicksburg National Military Park

CHICKASAW BAYOU BATTLEFIELD

Sherman Ave

**8** U.S.S. Cairo Museum Information

**7** Battery Selfridge

Vicksburg National Cemetery

Thayer's Approach **6**

Confederate Ave

Union Ave

Sherman Circle

Grant Ave

Grant's Headquarters Area

**9** Fort Hill

Graveyard Rd

Stockade Redan Attack **5**

**10** Stockade Redan

Cedar Hill Cemetery (Confederate Section)

Sky Farm Ave

Ransom's Gun Path **4**

Jackson Rd (modern)

Mission 66 Rd

Martin Luther King Jr Blvd

Third Louisiana Redan

**3**

**2** Shirley House

Great Redoubt **11**

Pemberton Ave

**1** Battery De Golyer

East Main St

Surrender Interview Site

Jackson St

Old Court House Museum (open to public)

Grove St

Pemberton Circle

Confederate Ave

Union Ave

BUS 61

Clay St

Second Texas Lunette **12**

Cherry St

Pemberton's Headquarters (open on a limited basis)

Baldwin Ferry Rd

**Visitor Center**

80

20

27

Railroad Redoubt **13**

**VICKSBURG**

HISTORIC SOUTHERN RR OF MISSISSIPPI

Hovey's Approach

Fort Garrott **14** **15**

Washington St

Fort Hill Dr

Connecting Ave

YAZOO RIVER DIVERSION CANAL

(DE SOTO POINT)

Indiana Ave

20

BUS 61

Halls Ferry Rd

Wisconsin Ave

LOUISIANA
MISSISSIPPI

**DELTA**

Grant's Canal (use Exit 186 to US-80)

80

20

MISSISSIPPI RIVER in 1863

**LOUISIANA CIRCLE** (Mississippi Overlook)

South Fort

Navy Circle

Washington St

N Frontage Rd

South Confederate Ave

Iowa Ave

MISSISSIPPI RIVER

20

BUS 61

61

**1** Auto Tour Stop

North ↑

0    1 Mile
0    2 Km

trains, defeating Gen. John Pemberton at the Battle of Port Gibson (May 1) and the Battle of Raymond (May 12). On May 14, Grant captured Jackson and scattered its defenders. He then turned west, following the Southern Railroad of Mississippi directly toward Vicksburg.

Two more battles with Pemberton's forces followed: the Confederates were defeated at the Battle of Champion Hill (May 16) and the Battle of the Big Black River Bridge (May 17). Grant reached Vicksburg on May 18, throwing a cordon around the city and sealing it off. Gen. William Tecumseh Sherman told his commander the operation had been "one of the greatest campaigns in history." Grant lost no time in assaulting the Vicksburg lines. But the "Gibraltar of the West," as Vicksburg was known, was not ready to surrender.

On May 19, 1863—convinced that Confederate morale had been shattered—Grant attacked. At 2:00 p.m., Sherman's corps advanced across the rugged terrain on either side of the Graveyard Road northeast of Vicksburg toward the Stockade Redan. Although a battalion from the 13th United States Infantry gained a brief toehold on the exterior slope of the fortress, the attack was repulsed with a loss of 942 men.

Grant tried again on May 22, expanding the assault over a three-mile front and leading the way with a thunderous four-hour bombardment. At 10:00 a.m., three Union corps advanced against the Confederate positions. Sherman attacked once again down the Graveyard Road, Gen. James McPherson's corps pressed the Confederate center along the Jackson Road, and Gen. John McClernand's corps targeted the Railroad Redoubt along the Baldwin Ferry Road. At the Railroad Redoubt, the few men who reached the defenses were hurled back with terrible losses. An officer in McClernand's command later wrote, "We passed through the mouth of hell. . . . Every third man fell, either killed or wounded." A few hundred yards to the north, the troops of Sherman and McPherson were also repulsed. The fighting on May 22 resulted in more than 3,000 Union casualties, making it the bloodiest day of the entire campaign.

**PREVIOUS SPREAD:** The sun peeks through Battery Benton in Navy Circle, adjacent to the Old Vicksburg Bridge.

**BELOW:** Remnants of field fortifications in Vicksburg National Military Park.

Reluctant to expend more lives on direct assaults against the city, Grant dug in for a long siege. Union troops built interlocking systems of zigzag trenches within yards of the Confederate fortifications, while Union artillery batteries on the land side and the gunboats of Adm. David Porter on the Mississippi River bombarded the city. The arrival of fresh Union divisions swelled Grant's force to about 70,000 men, further tightening the ring around the city.

The daily bombardments not only forced the Confederate defenders to hunker down in their fortifications, but also forced much of the city's civilian population underground. Eventually, about 500 caves were dug into the hillsides across Vicksburg. By mid-June, most of the city's food supply was also exhausted, and both troops and civilians were on the verge of starvation. Pemberton knew by late June that he must soon "capitulate upon the best attainable terms." On July 3 he met with Grant to discuss the terms. On the following morning, July 4, 1863, Vicksburg finally surrendered, bringing the 47-day siege to an end.

Grant, predictably unyielding, had initially demanded unconditional surrender. But after he met with Pemberton he softened his terms, agreeing to parole the Confederate troops and requiring them to sign an oath not to fight again until Union captives were freed in exchange. Grant later explained: "Had I insisted upon unconditional surrender, there would have been over thirty-odd thousand men to transport to Cairo, very much to the inconvenience of the army on the Mississippi." While the hungry, beaten Confederates marched out of Vicksburg and gave up their weapons, Federal troops, in a show of compassion and restraint, kept strict silence. "It was a strange sight," wrote Lt. Samuel Byers of the 5th Iowa, "those two armies that only a few hours before had been hurling destruction and death at each other, now walking in silence, side by side."

Elation at the fall of Vicksburg in the North was matched by despair in the South. Confederate Ordnance Chief Josiah Gorgas wrote: "Yesterday we rode on the pinnacle of success—today absolute ruin seems our portion. The Confederacy totters to its destruction." Lincoln, along with the rest of the Union, hailed Grant as a hero: "I write this now as a grateful acknowledgment for the almost inestimable service you have done the country."

PREVIOUS SPREAD: Big Black River Bridge, Hinds County, Mississippi. A Union victory at the Battle of the Big Black River Bridge, fought on May 17, 1863, forced the Confederates to retreat into Vicksburg.

LEFT, TOP: Stockade Redan. On May 19, 1863, a Union assault here was repulsed with heavy losses.

LEFT, BOTTOM: Artillery piece on the old Jackson Road.

OPPOSITE: The Illinois State Memorial, which was dedicated on October 26, 1906.

FOLLOWING SPREAD: Tunnel at Thayer's Approach. To protect Union troops from exposure to Confederate gunfire, a short tunnel was excavated through the ridgeline here.

# VICKSBURG Battlefield Hikes

Vicksburg National Military Park, which contains 1,325 monuments and markers and has more than 20 miles of original trenches and earthworks, offers several good hikes. All but one of the loop trails described below follow park roads across the battlefield. The city's historic defenses sit on top of a series of ridges bordered by steep ravines, making some of the hikes moderate to strenuous. All trails start at the visitor center on Clay Street, where maps and trail guides are available.

**Grant's Generosity Trail** (2.8 miles)
This hike follows Confederate Avenue north past the Second Texas Lunette and Great Redoubt, passes the Surrender Interview Site on Pemberton Avenue, and returns to the visitor center along Union Avenue. The lunette, manned by the 2nd Texas Volunteer Infantry, furiously repulsed repeated Union attacks during the fighting on May 22.

**Shirley's Hospitality Trail** (3.5 miles)
This hike follows Confederate Avenue north past the Second Texas Lunette to the historic Jackson Road just beyond the Great Redoubt. This massive Confederate earthwork guarded the old Jackson Road, and was under almost continuous bombardment during the siege. Hikers can turn right on the historic trace and continue past the Third Louisiana Redan, Illinois Monument, and

Shirley House. The house is the only surviving wartime structure in the park. The trail returns south on Union Avenue past Battery De Golyer to the visitor center.

**Forlorn Hope Trail** (6.0 miles)
This trail follows Confederate Avenue north past the Second Texas Lunette, Great Redoubt, and Stockade Redan to Graveyard Road. The failure of Union assaults against Stockade Redan on May 19 and 22 were major factors in Gen. Ulysses S. Grant's decision to avoid any more direct attacks on the Confederate defenses around Vicksburg. Hikers can turn right on Graveyard Road and walk to Union Avenue, then continue south past the Stockade Redan Attack site, Ransom's Gun Path, Shirley House, and Battery De Golyer on the way back to the visitor center.

**Pemberton's Revenge Trail** (10.4 miles)
This trail traverses the entire battlefield north of the visitor center, following Confederate and Union Avenues. Visitors can see the Second Texas Lunette, Great Redoubt, Stockade Redan, Fort Hill, Battery Selfridge, Thayer's Approach, the Stockade Redan Attack site, Ransom's Gun Path, Shirley House, and Battery De Golyer. Confederate batteries on Fort Hill anchored the northern flank of the Confederate lines and helped sink the Federal gunboat *Cincinnati* on May 27, 1863.

**Garrott's Promotion Trail** (3.0 miles)
This trail follows the park's South Loop on the south side of Clay Street past the Railroad

Redoubt, Fort Garrott, and Hovey's Approach. A restored section of Union trenches, dug by Gen. Alvin Hovey's Union troops, demonstrate how the siege was conducted. The zigzag design of the approach trenches helped to nullify the effects of Confederate enfilading fire and minimized Federal casualties.

### Al Scheller Hiking Trail (12.5 miles)

This trail follows a more physically demanding, off-road route across the entire battlefield, traversing the most rugged and natural areas of the park. The trail provides an excellent perception of the obstacles and difficult terrain faced by soldiers during the siege of Vicksburg. Designed as a compass course by the Boy Scouts of America, it winds through open fields, across the bottoms of steep ravines, into wooded areas, across several streambeds, and past locations of historical and natural interest. Hikers can obtain a copy of the trail guide at the visitor center.

OPPOSITE: Sunrise behind the Shirley House, the only surviving wartime structure in Vicksburg National Military Park.

ABOVE: Vicksburg National Cemetery.

# PORT HUDSON
## BATTLEFIELD

LOUISIANA  Port Hudson State Historic Site

WHEN VICKSBURG FELL ON JULY 4, 1863, PORT HUDSON—178 MILES downriver—was the last bastion of the Confederacy on the Mississippi River. Here Gen. Franklin Gardner, with just 6,800 Confederate defenders, held off Gen. Nathaniel Banks and some 30,000 Union troops. Banks, a Republican with strong abolitionist views, had served as speaker of the US House of Representatives and then governor of Massachusetts before the Civil War. At the outbreak of the war, President Abraham Lincoln appointed him one of his first political major generals. Banks was badly outfoxed and outfought by Gen. Thomas "Stonewall" Jackson during the 1862 Shenandoah Valley campaign, and fared little better at the Battle of Cedar Mountain during the Second Manassas campaign. He was subsequently transferred to the Department of the Gulf in New Orleans, where he replaced Benjamin Butler as commander.

In the spring of 1863, Banks was ordered to ascend the Mississippi River, secure Port Hudson, and then join Grant at Vicksburg. But like Vicksburg, Port Hudson was not ready to surrender. The place was situated on an 80-foot bluff on the east bank of the Mississippi above a hairpin turn in the river. The hills and ridges here consisted of extremely rough terrain surrounded by a maze of deep, thickly forested ravines, streams, and swamps. On the bluffs facing the river, the Confederates had planted 19 heavy guns. To the north, south, and east, Gardner had built an arc of trenches, redans, redoubts, and gun emplacements.

On May 27, 1863, Banks prepared to attack these fortifications. Most of his generals opposed a direct assault, but Banks was anxious to subdue Port Hudson as quickly as possible so he could proceed to Vicksburg and support Grant. With a four-to-one advantage in troop strength, Banks was confident he would easily force a Confederate surrender. But Gardner had no such plans.

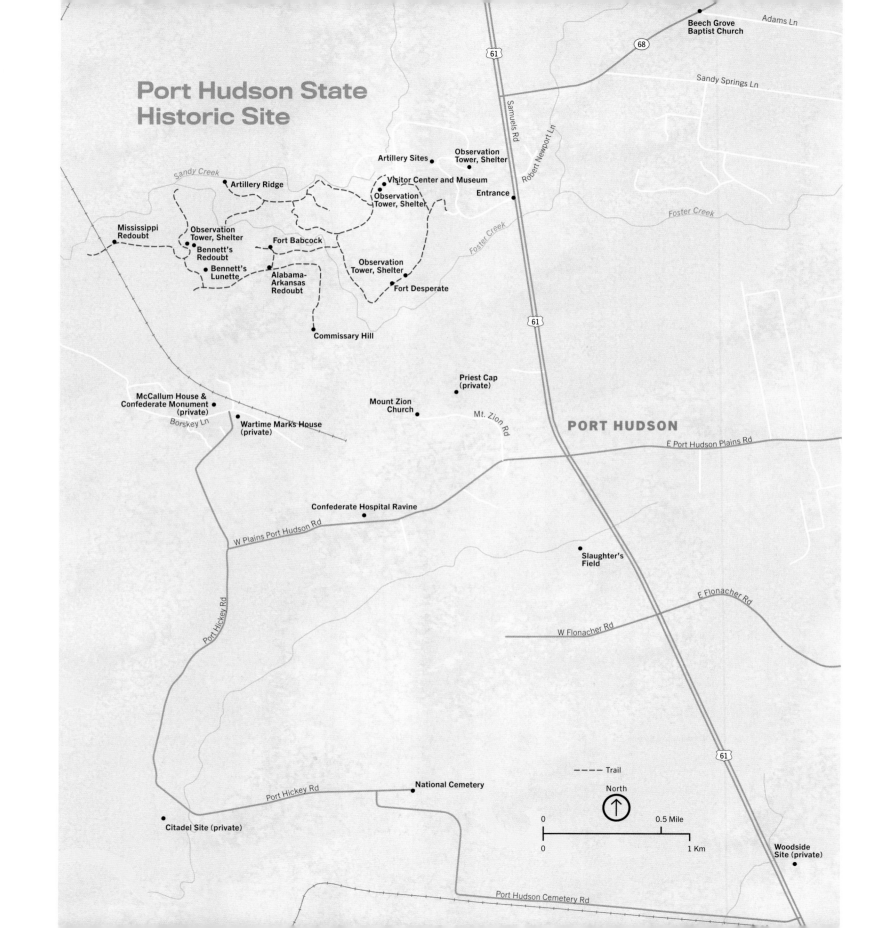

# Port Hudson State Historic Site

Beech Grove
Baptist Church

Adams Ln

68

Sandy Springs Ln

61

Samuels Rd

Robert Newport Ln

Foster Creek

Sandy Creek

Artillery Sites

Observation
Tower, Shelter

Artillery Ridge

Visitor Center and Museum

Observation
Tower, Shelter

Entrance

Mississippi
Redoubt

Observation
Tower, Shelter

Bennett's
Redoubt

Fort Babcock

Foster Creek

Bennett's
Lunette

Alabama-
Arkansas
Redoubt

Observation
Tower, Shelter

Fort Desperate

Commissary Hill

Priest Cap
(private)

McCallum House &
Confederate Monument
(private)

Mount Zion
Church

PORT HUDSON

Mt. Zion Rd

61

Borskey Ln

Wartime Marks House
(private)

E Port Hudson Plains Rd

Confederate Hospital Ravine

W Plains Port Hudson Rd

Slaughter's
Field

Port Hickey Rd

E Flonacher Rd

W Flonacher Rd

61

- - - Trail

North

National Cemetery

Citadel Site (private)

0                    0.5 Mile

0                          1 Km

Woodside
Site (private)

Port Hickey Rd

Port Hudson Cemetery Rd

Four assault groups were deployed, but Banks did not specify a time for the attack, simply ordering his generals to " . . . commence at the earliest hour practicable." Gen. Godfrey Weitzel and Gen. Cuvier Grover advanced at dawn, while the remaining divisions under Gen. Christopher Augur and Gen. Thomas Sherman didn't commence their attacks until noon. The piecemeal and sporadic assaults through steep-sided ravines and dense vegetation were easily repulsed. Union forces caught in rebel cross fire from salients in the strong defense works were cut to pieces.

Seeing that the Union advance had been stopped, Gen. William Dwight ordered the 1st and 3rd Louisiana Native Guards, two African American regiments, forward into the attack. Despite the heavy cross fire, the black regiments advanced with determination and courage. Taking heavy losses, the attackers were forced to retreat to avoid annihilation. Port Hudson was the first time African American soldiers were used in a major Civil War battle, and their fearless advance did much to enhance their reputation in combat.

The May 27 fighting ended around 5:00 p.m., when the commander of the 159th New York raised a white flag to signal a truce in order to remove the wounded and dead from the field. None of the Union attacks had even made it to the Confederate parapets.

Undaunted, Banks ordered a second attack for June 14. Again, uncoordinated assaults by the Union divisions were repulsed with severe losses. By the end of the day, Union forces suffered 1,792 casualties compared to 47 Confederates killed or wounded. Just as Grant had done at Vicksburg, Banks now turned his full attention to siege operations. Soon the Confederate defenders—already reduced by disease and sickness— were desperately short of food, water, and ammunition.

When Gardner learned that Vicksburg had surrendered on July 4, 1863, he realized his situation was hopeless. Terms of surrender were negotiated, and on July 9, 1863, the Confederates laid down their weapons. The 48-day siege was finally over, and the Confederacy was now split in two. "The Father of Waters," exclaimed Lincoln, "again goes unvexed to the sea."

PREVIOUS SPREAD: View of Port Hudson Battlefield.

ABOVE, LEFT: Battery overlooking the Mississippi River at Port Hudson.

ABOVE, RIGHT: Battered artillery and field fortifications inside Port Hudson after the 1863 siege.

# PORT HUDSON Battlefield Hike

This hike begins at the battlefield museum, where a trail map is available. Due to the hilly, uneven terrain, the trails are steep in some places.

### Port Hudson Battlefield Trail (6.0 miles)

Hikers can explore Port Hudson Battlefield along six miles of well-marked interconnecting trails. The battery positions and earthworks along these trails comprise the northern portion of the Port Hudson Battlefield (the southern portion of the battlefield is not part of the state historic site). The trails provide access to five major Confederate defensive breastworks and much of the area used by Union troops to attack these positions. Interpretive signs along the trails explain much of the action during the 48-day siege.

OPPOSITE: Boardwalk trail through Port Hudson Battlefield.

ABOVE: Naval gun at Port Hudson Battlefield.

KENTUCKY
EAST TENNESSEE
GEORGIA

# PERRYVILLE
# BATTLEFIELD

IN AUGUST 1862, CONFEDERATE GEN. BRAXTON BRAGG LAUNCHED AN invasion into the key border state of Kentucky. He was convinced that Kentuckians would rally to the Confederate cause. For President Abraham Lincoln, who was born in Kentucky, the state was just as vital to the North. "I think to lose Kentucky is nearly to lose the whole game," he wrote in September 1861. With an army of 22,000 men, Bragg slipped around Gen. Don Carlos Buell's Army of the Ohio near Nashville, Tennessee, and raced toward Louisville on the Ohio River. Buell's army headed north in pursuit.

While Bragg halted his advance to capture a Union fort at Munfordville, Buell arrived in Louisville. Here the Army of the Ohio was resupplied with thousands of new recruits. On October 1, 1862, Buell marched his army out of Louisville in four columns. Three columns, numbering nearly 57,000 men, converged on the small Kentucky town of Perryville. A fourth column, acting as a diversion, marched toward the state capital at Frankfurt.

The ruse worked. Bragg sent a quarter of his army north to meet the threat at Frankfurt, leaving only 16,000 men to fight at Perryville. Both armies had converged on the small town for two reasons: it was an important crossroads, and there was water. Kentucky was in the throes of a major drought during the summer of 1862. Just west of Perryville, thirsty troops found water in the stagnant pools of Doctor's Creek and the Chaplin River. On the morning of October 8, the Union Third Corps, commanded by Gen. Charles Gilbert, attacked a brigade of Arkansas troops and secured the area near Doctor's Creek. Gen. Philip Sheridan then seized Peter's Hill, where he was ordered to halt and await the arrival of the other Union columns.

The Confederate plan was to attack what they believed was a small Union force. Shifting their troops to the northwest of Perryville, they prepared to launch a flank attack down the valley of Doctor's Creek. At

# Perryville Battlefield State Historic Site

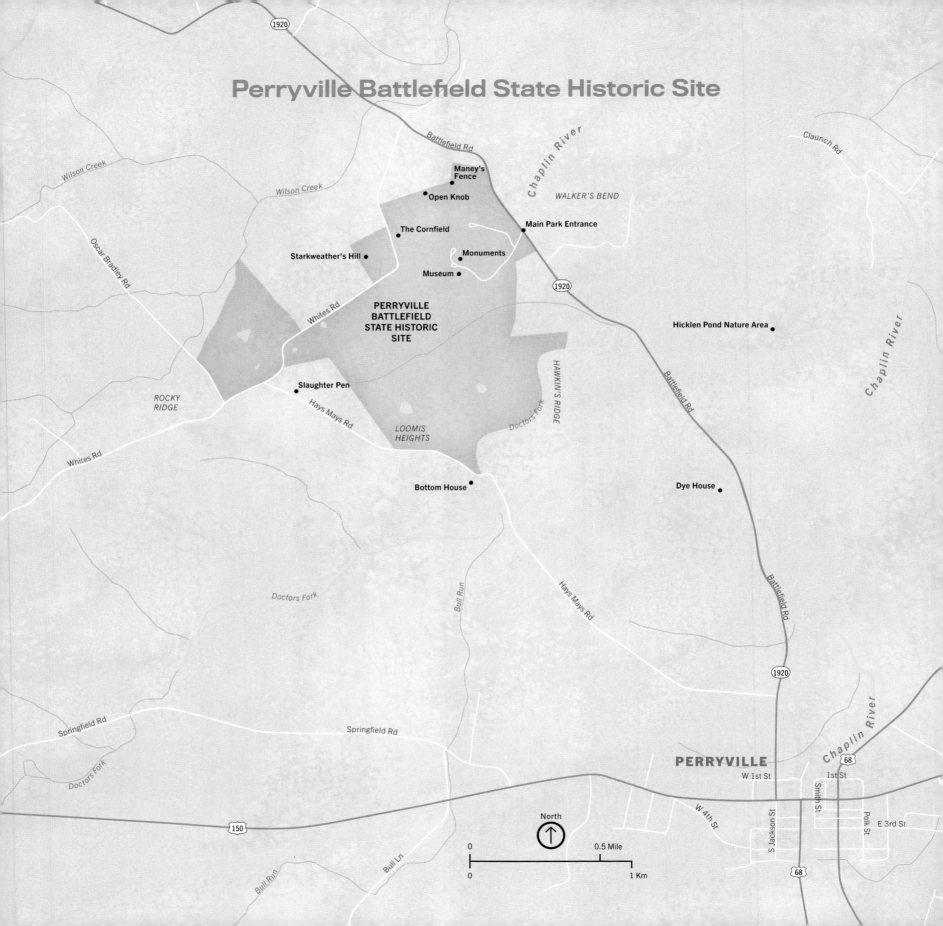

1920

Battlefield Rd

Chaplin River

Wilson Creek

Wilson Creek

WALKER'S BEND

Maney's Fence

Open Knob

The Cornfield

Main Park Entrance

Oscar Bradley Rd

Starkweather's Hill

Monuments

Museum

1920

PERRYVILLE
BATTLEFIELD
STATE HISTORIC
SITE

Hicklen Pond Nature Area

Whites Rd

HAWKIN'S RIDGE

Battlefield Rd

Chaplin River

ROCKY
RIDGE

Slaughter Pen

Hays Mays Rd

Doctors Fork

LOOMIS
HEIGHTS

Whites Rd

Bottom House

Dye House

Doctors Fork

Bull Run

Hays Mays Rd

1920

Springfield Rd

Springfield Rd

Doctors Fork

PERRYVILLE

Chaplin River

W 1st St

1st St

150

Smith St

68

W 4th St

S Jackson St

Polk St

E 3rd St

North

↑

0                    0.5 Mile

0                                1 Km

Bull Run

Bull Ln

68

2:00 p.m. on the afternoon of October 8, Gen. Benjamin Cheatham's division began the main assault. The Southerners pushed the Union line back across Open Knob and through a cornfield, threatening to crush the Union left flank. Only a gallant defense made by the 28th Brigade of Col. John Starkweather along a ridge west of The Cornfield saved Buell's army. With 2,200 men and 12 guns, Starkweather repulsed several Confederate assaults. Confederate Private Sam Watkins of the 1st Tennessee Infantry later wrote, "We were soon in a hand-to-hand fight—every man for himself—using the butts of our guns and bayonets. . . . Such obstinate fighting I never had seen before or since. The guns were discharged so rapidly that it seemed the earth itself was in a volcanic uproar. The iron storm passed through our ranks, mangling and tearing men to pieces."

The assault by the Confederates on Starkweather's line, which lasted more than three hours, was the bloodiest of the battle. Historian Kenneth Noe described the final Confederate repulse as the "high-water mark of the Confederacy in the western theater, no less important than the Angle at Gettysburg." The ridge is known today as Starkweather's Hill.

At the south end of the battlefield, around 4:00 p.m., Bragg ordered a Confederate infantry brigade to advance west on the Springfield Pike and silence a Union artillery battery. Rather than encountering an isolated battery, however, the rebels ran into Sheridan's entire division. The Confederates were repulsed and fell back into Perryville. A brigade of Union infantry pursued them into town, where street fighting continued into the evening. By 11:00 p.m. the fighting was over. The battle, the largest fought in Kentucky during the Civil War, cost the Union army 4,276 casualties; the Confederates lost 3,401 men. Bragg, finally realizing that he was facing a far larger army, withdrew from Perryville during the night. The Confederate offensive was over, and the North now firmly controlled Kentucky.

PREVIOUS SPREAD: Artillery piece on the Perryville Battlefield.

ABOVE, LEFT: View looking northwest toward Maney's Fence and Open Knob.

ABOVE, RIGHT: The Squire Bottom House, which was owned by Henry P. "Squire" Bottom, a slave-owning Unionist, during the Battle of Perryville.

# PERRYVILLE
# Battlefield Hikes

Twenty miles of interconnected trails crisscross Perryville Battlefield, providing access to virtually every part of this state historic site. The trail system has no specific trailheads or destinations; hikers may choose to follow any of the interconnecting trails to any part of the battlefield, hiking for just a few minutes or for several hours.

## Perryville Battlefield Trails (20.0 miles)

The trails of this system consist primarily of mowed paths through grassy fields, with a few wooded areas. A particularly good one-hour, 1.7-mile loop passes across a part of the battlefield where some of the fiercest fighting took place. Hikers should start at the visitor center and walk counterclockwise to the following points of interest: Cemetery Area, Opening Attack, Stewart's Advance, Turner's Battery, Maney's Fence, Open Knob, The Cornfield, Starkweather's Hill, Act of Mercy, Bloodbath at the Crib, and Valley of Death. Interpretive wayside exhibits provide in-depth information at each of the sites on the trail map, which can be obtained at the visitor center.

View looking north from Whites Road toward The Cornfield. Perryville Battlefield is one of the best-preserved Civil War sites in the nation.

# STONES RIVER
## BATTLEFIELD

TENNESSEE  Stones River National Battlefield

FOLLOWING THE BATTLE OF PERRYVILLE, CONFEDERATE GEN. BRAXTON
Bragg abandoned his invasion of Kentucky. On November 20, 1862, his reorganized Army of Tennessee took up
a defensive position northwest of Murfreesboro, Tennessee, along the West Fork of the Stones River. Bragg had
withdrawn from Kentucky over the vehement objections of his generals, who had pleaded with him to press the
attack against Union Gen. Don Carlos Buell. One observer noted that Bragg displayed "a perplexity and vacillation
which had now become simply appalling," prompting his subordinates to petition Richmond to have him replaced.
Confederate President Jefferson Davis, however, stood by his old friend, and Bragg retained his command.

On the Union side, President Abraham Lincoln had become frustrated with Buell's own passivity and inac-
tion. As 1862 drew to a close, Lincoln was desperate for a military victory. His armies were stalled, and the terrible
defeat at Fredericksburg spread a pall of defeat across the North. There was also the Emancipation Proclamation
to consider. The nation needed a victory to bolster morale and support the proclamation when it went into effect
on January 1, 1863. Buell was replaced by Gen. William Rosecrans, who was told in no uncertain terms, ". . . the
Government demands action, and if you cannot respond to that demand someone else will be tried."

On December 26, 1862, Rosecrans led the Army of the Cumberland out of Nashville to seek the victory
Lincoln demanded. The Union army totaled approximately 43,000 men. Bragg's Army of Tennessee fielded
about 35,000 troops. By the evening of December 30, the two armies faced each other in the fields and forests
along the Stones River. While both generals prepared their battle plans, the men lay down amid the cold mud
and rocks to get some sleep. The bands of both armies played tunes to raise the soldiers' spirits, leading up to
one of the war's most poignant moments. Sam Seay of the 1st Tennessee Infantry described what happened:

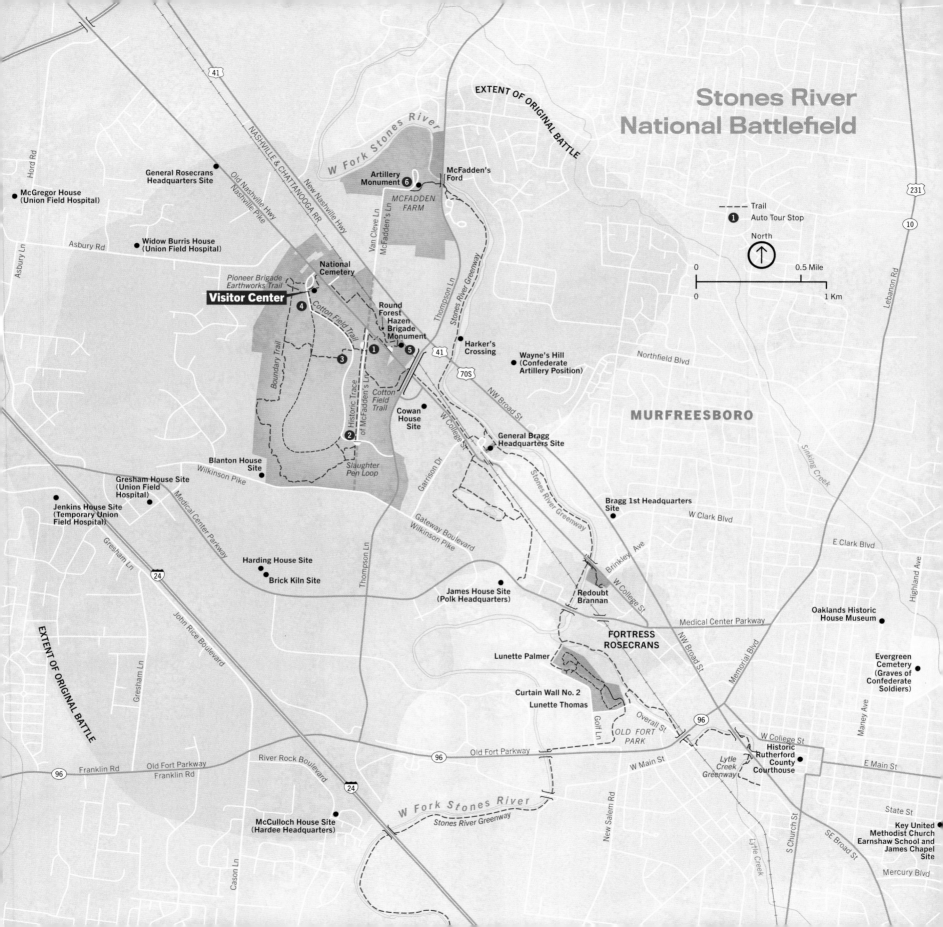

# Stones River
# National Battlefield

EXTENT OF ORIGINAL BATTLE

MURFREESBORO

- - - Trail
**1** Auto Tour Stop

North
↑

0          0.5 Mile

0                    1 Km

McGregor House
(Union Field Hospital)

General Rosecrans
Headquarters Site

Widow Burris House
(Union Field Hospital)

W Fork Stones River

Artillery
Monument  **6**

McFadden's
Ford

MCFADDEN
FARM

National Cemetery

Pioneer Brigade
Earthworks Trail

**Visitor Center**

**4**

Cotton Field Trail

Round
Forest
Hazen
Brigade
Monument

**1**        **5**

**3**

Boundary Trail

Harker's
Crossing

Wayne's Hill
(Confederate
Artillery Position)

Northfield Blvd

Historic Trace
of McFadden's Ln

Cotton
Field
Trail

**2**

Cowan House
Site

General Bragg
Headquarters Site

Slaughter
Pen Loop

Blanton House
Site

Wilkinson Pike

Gresham House Site
(Union Field Hospital)

Jenkins House Site
(Temporary Union
Field Hospital)

Gateway Boulevard
Wilkinson Pike

Bragg 1st Headquarters
Site

W Clark Blvd

E Clark Blvd

Harding House Site

Brick Kiln Site

James House Site
(Polk Headquarters)

Redoubt
Brannan

Medical Center Parkway

Oaklands Historic
House Museum

FORTRESS
ROSECRANS

Lunette Palmer

Curtain Wall No. 2
Lunette Thomas

Evergreen
Cemetery
(Graves of
Confederate
Soldiers)

OLD FORT
PARK

Historic
Rutherford
County
Courthouse

Lytle
Creek
Greenway

McCulloch House Site
(Hardee Headquarters)

W Fork Stones River

Stones River Greenway

Old Fort Parkway

W Main St

New Salem Rd

Key United
Methodist Church
Earnshaw School and
James Chapel
Site

*Just before "tattoo" the military bands on each side began their evening music. The still winter night carried their strains to great distance. At every pause on our side, far away could be heard the military bands of the other. Finally one of them struck up "Home Sweet Home." As if by common consent, all other airs ceased, and the bands of both armies as far as the ear could reach, joined in the refrain. Who knows how many hearts were bold next day by reason of that air?*

At dawn on December 31, 1862, the Confederates struck first, assaulting the Federal right flank. Bragg's plan was to swing around the Union line in a right wheel and drive them back to the Stones River, cutting them off from their lines of supply on the Nashville Pike and Nashville and Chattanooga Railroad. The surprised Federals were pushed back in confusion. One soldier of the 14th Texas Infantry wrote, "Many of the Yanks were either killed or retreated in their night-clothes." Union commanders tried to halt and resist at every fence and tree line, but the Confederate attack was too powerful to stop.

Only the actions of Gen. Philip Sheridan prevented a Union rout. Suspecting an imminent attack, he had ordered his men to rise before dawn and form a strong battle line. Fighting amid thick stands of cedar on ground marked by limestone outcroppings, deep crevices, and large boulders, his troops repulsed several enemy assaults, slowing the Confederate advance and allowing for an orderly retreat. But the cost to the Federals was appalling—in four hours of fighting all three of Sheridan's brigade commanders were killed or mortally wounded, and more than one third of his men were casualties. Sam Watkins of the 1st Tennessee Infantry described the carnage: "I cannot remember now of ever seeing more dead men and horses and captured cannon, all jumbled together . . . the ground was literally covered with blue coats dead." By the end of the day, this cedar forest became known as the "Slaughter Pen."

While fighting raged in the Slaughter Pen, Rosecrans worked furiously to save his army. He and Gen. George Thomas organized reserves and rallied fleeing troops into a strong line along the Nashville Pike, backed up by massed artillery. Again the woods helped the Union side. Confederate organization fell apart as the troops struggled through the dense forest

and across the rocky ground. Each wave of the enemy's attack along the pike was repulsed by Federal artillery that now commanded the field.

Bragg tried to revive his sputtering offensive by attacking the Round Forest. This wooded area, situated between the Stones River and the Nashville Pike, anchored the left of the Union line. Here the brigade of Col. William Hazen stood its ground against four separate attacks, leaving hundreds of Confederates dead or wounded. The carnage was described by J. Morgan Smith of the 32nd Alabama Infantry, who wrote, "We charged in fifty yards of them and had not the timely order of retreat been given—none of us would now be left to tell the tale. . . . Our regiment carried two hundred and eighty into action and came out with fifty eight."

The Union stand in "Hell's Half Acre," as this ground became known, gave Rosecrans a solid anchor for his Nashville Pike line that finally stopped the Confederate tide. As night approached, the Union army was bloody and battered, but it retained control of the pike and its vital lifeline to Nashville. On the Confederate side, Bragg was certain that he had won a victory. He sent a telegram to Richmond before he went to bed: "The enemy has yielded his strong position and is falling back. We occupy [the] whole field and shall follow him. . . . God has granted us a happy New Year."

**PREVIOUS SPREAD:** Troops on both sides used the rocky terrain in this cedar thicket for cover in what would become known as the Slaughter Pen.

**BELOW:** Stones River Artillery Monument.

To Bragg's utter surprise, on New Year's Day, January 1, 1863, Union forces still held their ground. Both armies spent the day reorganizing and tending to their wounded. Even more troubling, Union troops were now deployed on a hill east of the Stones River, threatening the Confederate right flank. On January 2, Bragg ordered Gen. John Breckinridge to seize this high ground. At about 4:00 p.m., 4,500 men attacked the hill, driving the Union defenders back across the Stones River at McFadden's Ford. But as they pressed their assault to the river, the Confederates encountered a deadly surprise. Massed Union artillery—57 cannon in all—cut the Southerners to pieces. In 45 minutes their concentrated fire killed or wounded more than 1,800 Confederates. Union troops soon crossed back over the river and reclaimed the heights.

With the failure of his assault, Bragg withdrew from Murfreesboro. In one of the costliest battles of the entire war, Union forces suffered 13,249 casualties while the Confederates lost 10,266 men. A relieved Lincoln thanked Rosecrans and his men for a "hard-earned victory, which, had there been a defeat instead, the nation could scarcely have lived over." Rosecrans renewed his advance against Chattanooga later that spring.

BELOW: View along the Slaughter Pen Trail, where some of the fiercest fighting of the battle raged.

OPPOSITE: Re-creation of Union artillery destroyed in the Slaughter Pen.

# STONES RIVER Battlefield Hike

Stones River National Battlefield features almost seven miles of hiking trails. The park trail system also connects to Murfreesboro's Greenway System, which boasts four and a half miles of paved trails along the Stones River and Lytle Creek. Hikers should start at the visitor center, where trail maps and interpretive information are available.

### Boundary Trail (3.5 miles)

This trail, which starts and ends at the visitor center, travels through the woods and across the rocky landscape that shaped much of the fighting at the Stones River Battlefield. The trail loops around the main battlefield area and crosses the old Nashville Pike to the site of the Round Forest, where the Hazen Brigade Monument—the oldest intact Civil War monument in the nation—marks the fighting on Hell's Half Acre. The trail also connects to several shorter side trails, including the Pioneer Brigade Earthworks Trail (0.25 miles), Slaughter Pen Loop (0.5 miles), and Cotton Field Trail (0.5 miles). The Cotton Field Trail is paved and fully accessible.

OPPOSITE: Wiard Cannon near the Slaughter Pen.
ABOVE: Hazen Brigade Monument, the oldest Civil War monument still standing in its original location.

# CHICKAMAUGA
## BATTLEFIELD

GEORGIA  Chickamauga and Chattanooga National Military Park

ON AUGUST 20, 1890, PRESIDENT BENJAMIN HARRISON SIGNED INTO law H.R. 6454, "An act to establish a national military park at the battle-field of Chickamauga." The legislation not only established the nation's first national military park, but also provided a framework for the preservation of other Civil War battlefields to follow. Equally important, the legislation mandated inclusion of both North and South in the commemoration of the site—the first Civil War battlefield to formally do so. At the park's dedication on September 20, 1895, Vice President Adlai Stevenson spoke to more than 10,000 veterans in attendance: "They meet, not in deadly conflict, but as brothers, under one flag—fellow citizens of a common country." What a marked contrast this was to some of the bloodiest fighting of the Civil War that took place here on September 18, 19, and 20, 1863.

The path to Chickamauga began in the spring of 1863, when Gen. William Rosecrans maneuvered his Army of the Cumberland, composed of some 58,000 Union soldiers, across eastern Tennessee. His objective was Chattanooga—an important Southern rail junction and gateway into northern Georgia. Once this small city was in Union hands, proclaimed President Abraham Lincoln, "I think the rebellion must dwindle and die."

Facing Rosecrans along the Duck River north of Chattanooga was Gen. Braxton Bragg. Bragg, who commanded the Army of Tennessee, was intent on using the natural river barrier to block Rosecrans's advance. But Rosecrans, moving his columns in a series of skillful feints, outfoxed Bragg and bypassed the flanks of the Confederate army, forcing Bragg to withdraw south. By July 3, 1863, Bragg's army had been pushed all the way to Chattanooga. The brilliant nine-day Union advance, known as the Tullahoma Campaign, succeeded at the astonishingly modest cost of just 560 Union casualties. Bragg confided to Confederate Army Chaplain

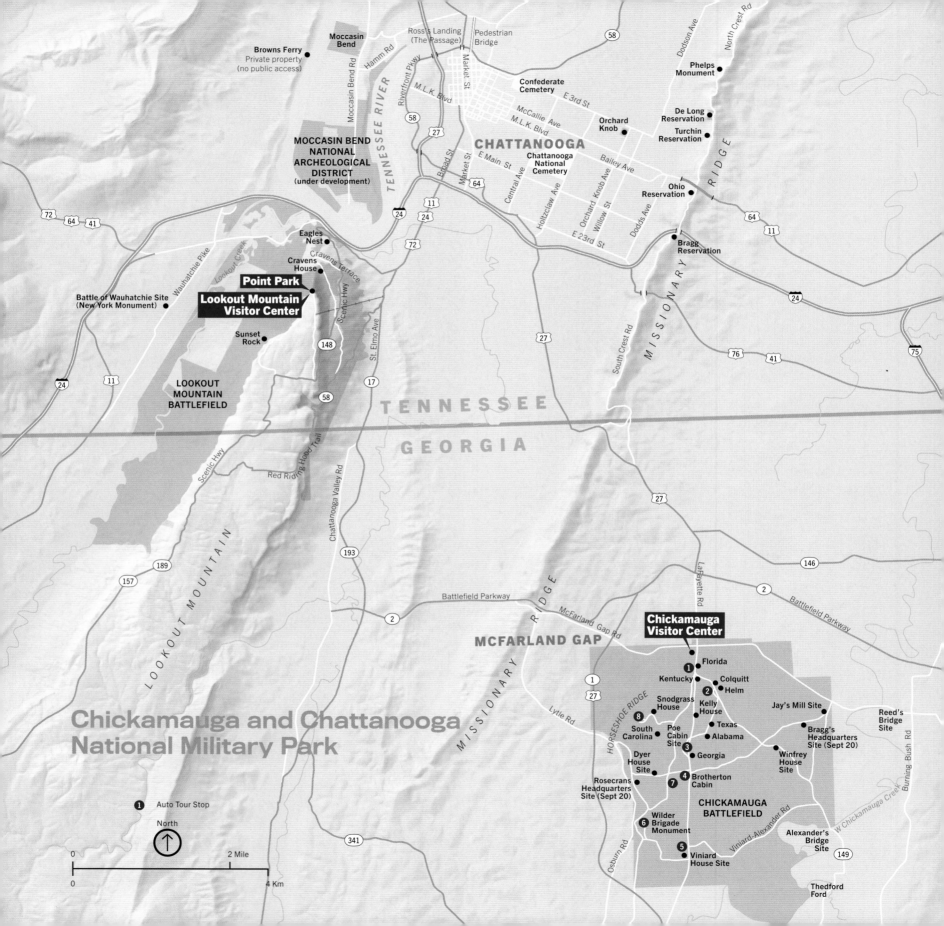

Browns Ferry
Private property
(no public access)

Moccasin
Bend

Ross's Landing
(The Passage)

Pedestrian
Bridge

Phelps
Monument

Confederate
Cemetery

De Long
Reservation

Turchin
Reservation

MOCCASIN BEND
NATIONAL
ARCHEOLOGICAL
DISTRICT
(under development)

CHATTANOOGA

Orchard
Knob

Chattanooga
National
Cemetery

Ohio
Reservation

TENNESSEE RIVER

Bragg
Reservation

Eagles
Nest

Cravens
House

**Point Park**

**Lookout Mountain
Visitor Center**

Battle of Wauhatchie Site
(New York Monument)

Sunset
Rock

LOOKOUT
MOUNTAIN
BATTLEFIELD

MISSIONARY RIDGE

**TENNESSEE**

**GEORGIA**

LOOKOUT MOUNTAIN

**Chickamauga and Chattanooga
National Military Park**

MISSIONARY RIDGE

MCFARLAND GAP

Battlefield Parkway

Battlefield Parkway

**Chickamauga
Visitor Center**

Florida

Reed's
Bridge
Site

Kentucky

Colquitt

Helm

Snodgrass
House

Kelly
House

Jay's Mill Site

South
Carolina

Poe
Cabin
Site

Texas

Bragg's
Headquarters
Site (Sept 20)

Alabama

Dyer
House
Site

Georgia

Winfrey
House
Site

Rosecrans
Headquarters
Site (Sept 20)

Brotherton
Cabin

**CHICKAMAUGA
BATTLEFIELD**

Wilder
Brigade
Monument

Alexander's
Bridge
Site

Viniard
House Site

Thedford
Ford

1 Auto Tour Stop

North

0        2 Mile

0        4 Km

Charles Quintard: "Yes, I am utterly broken down. This is a great disaster." Quintard's reply was more confident: "General, don't be disheartened, our turn will come next." That turn would come just a few weeks later along Chickamauga Creek, south of Chattanooga.

But at the moment, the Confederates were dug in around Chattanooga, nestled in a bend along the Tennessee River. Undaunted, Rosecrans crossed the river 20 miles west of the city on September 4, 1863. He directed two columns to cross separate gaps in Lookout Mountain—an imposing ridge extending 30 miles southwest from Chattanooga—wheel north, and imperil Bragg's southern flank and line of supply. The maneuver worked, and once again Bragg was forced to retreat, abandoning Chattanooga and withdrawing into Georgia. Rosecrans dispatched a triumphant message to Washington: "Chattanooga is ours without a struggle." He was convinced Bragg's army was demoralized and fleeing south in disorder.

Instead, Bragg conducted an orderly retreat, reorganizing his forces around LaFayette, Georgia, 26 miles south of Chattanooga. Bragg's army was soon bolstered with fresh reinforcements—8,000 men from Knoxville, Tennessee; 11,500 men from Mississippi; and two divisions dispatched from the Army of Northern Virginia under the command of Gen. James Longstreet. By the middle of September, Bragg counted more than 66,000 troops—a rare occasion during the Civil War when Confederate forces outnumbered the Union troops arrayed against them.

By September 16, 1863, the two armies were deployed along either side of Chickamauga Creek, south of Chattanooga. Preparing for battle, Bragg issued General Orders, No. 180, concluding with an impassioned plea to his troops: "Trusting in God and the justice of our cause, and nerved by the love of the dear ones at home, failure is impossible and victory must be ours."

On September 18, Confederate troops attempted to cross West Chickamauga Creek at Reed's Bridge and Alexander's Bridge. Bragg was determined to strike the left flank of Gen. Thomas Crittenden's Twenty-First Corps near Lee and Gordon's Mills at the north end of the Federal line. If the attack succeeded, the Confederates would wedge themselves between the Union army and Chattanooga, cutting off its line of retreat. But fierce fighting by Union cavalry stalled the advance for several hours. Col. John Wilder's mounted Union infantry brigade, armed with Spencer seven-shot repeating rifles, put up an especially effective fight. The cavalry eventually retired, and during the night Bragg succeeded in getting most of his army across the creek. But he had lost an entire day, giving Rosecrans enough time to counter the threat and strengthen his northern flank.

On the morning of September 19, skirmishing along the creek erupted into full-scale battle. Confederate troops poured into the fight from the east, while Union reinforcements moved in from the north and south. The wooded terrain across the battlefield concealed troop movements and positions, leading to chaos as units blindly attacked each other. The battle seesawed furiously back and forth through the woods east of the LaFayette Road all day long, but neither side could gain an advantage. By nightfall, Bragg's men had gained ground, but could not break the Union line despite several ferocious assaults. Corp. William Miller of the 75th Indiana Infantry described the horrific fighting:

> *Our men kept falling back as the Rebels pressed them and finally came out into the open field . . . They kept up the fight until darkness put a stop to it. There was heavy firing to our left until nine o'clock tonight. . . . This has been a terrible day to the American Nation and many bitter tears will be shed North and South for the dead of Chickamauga. There are thousands of men in the prime of life who this morning thought they were destined to live to a ripe old age who tonight are lying on the battlefield . . .*

Nightfall brought little rest to troops on either side. Anticipating another day of fierce fighting, Federal units were repositioned, battle lines were shored up, and trees were felled to make breastworks. At the Confederate headquarters, Bragg reorganized his army into two wings. Gen. Leonidas Polk was put in charge of the right wing to the north, while Longstreet commanded the left wing to the south. The change required considerable shifting of troops during the night, which caused a delay in Bragg's attack the next morning.

About 9:30 a.m. on September 20, Bragg finally renewed his attack, still bent on turning Rosecrans's left flank and blocking the road to Chattanooga. Polk's forces hammered the Federal positions with several

PREVIOUS SPREAD: Brotherton Cabin. Some of the heaviest fighting of the battle occurred here.

LEFT, TOP: Lee and Gordon's Mill on West Chickamauga Creek near the Chickamauga Battlefield.

LEFT, BOTTOM: Alexander's Bridge over West Chickamauga Creek.

OPPOSITE: Monument to the 11th Michigan Infantry on Horseshoe Ridge.

coordinated assaults. Furious fire from Union troops behind their new log breastworks repelled the attacks, but help was needed. Gen. George Thomas, commander of the Union Fourteenth Corps, sent Rosecrans an urgent message to order up reinforcements. In responding to the request, Rosecrans made a fatal mistake.

While units were being repositioned, a staff officer riding behind the lines reported a large gap near the center of the Union line. There was no gap—Gen. John Brannan's division was there, hidden in the trees. Rosecrans failed to confirm the report, however, and ordered Gen. Thomas Wood's division to fill the gap. Wood knew no such gap existed, and that moving his division would, in turn, open up a quarter-mile hole in the Federal line. But Wood had already been

OPPOSITE: Union artillery along Snodgrass Hill.

BELOW: 2nd Minnesota Infantry Regiment Monument on Snodgrass Hill.

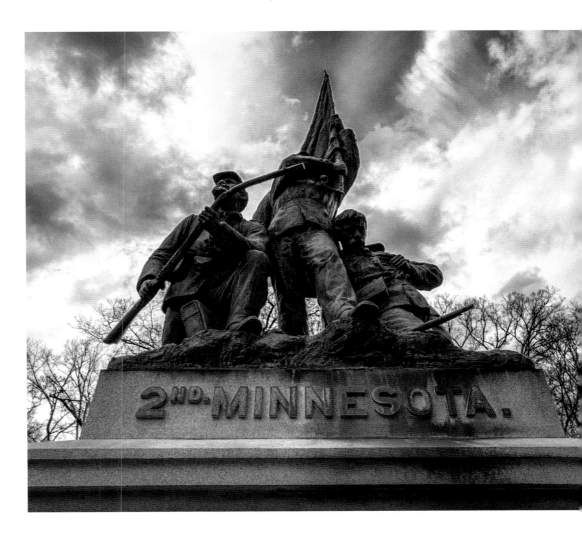

reprimanded earlier that day for not promptly obeying an order and was not inclined to question this one. He pulled his division out of the line and set it in motion. At about the same time, Longstreet had massed a force of 10,000 men for a ferocious Confederate assault on the Union front.

At 11:10 a.m., three Southern divisions, with eight brigades arranged in five lines, launched their attack, striking at precisely the point where Wood's division was pulling out of the line. The effect was catastrophic, and resistance at the southern end of the battlefield evaporated as Federal troops, including Rosecrans himself, fled from the field. Col. Gates Thruston, a Union staff officer, recalled the scene: "All became confusion. No order could be heard above the tempest of battle. With a wild yell the confederates swept on far to their left. They seemed everywhere victorious."

Thomas, however, wasn't prepared to join the flight. In a move that would earn him the nickname "Rock of Chickamauga," Thomas began consolidating the scattered Union forces on Horseshoe Ridge and Snodgrass Hill. Here he formed a strong defensive position, throwing back furious Confederate assaults with murderous volleys. Capt. Israel Webster of the 10th

Kentucky Infantry described the action: "After several attempts of the rebs to take this hill it seems they had determined to have it. . . . Our artillery support gave way and came scampering down on our side of the hill. Gen. Thomas had not ceased his vigilance. He saw it all, and in a moment he drew his sword, rose in his stirrups and rode among his men, shouting to them: 'Go back! Go back! This hill must be held at all hazards!'"

Confederate attacks pressed within feet of the Union line, but the defenders held. As darkness fell over the battlefield, Thomas managed an orderly withdrawal, sending his beleaguered units one by one north toward Chattanooga. He had saved the Union army from utter destruction. Bragg, his own army battered by three days of fighting, refused to pursue the beaten Federals. He instead occupied the heights surrounding Chattanooga, blocking the Federal supply lines and setting the stage for another fight just two months later.

The results of the battle were staggering. Although the Confederates had won a decisive victory, Bragg's losses actually outnumbered those of Rosecrans. With more than 18,000 Confederate and 16,000 Union casualties, the fighting at Chickamauga resulted in the highest losses of any battle in the Western Theater.

BELOW, LEFT: Site of Gen. James Longstreet's breakthrough at Chickamauga.

BELOW, RIGHT: Monument to the 3rd Independent Battery, Wisconsin Light Artillery.

OPPOSITE: The dense wooded terrain across the Chickamauga Battlefield led one Union general to describe the fighting as "bushwhacking on a grand scale."

# CHICKAMAUGA Battlefield Hikes

The trail network at Chickamauga uses a number of the old roads and paths through the battlefield that were used by the families who lived here before the battle. Though they don't follow the flow of the battle itself, they do provide an understanding of the terrain and obstacles that caused one Union commander to call the battle "bushwhacking on a grand scale." Hikers should start at the visitor center, where maps and trail guides are available.

## Cannon Trail (14.0 miles)

There were six principal types of cannons used in the Battle of Chickamauga; this trail takes hikers around the battlefield to see examples of these artillery pieces, including some rarer models. Chickamauga was a nightmare for artillerymen, who found themselves fighting at close range and, as a consequence, suffering heavy losses.

## Confederate Line Trail (6.0 miles)

This trail goes through the heart of the battlefield where some of the fiercest fighting occurred on both September 19 and 20. The trail passes through the Confederate lines where Gen. James Longstreet's divisions formed up for their breakthrough on September 20, as well as the lines of Gen. Leonidas Polk's morning attacks on the same day. It also traverses Viniard Field, where the Federals launched several unsuccessful counterattacks late on the afternoon of September 20 to regain the ground around the Viniard House—some of the bloodiest fighting of the entire war.

## General Bragg Trail (5.0 miles)

This trail traverses part of the field where the opening actions of the fighting on September 19 occurred.

## Historical Trail (11.0 miles)

This trail covers the areas that witnessed the heaviest fighting of the battle, from the opening shots fired on September 18 to the last stand of the Union army on Snodgrass Hill on September 20.

## Memorial Trail (9.0 miles)

There are 666 monuments and markers on the battlefield; this trail takes hikers around to the markers for six brigade commanders killed or mortally wounded during the battle—three on each side. Among these commanders were President Abraham Lincoln's brother-in-law, Confederate Gen. Benjamin Helm; Confederate Gen. Preston Smith, a Memphis lawyer turned soldier; and Gen. William Lytle, the poet general and highest-ranking officer killed on the Union side.

Monuments cover the landscape on Kelly Field.

# LOOKOUT MOUNTAIN
## BATTLEFIELD

FOLLOWING HIS DEFEAT AT THE BATTLE OF CHICKAMAUGA, GEN. WILLIAM Rosecrans pulled his Union troops back into Chattanooga, Tennessee. The Confederates quickly encircled the city, cutting off all practical lines of supply to the beleaguered Union army. Through most of October 1863, Confederate troops perched high atop Lookout Mountain could observe the Federal forces down below. Artillery on the point of the mountain choked off supply routes and was within range of Union positions on Moccasin Bend, where the Tennessee River makes a wide turn beneath Lookout Mountain.

Aware of Rosecrans's plight, President Abraham Lincoln sent reinforcements. Gen. Joseph Hooker was sent from the Army of the Potomac in Virginia with 20,000 men. Gen. William Tecumseh Sherman brought 16,000 troops from Mississippi. Lincoln urged Rosecrans to take action, but nothing could rouse the demoralized general. Exasperated, Lincoln concluded that Rosecrans was "confused and stunned, like a duck hit on the head." Finally, Secretary of War Edwin Stanton ordered Gen. Ulysses S. Grant to go to Chattanooga. On October 17, 1863, Grant was promoted to commander of the newly created Military Division of the Mississippi, bringing all of the territory from the Appalachian Mountains to the Mississippi River under a single commander for the first time. On October 23, the hero of Vicksburg rode into Chattanooga.

Grant's first order of business was to open a reliable supply route into the city and break the Confederate siege. On October 28, Union forces opened the "Cracker Line," a dependable line of supply across Raccoon Mountain and along the Brown's Ferry-Wauhatchie Road west of Lookout Mountain. In just five days, Grant had completely changed the strategic situation. Confederate Gen. Braxton Bragg knew the siege was effectively broken.

With the arrival of Sherman's 16,000 men in mid-November 1863, Grant prepared for offensive operations. On November 23, Federal forces drove the Confederates from Orchard Knob, a small 100-foot-high knoll on the east side of Chattanooga. The following day, Grant ordered Hooker to move against Lookout Mountain with three divisions—about 10,000 men. Grant instructed Hooker to "take the point only if his demonstration should develop its practicability." Fighting Joe Hooker, however, chose to be much more aggressive, ordering Gen. John Geary "to cross Lookout Creek and to assault Lookout Mountain, marching down the valley and sweeping every rebel from it."

Bragg's forces on Lookout Mountain numbered about 7,000, but they were widely scattered. Only a fraction of his men were in position to defend the northern end of the long ridge. On November 24, 1863, Geary's men crossed Lookout Creek and swept northeast along the base of Lookout Mountain, pushing the badly outnumbered Confederate defenders back to the Cravens House, just below the northern end of the mountain. On top of Lookout Mountain, Capt. Max Van Den Corput's Georgia Battery—composed of four 12-pounder Napoleons—could do little to stop the Union assault, being unable to lower their guns' barrels enough to fire on the attackers.

By about 3:00 p.m., thick fog enveloped the mountain. The two sides blazed away blindly at one another in a fierce firefight that became known as the "Battle Above the Clouds." Bragg's battered troops still held their ground as darkness settled in, but Hooker, in a message to Grant, predicted, "In all probability the enemy will evacuate tonight." He was right. Realizing his troops were badly outnumbered and that the battle was lost, Bragg ordered the position abandoned. Capt. John Wilson of the 8th Kentucky Infantry wrote that on the following morning, "We crept cautiously upward, clutching at rocks and bushes, supporting each other, using sticks and poles and such other aids as we could gather. At every step we expected to be greeted with deadly missiles of some sort from the enemy. But fortune favored us, and before sunup I, in front, reached the summit and planted the flag on top of Lookout Mountain." The towering ridge was now in Federal hands.

Missionary Ridge, an imposing rise of about 300 feet along the eastern edge of Chattanooga, was now the last Confederate stronghold. Here Bragg had concentrated most of his army. On November 25, Grant launched Sherman's troops against the Confederate right flank on the north end of the ridge, while Hooker's men assaulted the ridge's south end. Gen. George Thomas's Army of the Cumberland, totaling 24,000 men, was deployed along the base of the ridge to provide support as needed. By 3:00 p.m. Hooker's forces had secured a foothold on the south end of Missionary Ridge, but their progress was slow. On the north end of the ridge, at Tunnel Hill, Sherman's assaults had stalled. Watching the battle unfold from Orchard Knob, Grant ordered Thomas forward.

The Federals advanced and quickly pushed the Confederates from their rifle pits below the crest of the ridge. But fire from Confederate positions near the top of the hill was taking a deadly toll on the Union ranks. Still, the great mass of blue uniforms surged forward. The Union advance was disorganized but effective, finally overwhelming and scattering what many thought would have been an impregnable Confederate line. By 4:30 p.m. the center of Bragg's line was broken and in full retreat. Grant wired the news to Washington: "Although the battle lasted from nearly dawn until dark this evening I believe I am not premature in announcing a complete victory over Bragg." The gateway to Georgia and the road to Atlanta were thrown wide open.

PREVIOUS SPREAD: Artillery piece overlooks the Tennessee River and Chattanooga from Point Park on Lookout Mountain.

OPPOSITE: Officers of the 16th US Colored Troops Infantry Regiment pose for a photograph on Point Lookout, a rocky outcrop atop Lookout Mountain.

BELOW: Numerous hiking trails traverse the slopes of Lookout Mountain.

# LOOKOUT MOUNTAIN Battlefield Hikes

Lookout Mountain offers more than 30 miles of interconnected trails along the crest and slopes of the mountain ridge. Many of these trails were originally cleared shortly after 1897, when much of the Lookout Mountain Battlefield was acquired by the government. The trails provide access to artillery batteries, monuments, historical tablets, spectacular views of the Tennessee River and surrounding valleys, and a wide array of natural features. Point Park at the summit of the mountain and across the street from the visitor center serves as the hub for many of these hikes. The entrance gate at Point Park, built in 1905 by the US Army Corps of Engineers, is the world's largest replica of the Corps insignia. Hiking on Lookout Mountain can include elevation changes and steep slopes and is often physically demanding. Hikers should start at the visitor center, where maps and trail guides are available. The visitor center also houses James Walker's enormous 13-by-30-foot painting, *The Battle of Lookout Mountain*.

ABOVE: Entrance to Point Park on Lookout Mountain, constructed in 1904 and modeled after the US Army Corps of Engineers insignia.

OPPOSITE: Umbrella Rock on Lookout Mountain.

### Battle of Lookout Mountain Hiking Tour (3.5 miles)

This hike begins at the Point Park Trailhead. This is a moderate, two-and-a-half-hour hike with an elevation change of 600 feet. The hike follows sections of the Bluff Trail, Cravens House Trail, Rifle Pits Trail, and Mountain Beautiful Trail. Highlights include Confederate Capt. Max Van Den Corput's artillery battery, the point on the mountain where volunteers from the 8th Kentucky Infantry planted the US flag, Confederate rifle pits, and the Cravens House. It was around this house that fog shrouded the fighting between Union and Confederate forces, inspiring the nickname the "Battle Above the Clouds."

### Blue Beaver Trail (7.5 miles)

This moderate to strenuous hike begins at the Kiddie Trailhead. Traveling from the foot of the mountain more than 600 feet up to Point Park, this hike in part follows an old Boy Scout route tracing the Union attack up Lookout Mountain. From the Kiddie Trailhead, the trail continues to the Skyuka Trail, and then up the Lower Gum Springs Trail to the Upper Truck Trail. Hikers can take the Rifle Pits Trail up to the Cravens House, and then hike to Point Park via the Cravens House Trail.

### Glenn Falls Trail (1.0 mile)

This trail starts at the Glenn Falls Trailhead. This is an easy hike along a trail constructed in the 1930s by the Civilian Conservation Corps. The trail leads from Ochs Highway to Glenn Falls.

### Point Park to Sunset Rock Trail (2.0 miles)

This trail starts at the Point Park Trailhead. The relatively flat hike along the Bluff Trail offers vistas of Lookout Valley and provides a perspective on ground fought over by soldiers during the battle. Constructed by the Civilian Conservation Corps as a fire trail in the 1930s, the path leads to Sunset Rock, where Gen. Braxton Bragg and Gen. James Longstreet watched Gen. Joseph Hooker's corps enter Lookout Valley on October 28, 1863.

### Skyuka Springs Trail (5.5 miles)

This moderate to strenuous hike begins at the Ochs Gateway Trailhead. From there, hikers can walk down to the Bluff Trail and turn south, then continue on the John Smartt Trail and hike to the bottom of the mountain. Skyuka Springs emerges from under a large boulder to join Lookout Creek.

# PICKETT'S MILL
## BATTLEFIELD

GEORGIA  Pickett's Mill Battlefield Historic Site

ACCORDING TO THE CIVIL WAR TRUST, PICKETT'S MILL IS THE BEST-preserved battlefield of the 1864 Atlanta Campaign. The site's historic roads, earthworks, and terrain features have changed little since the May 27, 1864, battle. Here visitors can visually connect with ground where the Union forces of Gen. William Tecumseh Sherman and Gen. Joseph Johnston's Confederates battled one another on the bloody road to Atlanta.

From May to September 1864, the Union army maneuvered south from Dalton to Atlanta, engaging in several fierce battles and almost daily skirmishing. Sherman's orders were to "move against Johnston's army, to break it up, and to get into the interior of the enemy's country as far as you can, inflicting all the damage you can against their war resources." Sherman made good use of his superior numbers—110,000 Union troops to just 65,000 Confederates—holding a broad front against Johnston's entrenched forces while sending a large column around one of their flanks. In this manner, Sherman tried to avoid blunt frontal attacks and instead concentrated on severing the Western and Atlantic Railroad— the principal Confederate supply line. For much of the campaign, Sherman's tactics succeeded. Day by day, Johnston's army was forced to retreat closer and closer to Atlanta. But on May 27, 1864, at Pickett's Mill—about 35 miles northwest of Atlanta—the Confederates succeeded in thwarting the Union advance with some of the bloodiest fighting of the campaign.

After being blocked by Johnston's army at New Hope Church, Sherman ordered Gen. Oliver Howard to dispatch a division from his Fourth Corps on an "arduous and dangerous task . . . to find the extreme right of the enemy's position, turn it, and attack him in flank." The job fell to Gen. Thomas Wood's division of 14,000 men. Johnston, aware of Sherman's intent, deployed Gen. Patrick Cleburne's division—about 10,000 strong—to

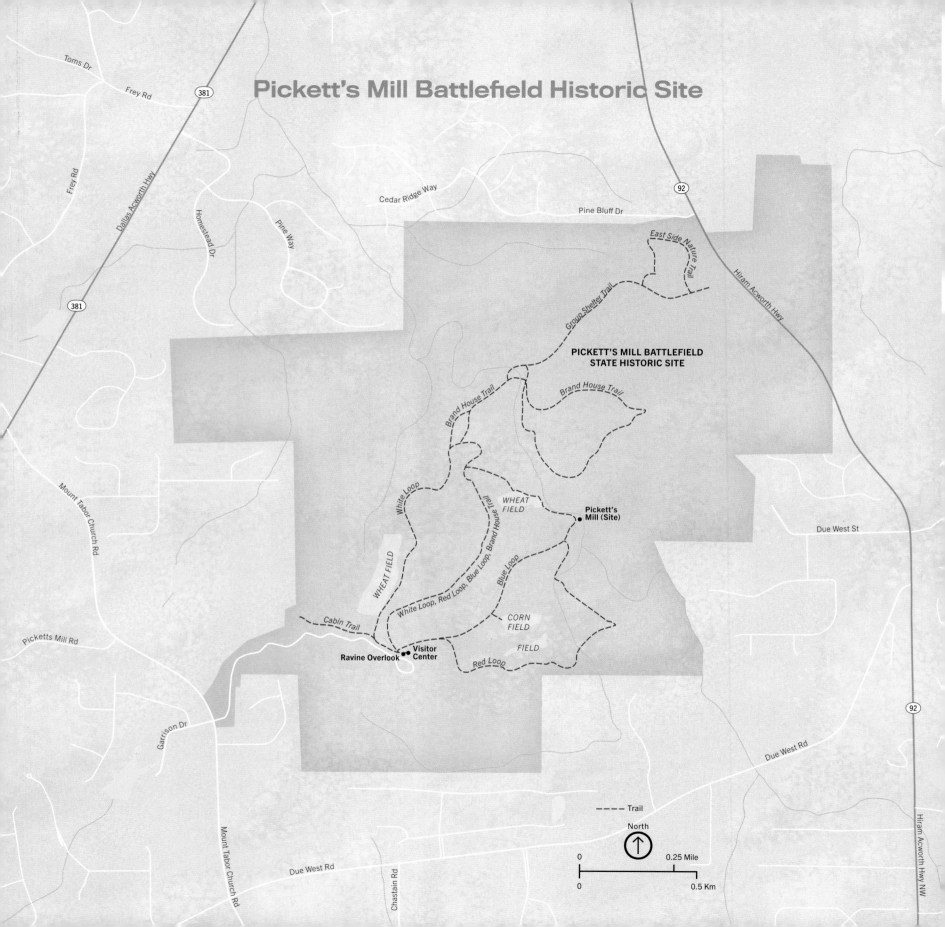

# Pickett's Mill Battlefield Historic Site

**PICKETT'S MILL BATTLEFIELD STATE HISTORIC SITE**

Toms Dr
Frey Rd
381
Frey Rd
Dallas Acworth Hwy
Homestead Dr
Pine Way
Cedar Ridge Way
Pine Bluff Dr
92
Hiram Acworth Hwy
East Side Nature Trail
Group Shelter Trail
Brand House Trail
Brand House Trail
Mount Tabor Church Rd
White Loop
WHEAT FIELD
WHEAT FIELD
White Loop, Red Loop, Blue Loop, Brand House Trail
Blue Loop
Pickett's Mill (Site)
Due West St
Cabin Trail
CORN FIELD
FIELD
Picketts Mill Rd
Ravine Overlook
Visitor Center
Red Loop
Garrison Dr
92
Mount Tabor Church Rd
Due West Rd
Chastain Rd
Due West Rd
Hiram Acworth Hwy NW

- - - Trail

North

0        0.25 Mile

0                    0.5 Km

counter the threat. Cleburne's men dug in on the extreme right of the Confederate line on a hilltop overlooking a farm and gristmill owned by the widow Martha "Fanny" Pickett, whose husband had been killed at Chickamauga.

At around 3:30 p.m. on May 27, Howard finally reported to Sherman, "I am now turning the enemy's right flank, I think." Maneuvering through the dense forest, he was clearly unsure if his troops had actually reached Johnston's flank. An impatient Sherman ordered him to attack anyway, and around 5:00 p.m. Gen. William Hazen's brigade began the assault. The Confederates were ready.

Hazen's brigade had to advance through a steep, densely overgrown ravine to reach the Confederate positions along the hilltop. For a time, the Federals threatened to overlap the Confederate right, but Cleburne shuttled troops to extend his line. Several Union assaults were pushed back with appalling losses. By 7:00 p.m., both Howard and Wood concluded that further attacks were pointless. Federal casualties totaled about 1,600; the Confederates had lost just 500 men. To Ambrose Bierce, an officer on Hazen's staff, the Union attack was a "crime"—it had gained nothing.

The following day, May 28, 1864, Sherman halted his westward flanking maneuvers and shifted his armies east toward Kennesaw Mountain and Marietta, Georgia. He was moving closer to Atlanta, but another battle in the bloody campaign was looming.

PREVIOUS SPREAD: Confederate trench line on the Pickett's Mill Battlefield. Natural, unspoiled landscape characterizes this state historic site.

RIGHT, TOP: Several miles of trails crisscross the battlefield.

RIGHT, BOTTOM: The pristine landscape of the battlefield.

# PICKETT'S MILL Battlefield Hikes

Visitors can explore the historic roads, earthworks, and terrain features of this well-preserved Civil War battlefield park along four miles of trails. All the loop trails follow the same route of the ill-fated Union assault through the ravine and back up to the visitor center. Hikers should begin at the visitor center, where maps and trail guides are available.

## White Trail (1.1 miles)

This trail leads from the ravine overlook at the visitor center to the left of the 1864 Confederate battle line. The trail passes along the once-flourishing Wheat Field down to the initial Federal position. From there the path follows the route of the Federals down into the ravine, tracing the route of their ill-fated assault back up the ravine. Along the way visitors will see original Civil War entrenchments, artillery emplacements, wagon roads, and beautiful, pristine forest.

## Blue Trail (1.5 miles)

This trail travels from the visitor center along the Confederate battle line down to Pickett's Mill. From the mill the trail follows the creek, traveling up a steep hill to the initial Federal position. From there, hikers can follow the route of the Federals down into the ravine, tracing the route of their ill-fated assault.

## Red Trail (2.0 miles)

This trail leads from the visitor center along the Confederate battle line toward Pickett's Mill, bearing right before the mill toward the infamous Corn Field, which almost caused the defeat of the Confederates. The trail continues down to Pickett's Mill. From the mill, the trail follows the creek, traveling up a steep hill to the initial Federal position. The trail then traces the route of the ill-fated Federal assault up the ravine.

## Brand House Trail (3.0 miles)

This trail leads from the ravine overlook at the visitor center to the left of the Confederate battle line. The path travels along the once-flourishing Wheat Field down to the initial Federal position. The trail then leads down past a Civil War field hospital across the creek to the former site of the Brand House. From the house site, the trail follows some of the best-preserved Civil War trenches down to the creek and back to the initial Federal position. From there, hikers can follow the route of the Federal assault up the ravine.

## Cabin Trail (0.5 miles one way)

Hikers can access this trail from the White Trail, which leads to a restored historic 1850s log cabin. The cabin was originally located several miles north of its current location, but the park rescued it from certain destruction and restored it. Today, it is used for interpretive programs for all ages. In addition to the restored cabin, there is also a corncrib and smokehouse at the site.

Pickett's Mill Creek bisects the battlefield.

# KENNESAW MOUNTAIN
## BATTLEFIELD

GEORGIA  Kennesaw Mountain National Battlefield Park

By the middle of June 1864, Gen. William Tecumseh Sherman had again sidestepped Gen. Joseph Johnston's Confederate army at Pickett's Mill, forcing Southern troops to withdraw once more—inching ever closer to Atlanta. This time, Johnston moved into a seven-mile-long prepared defensive position anchored by the twin peaks of Kennesaw Mountain, a high ridge with steep, rocky slopes just 15 miles northwest of Atlanta. Here Confederate engineers had laid out elaborate earthworks and trenches, commanding all approaches with artillery and rifle fire.

Anxious to avoid costly frontal assaults against his entrenched enemy, Sherman again extended his lines to the south to get around the Confederate flank. Once again, Johnston countered, shifting 11,000 men under Gen. John Hood to meet the threat. At Kolb's Farm on June 22, 1864, Hood struck Gen. Joseph Hooker's Twentieth Corps. The Confederate assault burst out of thick woods into an open plain, running straight into the massed fire of more than 40 Union artillery pieces. The attack was repulsed, and Hood was forced to pull back into his defensive positions. Total Confederate casualties, which one historian referred to as "more a one-sided slaughter than a battle," were approximately 1,500 men.

Sherman became convinced that Johnston had stretched his line too thin, believing that one sharp thrust might break through. He devised a two-pronged attack. Three brigades of Gen. James McPherson's Army of the Tennessee—about 5,500 men—would advance against the fortifications on Pigeon Hill south of Kennesaw Mountain. Gen. George Thomas would attack a salient in the Confederate line nearly three miles south of Pigeon Hill with two divisions from his Army of the Cumberland. Finally, Gen. John Schofield's Army of the Ohio would launch a diversion south of Kolb's Farm to force Johnston to keep extending his line.

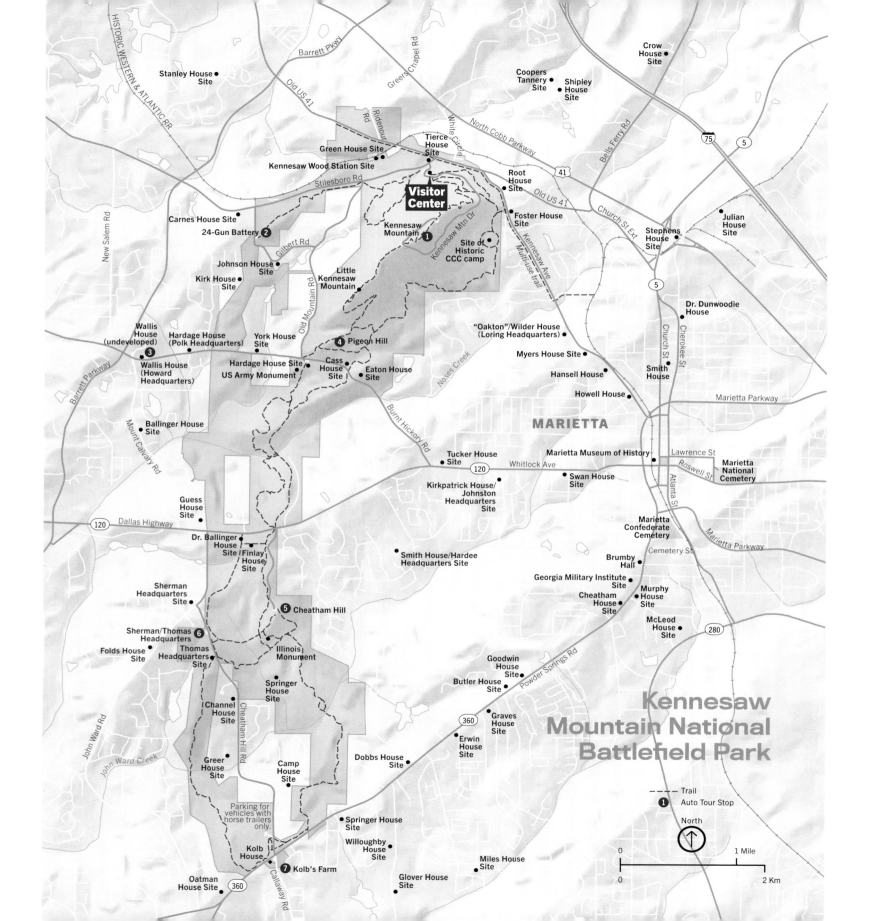

Stanley House Site

Crow House Site

Coopers Tannery Site

Shipley House Site

HISTORIC WESTERN & ATLANTIC RR

Barrett Pkwy

Greers Chapel Rd

Old US 41 Rd

Ridenour

North Cobb Parkway

Bells Ferry Rd

75

5

Green House Site

Tierce House Site

Kennesaw Wood Station Site

Stilesboro Rd

White Circle

41

Root House Site

Old US 41

Church St Ext

Julian House Site

Visitor Center

Carnes House Site

24-Gun Battery  2

Kennesaw Mountain  1

Kennesaw Mtn Dr

Foster House Site

Stephens House Site

Multi-use trail

5

Site of Historic CCC camp

Gilbert Rd

Johnson House Site

Little Kennesaw Mountain

Dr. Dunwoodie House

Kirk House Site

Old Mountain Rd

"Oakton"/Wilder House (Loring Headquarters)

Kennesaw Ave

Cherokee St

Church St

Wallis House (undeveloped)

Hardage House (Polk Headquarters)

York House Site

Pigeon Hill  4

Myers House Site

Smith House

Barrett Parkway

Wallis House (Howard Headquarters)  3

Hardage House Site

US Army Monument

Cass House Site

Eaton House Site

Noses Creek

Hansell House

Howell House

Marietta Parkway

Ballinger House Site

MARIETTA

Mount Calvary Rd

Burnt Hickory Rd

Tucker House Site

Marietta Museum of History

Lawrence St

120

Whitlock Ave

Swan House Site

Marietta National Cemetery

Roswell St

Guess House Site

120  Dallas Highway

Kirkpatrick House/ Johnston Headquarters Site

Atlanta St

Marietta Parkway

Marietta Confederate Cemetery

Cemetery St

Dr. Ballinger House Site

Finlay House Site

Smith House/Hardee Headquarters Site

Brumby Hall

Georgia Military Institute Site

Sherman Headquarters Site

Cheatham House Site

Murphy House Site

280

Cheatham Hill  5

Sherman/Thomas Headquarters  6

McLeod House Site

Folds House Site

Thomas Headquarters Site

Illinois Monument

Goodwin House Site

Powder Springs Rd

John Ward Rd

Cheatham Hill Rd

Springer House Site

Butler House Site

Channel House Site

360

Graves House Site

John Ward Creek

Greer House Site

Camp House Site

Dobbs House Site

Erwin House Site

Parking for vehicles with horse trailers only.

Springer House Site

Willoughby House Site

Miles House Site

Trail

1  Auto Tour Stop

Kolb House

Kolb's Farm  7

Callaway Rd

Oatman House Site

360

Glover House Site

**Kennesaw Mountain National Battlefield Park**

North

0 ——— 1 Mile

0 ——— 2 Km

The attacking brigades moved into position before dawn on June 27, 1864. At 8:00 a.m., after a short but ferocious artillery bombardment with more than 200 guns, the first wave of Federal troops surged forward. McPherson's three brigades succeeded in overrunning several rifle pits, but became mired in the undergrowth and were punished by sheets of musket fire as they attempted to ascend the steep slopes of Pigeon Hill. At the center of the Union line, along either side of the Dallas Road, the two armies were only 400 yards apart. Here the Confederates of Gen. Patrick Cleburne's division had built abatis—sharp wooden stakes driven into the ground—and strengthened their entrenchments with headlogs. On a nearby rise now known as Cheatham's Hill, the trenches of Gen. Frank Cheatham's division jutted forth in a V-shaped salient. Thomas sent his two divisions—about 8,000 Union infantry—against these entrenched positions. Some of the men advanced to close quarters, and for a few minutes brutal hand-to-hand fighting occurred on top of the Confederate earthworks. Eventually the Union troops were forced to retreat and find cover. Both sides later called this bloody battleground the "Dead Angle."

By late morning, both Union attacks had failed. The frontal assault cost Sherman 3,000 men in just more than three hours. Confederate losses totaled about 1,000. Private Sam Watkins of Company H, 1st Tennessee Infantry, later described the fighting at the Dead Angle: "I've heard men say that if they ever killed a Yankee during the war they were not

PREVIOUS SPREAD: Artillery piece near the park visitor center.

BELOW: Confederate artillery position on the summit of Big Kennesaw Mountain.

aware of it. I am satisfied that on this memorable day, every man in our regiment killed from . . . twenty to a hundred each. All that was necessary was to load and shoot. Afterward, I heard a soldier say he thought 'hell had broke loose in Georgia, sure enough.'"

Chastened to the futility of his blunt frontal assaults, Sherman resumed his flanking strategy. Schofield's June 27 diversionary attack, along with an advance by Gen. George Stoneman's cavalry division, put Union troops within five miles of the Chattahoochee River—closer to the last river protecting Atlanta than any unit in Johnston's army. On July 2, Sherman surprised Johnston by sending a small force across the river, again threatening the Confederate supply line. Johnston was forced to abandon his Kennesaw lines and fall back across the river. Still, it would take two more months of fierce fighting to capture Atlanta. When the city finally fell on September 1, 1864, another vital Confederate rail junction and manufacturing center came into Union hands, further crippling the South's ability to wage war.

OPPOSITE: Earthwork remains on the Kennesaw Mountain Battlefield.

BELOW: Well-concealed artillery position on the Kennesaw Mountain Battlefield.

# KENNESAW MOUNTAIN Battlefield Hikes

Kennesaw Mountain National Battlefield has 22 miles of trails, offering both short walks and long hikes. From the visitor center, there are round-trip hikes of two, six, 11, and 17 miles. Most trails include cutoffs or intersections to create shorter loop hikes. All the park trails include moderate to strenuous climbs, and many trails offer a pleasant mix of flora and fauna. Drinking water is limited, and neither food nor shelter is available along the trails. Visitors should wear sturdy shoes and stay on the park trails. Hikers should start at the visitor center, where maps and trail guides are available.

### Environmental Loop Trail (1.33 miles)

This hike starts at the visitor center. The loop trail explores the natural landscape on Kennesaw Mountain's northwestern slope. Interpretive markers provide information about the trees, wildlife, habitats, food chains, creek systems, geology, human impacts, and forest conservation.

### 24-Gun Trail (1.5 miles one way)

This hike starts by following the Environmental Loop Trail west from the visitor center. The 24-Gun Trail passes through rolling forest, across several small creeks, and along a line of earthworks used by Union troops during the battle. The 24-Gun Battery is located on a small, wooded rise facing Little Kennesaw and

Pigeon Hill. This Federal gun emplacement accommodated four batteries, each containing six artillery pieces. These guns bombarded Confederate positions on Kennesaw Mountain on and off for 10 days.

### Kennesaw Mountain Trail (2.0 miles)

Hikers can follow the Kennesaw Mountain Trail, which climbs from the visitor center to the top of Kennesaw Mountain (elevation 1,808 feet). The mountaintop offers great views of Cobb County and Atlanta to the south, and Kennesaw and beyond to the north. Along the way hikers can see the old Confederate earthworks that ran the length of the mountain. There are several cannon on display at the top of the mountain, as well as rocks where Civil War soldiers etched their names.

### Pigeon Hill Trail (5.8 miles)

This trail is an extension of the Kennesaw Mountain Trail. Hikers can continue on the Red Loop from the summit of Kennesaw Mountain along the Little Kennesaw Mountain Trail (Little Kennesaw Mountain, elevation 1,610 feet), Pigeon Hill Trail (Pigeon Hill, elevation 1,247 feet), Pigeon Hill Cutoff, and Camp Brumby Trail, where the loop dips to its lowest elevation of 1,097 feet. Confederate earthworks are still visible on Pigeon Hill, where one of Sherman's two major attacks was repulsed. The entire 5.8-mile loop starts and ends at the visitor center.

### Noses Creek Trail (3.7 miles)

The Yellow Loop explores the central section of the Kennesaw Mountain Battlefield, and includes both the Noses Creek Trail and Hardage Mill Trail. Elevations range from a low point of 961 feet to a high point of 1,124 feet. Start and end this hike at the information kiosk and parking area on Burnt Hickory Road.

### Cheatham Hill / Kolb Farm Loop Trail (5.5 miles)

The Blue Loop explores the southern section of the Kennesaw Mountain Battlefield along the Kolb Farm West Trail, Kolb Farm East Trail, and Kolb Farm Connector. Elevations range from a low point of 949 feet to a high point of 1,126 feet. The trail passes Kolb's Farm, where Union forces repulsed Confederate Gen. John Hood's ill-fated attack just north of Powder Springs Road. The trail also crosses over Cheatham Hill, where the fiercest fighting of the battle raged at what came to be called the Dead Angle. Hikers can see Confederate earthworks and markers where Union soldiers fell. This hike starts and ends at the information kiosk and parking area on Cheatham Hill Road near the Sherman/Thomas Headquarters (Auto Tour Stop 6).

OPPOSITE: Restored cabin on Kolb's Farm.

ABOVE: Cheatham Hill.

# OTHER REGIONS

# WILSON'S CREEK
## BATTLEFIELD

MISSOURI  Wilson's Creek National Battlefield

FROM THE OUTSET OF THE CIVIL WAR, MISSOURI'S ALLEGIANCE TO THE Union was of vital concern. The state's strategic location on the Missouri and Mississippi Rivers and its abundance of manpower and natural resources made it imperative that it remain loyal to the North. Most of the state's population desired neutrality, but many, including the governor, Claiborne Jackson, held strong Southern sympathies and supported the Confederacy's bid for independence.

When President Abraham Lincoln called for troops to put down the Rebellion on April 15, 1861, Missouri was asked to supply four regiments. Jackson refused the request. Instead, he ordered state militia units to muster at Camp Jackson outside St. Louis and prepare to seize the US arsenal in the city. The arsenal's commander, Capt. Nathaniel Lyon, a West Point graduate and staunch opponent of slavery, had most of the weapons moved secretly to Illinois. On May 10, he marched 7,000 men out to Camp Jackson and forced the militia to surrender. But when he marched the prisoners through the streets to the St. Louis Arsenal, taunts from angry members of the crowd led to gunfire. Lyon's troops opened fire on the crowd, injuring at least 75 and killing 28. The Civil War had come to Missouri.

Lyon, promoted to brigadier general, succeeded in installing a pro-Union state government and moved the capital from Jefferson City to St. Louis. Pro-Confederate forces, meanwhile, gathered about 75 miles southwest of Springfield, Missouri. By the end of July 1861, 5,200 men of the Missouri State Guard, commanded by Gen. Sterling Price, were reinforced by Confederate Gen. Benjamin McCulloch and Arkansas state militia Gen. N. Bart Pearce. The mixed force of Confederate soldiers and state militiamen now totaled 12,000. Lyon commanded just 6,000 Union soldiers in Springfield. These troops included regiments from Missouri, Iowa,

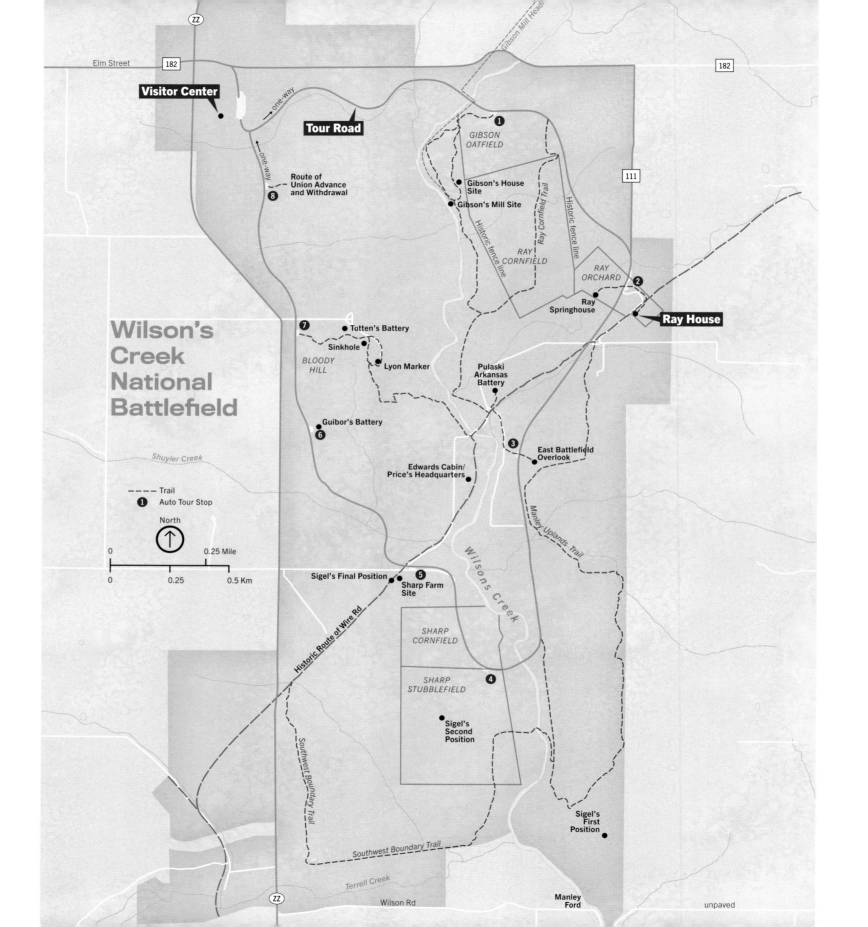

# Wilson's Creek National Battlefield

Visitor Center

Tour Road

Route of Union Advance and Withdrawal

GIBSON OATFIELD

Gibson's House Site

Gibson's Mill Site

Historic fence line

RAY CORNFIELD

Ray Cornfield Trail

Historic fence line

RAY ORCHARD

Ray Springhouse

Ray House

Totten's Battery

Sinkhole

Lyon Marker

BLOODY HILL

Pulaski Arkansas Battery

Guibor's Battery

East Battlefield Overlook

Edwards Cabin/ Price's Headquarters

Manley Uplands Trail

Shuyler Creek

Wilsons Creek

**Trail** - - - -

❶ Auto Tour Stop

North ↑

0          0.25 Mile
0     0.25     0.5 Km

Sigel's Final Position

Sharp Farm Site

Historic Route of Wire Rd

SHARP CORNFIELD

SHARP STUBBLEFIELD

Sigel's Second Position

Southwest Boundary Trail

Southwest Boundary Trail

Sigel's First Position

Terrell Creek

Wilson Rd

Manley Ford

unpaved

Elm Street

one-way

one-way

and Kansas, as well as several companies of Regular Army infantry and cavalry.

By August 6, the Confederates were encamped near Wilson's Creek, just 10 miles southwest of Springfield. Despite his inferior numbers, Lyon decided to attack, hoping to surprise the rebel forces. Marching out of Springfield on the night of August 9, Lyon planned a pincer movement. With 5,400 men, he would strike the Confederate camp from the north while Col. Franz Sigel would swing wide to the south, flanking the enemy's right with his own force of 1,200 men. Success hinged on the element of surprise.

At first light on the morning of August 10, 1861, Lyon's attack caught the Southerners off guard, driv-ing them back and taking the high ground west of Wilson's Creek. On the east side of the creek, the Pulaski Arkansas Battery opened fire on the Northerners, check-ing their advance and giving Price's Missouri militia-men time to form a battle line. Farther south, Sigel's flanking attack was successful at first, advancing into the Confederate rear soon after dawn. McCulloch, however, was able to rally several Confederate units and lead a counterattack. At this very early stage of the Civil War, uniforms were a haphazard mix of old state militia col-ors and standard US military attire worn by both sides. Sigel's men mistook the 3rd Louisiana for the 1st Iowa Infantry, who happened to also be wearing gray uni-forms. The Union troops withheld their fire until it was

**PREVIOUS SPREAD:** Capt. James Totten's Union Battery.

**ABOVE:** Union Col. Franz Sigel's last line.

too late. The rebel assault devastated Sigel's flank, and his men fled the field, leaving Lyon's force without any additional support.

Back at the northern end of the battlefield, on ground that would become known as the "Bloody Hill," Price's infantry regrouped and counterattacked the Union line. For more than five hours, the battle raged along the high ground here. Fighting was often at close quarters, and the tide turned with each charge and countercharge. At about 9:30 a.m., Lyon, who had been wounded twice already, was killed while leading the 2nd Kansas Infantry in a countercharge. Maj. Samuel Sturgis assumed command of the Federal forces. Around 11:00 a.m., with their ammunition nearly exhausted, Sturgis ordered a withdrawal back to Springfield. The Battle of Wilson's Creek was over.

Losses were heavy on both sides. Union casualties totaled 1,317, while the Confederates lost 1,222 men. Lyon was also the first Union general killed in the war. Although the Union army was defeated at Wilson's Creek, Lyon's quick and decisive action had neutralized the effectiveness of pro-Southern forces in Missouri, and the state remained under Union control. Still, for the next three and a half years, Missouri was the scene of fierce fighting—mostly guerrilla warfare—with small bands of mounted raiders destroying anything military or civilian that could aid the enemy. By the time the Civil War was over, Missouri had witnessed so many battles and skirmishes that it ranked as the third most fought-over state during the war.

Gibson's Mill site on Wilson's Creek, which bisects the Wilson's Creek Battlefield.

# WILSON'S CREEK Battlefield Hikes

Seven miles of trails crisscross the Wilson's Creek Battlefield. The landscape here is characterized by rolling hills, broken in places by ravines, with Wilson's Creek running north to south between high banks. Hikers should start at the visitor center at the north end of the park, where trail maps and information are available.

## Gibson's Mill Loop (0.8 miles)

This hike starts at Auto Tour Stop 1 and explores the area where Union forces first entered the battlefield. Gen. James Rains of the Missouri State Guard was encamped with his 2,500-man division near Gibson's Mill. Gen. Nathaniel Lyon's early morning attack drove the Missouri militiamen south down the creek. Interpretive wayside exhibits tell the story of the Gibson family and the mill, which is no longer standing.

## Ray Cornfield Trail (1.9 miles)

This hike also starts at Auto Tour Stop 1 and explores the area where the only major fighting on the east side of Wilson's Creek took place. Two Confederate infantry regiments engaged Capt. Joseph Plummer's Union forces, who had been ordered to cross Wilson's Creek and protect the Union left flank here in the Ray Cornfield. The Federals were forced back across the creek, ending the fighting on this part of the battlefield.

## Ray House and Ray Springhouse Trail (0.5 miles)

This hike starts at Auto Tour Stop 2 and leads to the Ray House, which served as a Confederate field hospital during the battle. Gen. Nathaniel Lyon's body was brought here when the fight was over. A short trail leads to the Ray Springhouse.

## Edwards Cabin via Wire Road Trail (0.7 miles one way)

This hike also starts at Auto Tour Stop 2 and leads to the William Edwards Cabin, which sat in the middle of the Confederate camp along Wilson's Creek. The present log structure, which was moved here from a site near the battlefield, is non-historic and was restored in 2005. Gen. Sterling Price, commander of the Missouri State Guard, established his headquarters near the original cabin.

## Pulaski Arkansas Battery and Edwards Cabin Trail (0.5 miles one way)

This hike starts at Auto Tour Stop 3 and explores the area where the Pulaski Arkansas Battery opened fire, stalling the Union assault on Bloody Hill and giving Confederate infantry time to form a battle line and counterattack. A single cannon now marks the location of the battery. The headquarters of Missouri State Guard commander Gen. Sterling Price was located near the William Edwards Cabin.

## Manley Uplands Trail (2.5 miles)

This hike also starts at Auto Tour Stop 3. The trail leads to Col. Franz Sigel's first position on the east side of Wilson's Creek on the morning of August 10, 1861. From this ridge, Sigel's Union artillery opened fire on 1,800 Southern cavalry camped in the field across the creek, sending them fleeing toward the woods to the north and west.

## Southwest Boundary Trail (3.9 miles)

This hike, which begins at Auto Tour Stop 5, includes the historic route of Wire Road and passes across both Sigel's second position and final position. At the second position, Sigel deployed his 1,200 men into a battle line to oppose Confederate cavalry gathering at the north end of the field. After a 20-minute artillery bombardment, the Southerners withdrew and Sigel continued his advance. At the final position, Sigel halted his advance on the hillside and formed up a battle line across the Wire Road. Here, Confederate troops that he mistook for a Federal regiment attacked and defeated him. This costly error turned the battle's tide in favor of the Southerners.

## Bloody Hill Loop (0.7 miles)

This hike starts at Auto Tour Stop 7. Bloody Hill saw most of the fighting during the Battle of Wilson's Creek. Here Gen. Nathaniel Lyon's men held the high ground against repeated Confederate assaults throughout the morning of August 10. As the fighting reached its peak, battle smoke covered the entire south slope of the hill. More than 1,700 Union and Confederate soldiers were killed or wounded here. The trail passes the site of Totten's Union Battery, the Lyon Marker—denoting the spot where Lyon was killed—and a sinkhole where 30 Union soldiers were hastily buried following the battle.

The Ray House, where John Ray watched the Battle of Wilson's Creek from his porch. The house served as a Confederate field hospital after the battle.

# PICACHO PEAK
## BATTLEFIELD

ARIZONA  Picacho Peak State Park

ON APRIL 15, 1862, THE WESTERNMOST BATTLE OF THE CIVIL WAR WAS fought on the flanks of Picacho Peak, a volcanic spire rising 3,374 feet above the Sonoran Desert about 50 miles northwest of Tucson, Arizona. The fight—really just a skirmish—pitted a band of Confederate Rangers under Capt. Sherod Hunter against a column of Federal troops under Col. James Carleton along the route of the Butterfield Overland Stagecoach Company. Mail and passenger service along the route, which had commenced in 1857, ceased when the Civil War began.

Hunter's force—about 120 cavalrymen—had traveled west from Texas. On February 28, 1862, they proclaimed Tucson the capital of the western district of the Confederate Arizona Territory, carving out land from what is now southern Arizona and southern New Mexico. The rangers hoped that sympathizers in southern California would join them and help extend the Confederacy from ocean to ocean. California Unionists, however, were intent on preventing this outcome. To thwart the Confederates, Carleton gathered 6,000 Union volunteers, known as the "California Column," and advanced east to Fort Yuma, California. Here he dispatched 276 men under the command of Capt. William Calloway to proceed to Tucson.

Calloway's men followed the old stagecoach route, advancing from water station to water station, each stop about 15 to 20 miles apart. As the column approached Picacho Station in the shadow of Picacho Peak, he devised a plan to surprise Confederate scouts he expected would be posted there. Calloway wanted prisoners so he could learn the disposition of the Confederate Rangers in Tucson. He ordered Lt. Ephraim Baldwin to circle the Picacho Mountains from the south with 13 cavalrymen. Lt. James Barrett was instructed to scout around the north side of the mountain with 12 troopers and a guide. The two small detachments would meet

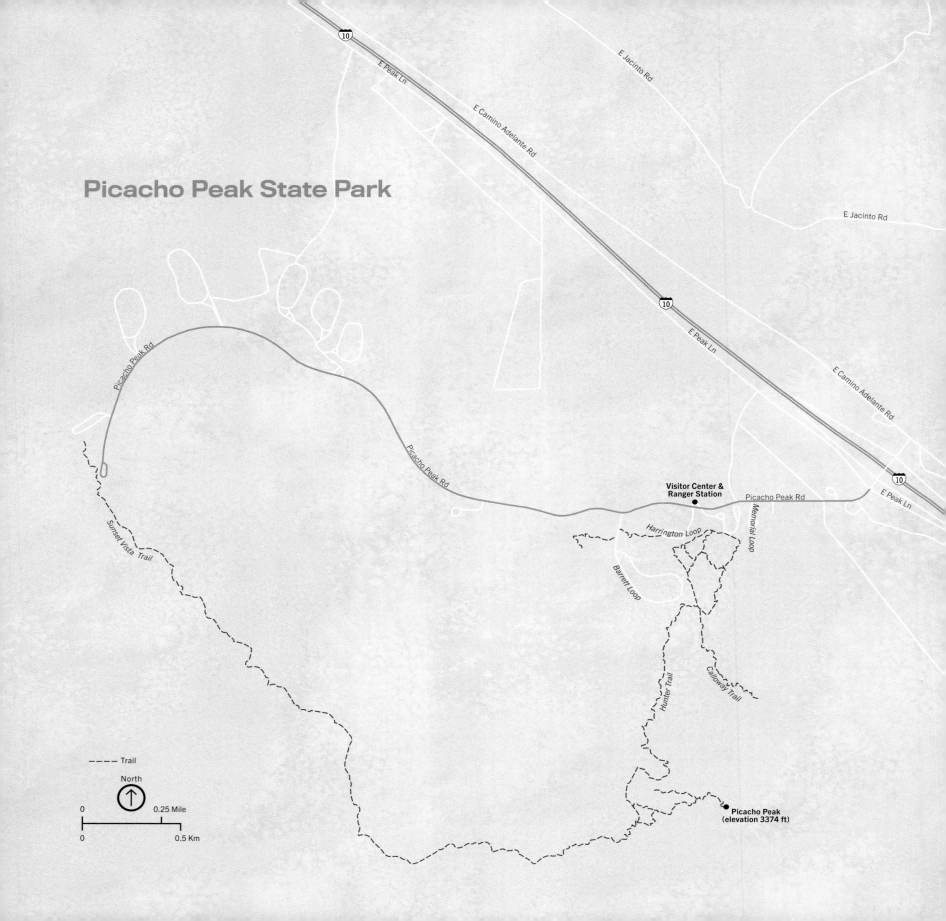

# Picacho Peak State Park

E Peak Ln

E Camino Adelante Rd

E Jacinto Rd

E Jacinto Rd

10

10

E Peak Ln

E Camino Adelante Rd

Picacho Peak Rd

Picacho Peak Rd

10

E Peak Ln

**Visitor Center &
Ranger Station**

Picacho Peak Rd

Sunset Vista Trail

Harrington Loop

Memorial Loop

Barrett Loop

Hunter Trail

Calloway Trail

**Picacho Peak
(elevation 3374 ft)**

- - - - Trail

North

0          0.25 Mile

0          0.5 Km

behind the rebels' position and cut off their escape while the main column of 250 men would come up directly in front of them.

On April 15, 1862, Barrett's 1st California Cavalry Volunteers reconnoitered Picacho Pass in advance of the main Union column. When he found the Confederate encampment around 2:00 p.m., however, he disobeyed his orders and immediately led a mounted charge. Three Confederates surrendered, but seven more fired on the cavalrymen. Barrett charged ahead, calling on his men to follow him, and was killed almost immediately. The two sides then exchanged gunfire for more than an hour in a fierce and confused melee among the mesquite and arroyos. Two more Union soldiers were killed and three men wounded. Exhausted and without their commander, the Californians finally broke off the fight and withdrew. Their only prizes were the three Confederate prisoners. According to Calloway's report, Barrett "surprised the rebels and should have captured them without firing a shot, if the thing had been conducted properly."

The Confederate Rangers carried word of the Union advance back to Tucson. But their victory only delayed the Union force. When Carleton's California Column advanced against the Confederates the following month, Hunter and his Confederate Rangers abandoned Tucson without a fight. The Confederacy had lost its tenuous hold on the Southwest. Several years later, US soldiers returned to search for the men who fell at Picacho Peak. The bodies of the two enlisted men were removed and buried in the National Cemetery at the Presidio in San Francisco, California, but Barrett's remains were never found.

PREVIOUS SPREAD: Civil War reenactors provide an artillery demonstration on the Picacho Peak Battlefield.

RIGHT: Union cavalry reenactors at the Picacho Peak Battlefield. Civil War images from the American Southwest remind us that fighting extended well beyond the Mississippi River.

# PICACHO PEAK
## Battlefield Hikes

Hiking trails at Picacho Peak State Park vary in difficulty, ranging from moderate to strenuous. Visitors should wear suitable hiking boots; bring a hat and sunscreen for sun protection; stock up on snacks such as trail mix, energy bars, and fruit; and bring at least two liters of water per person. Gloves are recommended for steep trail sections with handrails and steel cables. Weather can be unpredictable. Hikers can pick up a trail map at the visitor center.

### Hunter Trail (2.0 miles one way)

This strenuous hike starts at the trailhead on the Barrett Loop Road. The trail leads to the 3,374-foot summit of Picacho Peak and includes steep, rocky sections of trail—both climbs and descents—with steel cables anchored into the rock where the surface is bare. The total elevation gain is 1,401 feet, and the summit provides a breathtaking 360-degree view of the surrounding Sonoran Desert.

### Sunset Vista Trail (3.1 miles one way)

This trail begins at the Sunset Vista Trailhead at the north end of the park. The path climbs moderately at first, and then becomes generally flat for the first two miles as it traverses the bajada—a broad slope of alluvial material at the foot of an escarpment—on the west side of the range. As the trail approaches Picacho Peak, it begins a steep climb up a series of switchbacks, including a few steep sections rigged with cables. The trail then joins the Hunter Trail and continues its climb to the summit of Picacho Peak.

Artillery piece on the Picacho Peak Battlefield.

# BENTONVILLE
## BATTLEFIELD

NORTH CAROLINA  Bentonville Battlefield State Historic Site

FOLLOWING HIS MARCH THROUGH GEORGIA FROM NOVEMBER 15 TO December 21, 1864, Union Gen. William Tecumseh Sherman turned northward. His plan was to march through the Carolinas, destroying railroads and disrupting supply lines before joining Gen. Ulysses S. Grant's army near Richmond, Virginia. During the late winter and early spring of 1865, the Federals cut a swath of destruction through South Carolina. On March 8, they crossed into North Carolina, advancing in two columns toward Goldsborough. Recognizing that the end of the war was now in sight, Sherman ordered his soldiers to "deal as moderately and fairly by the North Carolinians as possible . . ."

In Sherman's path was a small Confederate army of about 22,000 men, cobbled together from several smaller forces and commanded by Gen. Joseph Johnston. Sherman's two wings, commanded by Gen. Henry Slocum and Gen. Oliver Howard, totaled 60,000 men. Johnston's only real hope for victory was to try to defeat each Union column in detail before they converged at Goldsborough. He chose Bentonville, North Carolina— about 50 miles south of Raleigh—to make a stand.

On March 19, 1865, Slocum's column encountered Confederate resistance on the Goldsborough Road. Believing he only faced cavalry, Slocum attempted to brush the Confederates aside. Instead, a division of rebel infantry under Gen. Robert Hoke attacked around 3:00 p.m., driving the Union left flank back in confusion, overrunning a Union field hospital, and putting Slocum's column in dire jeopardy. Only a ferocious stand by the Union 2nd Division of Gen. James Morgan stopped the onslaught. Reinforcements finally arrived and checked the Confederate advance. The weary rebels pulled back to their entrenched positions, and nightfall brought the first day's fighting to a close.

# Bentonville Battlefield State Historic Site

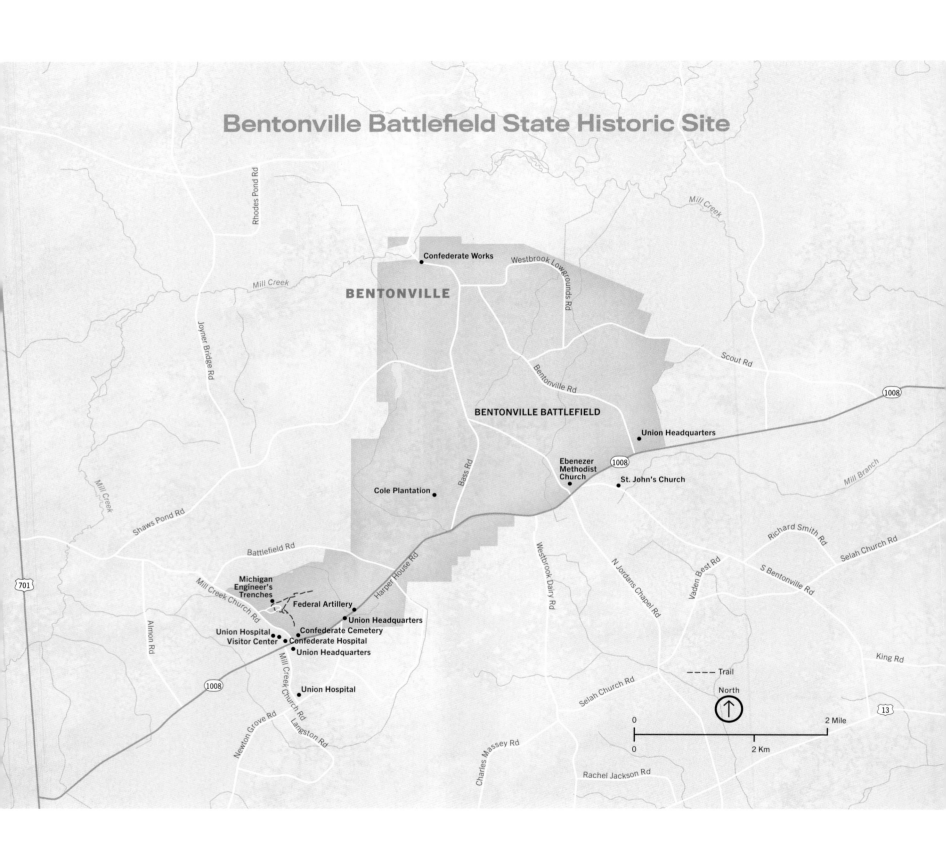

BENTONVILLE

BENTONVILLE BATTLEFIELD

Confederate Works

Union Headquarters

Ebenezer Methodist Church

St. John's Church

Cole Plantation

Michigan Engineer's Trenches

Federal Artillery

Union Headquarters

Union Hospital

Visitor Center

Confederate Cemetery

Confederate Hospital

Union Headquarters

Union Hospital

Rhodes Pond Rd

Mill Creek

Mill Creek

Westbrook Lowgrounds Rd

Scout Rd

Joyner Bridge Rd

Bentonville Rd

1008

Bass Rd

Mill Branch

Mill Creek

Shaws Pond Rd

1008

Richard Smith Rd

Selah Church Rd

Battlefield Rd

Harper House Rd

Westbrook Dairy Rd

N Jordans Chapel Rd

Vaden Best Rd

S Bentonville Rd

701

Mill Creek Church Rd

Almon Rd

King Rd

Trail

North

1008

Newton Grove Rd

Langston Rd

Mill Creek Church Rd

Selah Church Rd

Charles Massey Rd

Rachel Jackson Rd

13

0     2 Mile

0     2 Km

On the following day, the arrival of Howard's column put the Confederates at a huge numerical disadvantage. Sherman expected Johnston to retreat, but his old foe still hoped to entice the Federals into attacking his entrenched position. Sherman declined, having learned his lesson during the march from Chattanooga to Atlanta the previous summer. With the Confederates still holding their position on March 21, Union Gen. Joseph Mower led a "little reconnaissance" toward the Mill Creek Bridge—Johnston's only means of supply and retreat. When Mower discovered the weakness of the Confederate left flank, however, the reconnaissance became a full-scale attack against the small force holding the bridge. Mower's men managed to come within a mile of the vital crossing when Sherman ordered them to pull back.

In his memoirs, Sherman admitted his order to pull back was a mistake and that he missed an opportunity to end the campaign then and there. Johnston's small army, heavily outnumbered and now threatened with annihilation, withdrew across Mill Creek on the night of March 21. Bentonville was the last battle between the two generals. In three days of fighting, the Confederates suffered nearly 2,600 casualties; the Union army lost 1,527 men. After regrouping at Goldsborough, Sherman pursued Johnston's army toward the North Carolina state capital at Raleigh. On April 18, 1865, Johnston signed an armistice with Sherman at the Bennett House, and on April 26, formally surrendered his army.

PREVIOUS SPREAD: State historic marker on the Bentonville Battlefield.

RIGHT, TOP: The Harper House, built in the late 1850s, served as a field hospital for Gen. William Tecumseh Sherman's Fourteenth Army Corps. The house now serves as the visitor center for the Bentonville Battlefield.

RIGHT, BOTTOM: Statue of Confederate Gen. Joseph Johnston.

# BENTONVILLE
## Battlefield Hikes

The trail system at the Bentonville Battlefield State Historic Site currently covers three and a quarter miles and is composed of two distinct trails. The trails feature interpretive wayside exhibits and markers that designate the positions of the various brigades during the battle. Trails close at 5:00 p.m. daily. Hikers should start at the park visitor center.

### Bentonville History Trail (1.75 miles)

This trail is divided into multiple sections with options for a quarter-mile or one-mile loop. The trail begins at the replica earthworks just east of the visitor center. The trail leads to authentic fieldworks dug by the 1st Michigan Engineers and mechanics from the US Army's Twentieth Corps. Here hikers are given the option of looping back toward the visitor center or continuing to follow the trench line across the battlefield. A right-hand turn at the next fork allows hikers to follow the trenches on a half-mile spur trail (0.5 miles one way). To continue the loop back toward the visitor center, hikers should go left at the fork and follow the brown arrows.

### Cole Plantation Loop Trail (1.5 miles)

This trail starts at a parking area located on a dirt road just north of Harper House Road, one and a half miles east of the visitor center. Hikers should step down the embankment from the parking area and walk north adjacent to the dirt road for approximately 100 yards. Here they will make a left turn onto a section of the trail that follows the trenches erected by the 1st Division of the US Army's Fourteenth Corps. The trail leaves the woods and proceeds north across fields that were once part of Willis Cole's plantation. Hikers will reenter the woods on the north side of the field, where they can see earthworks constructed by the Confederate Army of Tennessee. The trail eventually leads back to the dirt road, and hikers can then walk a half mile south to return to the parking area.

The Cole Plantation, where on March 19, 1865, Confederate forces attacked advancing Union troops. Only a ferocious stand by the 2nd Division of Gen. James Morgan prevented a Union disaster.

# Battlefield Sites

## Eastern Virginia

**Manassas National Battlefield Park**
Henry Hill Visitor Center
6511 Sudley Road
Manassas, VA 20109
www.nps.gov/mana

**Fredericksburg and Spotsylvania National Military Park**
Fredericksburg Battlefield Visitor Center
1013 Lafayette Boulevard
Fredericksburg, VA 22401
www.nps.gov/frsp

**Slaughter Pen Farm Battlefield Trail**
11190 Tidewater Trail
Fredericksburg, VA 22408

**Fredericksburg and Spotsylvania National Military Park**
Chancellorsville Battlefield Visitor Center
9001 Plank Road
Spotsylvania, VA 22553
www.nps.gov/frsp

**Fredericksburg and Spotsylvania National Military Park**
Wilderness Battlefield Exhibit Shelter
35347 Constitution Highway
Locust Grove, VA 22508
www.nps.gov/frsp

**Fredericksburg and Spotsylvania National Military Park**
Spotsylvania Battlefield Exhibit Shelter
9950 Grant Drive West
Spotsylvania, VA 22553
www.nps.gov/frsp

**Richmond National Battlefield Park**
Gaines' Mill Battlefield Parking Area
6283 Watt House Road
Mechanicsville, VA 23111
www.nps.gov/rich

**Richmond National Battlefield Park**
Malvern Hill Battlefield Parking Area
9175 Willis Church Road
Richmond, VA 23231
www.nps.gov/rich

**Richmond National Battlefield Park**
Cold Harbor Visitor Center
5515 Anderson-Wright Drive
Mechanicsville, VA 23111
www.nps.gov/rich

**Brandy Station Battlefield**
Graffiti House
19484 Brandy Road
Brandy Station, VA 22714
www.brandystationfoundation.com

**Brandy Station Battlefield**
Fleetwood Hill Walking Trail
20362 Fleetwood Heights Road
Brandy Station, VA 22714
www.brandystationfoundation.com

**Petersburg National Battlefield**
Eastern Front Visitor Center
5001 Siege Road
Prince George, VA 23875
www.nps.gov/pete

**Hatcher's Run Battlefield Trail**
Entrance is across the street from:
9221 Duncan Road
Petersburg, VA 23803

**Petersburg National Battlefield**
Five Forks Battlefield Visitor Center
9840 Courthouse Road
Dinwiddie, VA 23841
www.nps.gov/pete

**Pamplin Historical Park**
6125 Boydton Plank Road
Petersburg, VA 23803
www.pamplinpark.org

**Appomattox Court House National Historical Park**
111 National Park Drive
Appomattox, VA 24522
www.nps.gov/apco

## Western Virginia and the Shenandoah Valley

**McDowell Battlefield Civil War Orientation Center**
161 Mansion House Road
McDowell, VA 24458
www.shenandoahatwar.org/visit/signature-sites
/augustahighland-sites/sitlingtons-hill

**Third Winchester Battlefield Visitor Center**
541 Redbud Road
Winchester, VA 22603
www.shenandoahatwar.org/visit/signature-sites
/winchester-area-sites/redbud-run-trails

**Ramseur's Hill Trail Parking Area**
601 Battlefield Road
Fishers Hill, VA 22645
www.shenandoahatwar.org/visit/signature-sites/signal
-knob-area-sites/fishers-hill-battlefield-ramsuers-hill

## West Virginia, Maryland, and Pennsylvania

**Harpers Ferry National Historical Park**
171 Shoreline Drive
Harpers Ferry, WV 25425
www.nps.gov/hafe

**Antietam National Battlefield**
5831 Dunker Church Road
Sharpsburg, MD 21782
www.nps.gov/anti

**Gathland State Park**
900 Arnoldstown Road
Jefferson, MD 21755
dnr2.maryland.gov/publiclands/pages/western
/gathland.aspx

**Gettysburg National Military Park**
1195 Baltimore Pike
Gettysburg, PA 17325
www.nps.gov/gett

**Monocacy National Battlefield**
5201 Urbana Pike
Frederick, MD 21704
www.nps.gov/mono

## West Tennessee, Mississippi, and Louisiana

**Fort Donelson National Battlefield**
120 Fort Donelson Park Road
Dover, TN 37058
www.nps.gov/fodo

**Shiloh National Military Park**
1055 Pittsburg Landing Road
Shiloh, TN 38376
www.nps.gov/shil
www.shilohmilitarytrails.org

**Vicksburg National Military Park**
3201 Clay Street
Vicksburg, MS 39183
www.nps.gov/vick

**Port Hudson State Historic Site**
236 US 61
Jackson, LA 70748
www.crt.la.gov/louisiana-state-parks/historic-sites/port
-hudson-state-historic-site

## Kentucky, East Tennessee, and Georgia

**Perryville Battlefield State Historic Site**
1825 Battlefield Road
Perryville, KY 40468
parks.ky.gov/parks/historicsites/perryville-battlefield

**Stones River National Battlefield**
3501 Old Nashville Highway
Murfreesboro, TN 37129
www.nps.gov/stri

**Chickamauga and Chattanooga National Military Park**
Chickamauga Battlefield Visitor Center
3370 LaFayette Road
Fort Oglethorpe, GA 30742
www.nps.gov/chch

**Chickamauga and Chattanooga National Military Park**
Lookout Mountain Visitor Center
110 Point Park Road
Lookout Mountain, TN 37350
www.nps.gov/chch

**Pickett's Mill Battlefield Historic Site**
4432 Mount Tabor Church Road
Dallas, GA 30157
gastateparks.org/PickettsMillBattlefield

**Kennesaw Mountain National Battlefield Park**
900 Kennesaw Mountain Drive
Kennesaw, GA 30152
www.nps.gov/kemo

## Other Regions

**Wilson's Creek National Battlefield**
6424 West Farm Road 182
Republic, MO 65738
www.nps.gov/wicr

**Picacho Peak State Park**
15520 Picacho Peak Road
Picacho, AZ 85241
azstateparks.com/Parks/PIPE

**Bentonville Battlefield State Historic Site**
5466 Harper House Road
Four Oaks, NC 27524
www.nchistoricsites.org/bentonvi

The sun rises over Union artillery at Fairview, Chancellorsville Battlefield, Fredericksburg and Spotsylvania National Military Park, Virginia.

# About the Civil War Trust

A century and a half has passed since a single cannon shot over Fort Sumter inaugurated the most bloody and tragic conflict in our country's history. For four years, armies in blue and gray roamed the countryside, clashing in battles that defined us as a nation and sounded the death knell of slavery. When the guns fell silent in 1865, more than 600,000 Americans had lost their lives on these blood-soaked battlefields.

Today, many Civil War battlefields are under siege. Year after year, thousands of acres of unprotected battlefield land are paved over, bulldozed, or otherwise erased from our national consciousness. Only about 20 percent of priority Civil War battlefield land is preserved—the rest is either unprotected or has been lost forever. The Civil War Trust is in a race against time to save these priceless treasures.

Twenty-five years ago, the looming threat of development on America's battlefields spurred the formation of two organizations determined to protect these hallowed grounds. The two groups merged in 1999, becoming the Civil War Trust, which continues that work as the nation's premier battlefield preservation organization. All told, the Civil War Trust has saved more than 43,000 acres of battlefield land in 23 states, including historic properties at Antietam, Bentonville, Chancellorsville, Chattanooga, Gettysburg, Manassas, Shiloh, Vicksburg, Wilson's Creek, and the Wilderness.

The Civil War Trust seeks help to continue its efforts so that future generations may also visit and learn from these living memorials to American courage and sacrifice. Working closely with partner groups, federal and state agencies, local governments and community-minded businesses, it strives to protect battlefield land and promote educational programs designed to teach Americans about the conflicts that shaped our history. With this imperative in mind, in November 2014 the Civil War Trust expanded its mission to include protection of hallowed ground associated with the Revolutionary War and War of 1812.

The Civil War Trust believes there is no better way to comprehend our nation's history than to walk in the footsteps of America's heroes. By creating walking trails, installing interpretive signs, and restoring the landscape to its wartime appearance, it works to transform these battlefields into genuine heritage tourism destinations. Through its website (www.civilwar.org), magazine, tours, and other events, the Civil War Trust seeks to be an invaluable source for government officials, educators, and history enthusiasts to share information about the conflicts that defined our national identity.

# Acknowledgments

I'm indebted to several individuals and organizations for their assistance and contributions to this project.

For his generous support, assistance, and feedback on all aspects of this book, I'm indebted to Garry Adelman of the Civil War Trust.

National Park Service staff at Civil War sites and at the media design center in Harpers Ferry, West Virginia, have been invaluable. These people include Tom Patterson and Marsha Wassel (Harpers Ferry Center); Dennis Frye (Harpers Ferry National Historical Park); Brian Eick (Appomattox Court House National Historical Park); Lee White (Chickamauga and Chattanooga National Military Park); Doug Richardson (Fort Donelson National Battlefield); Greg Mertz and Gregg Kneipp (Fredericksburg and Spotsylvania National Military Park); Christopher Gwinn (Gettysburg National Military Park); Tracy Evans (Monocacy National Battlefield); Grant Gates (Petersburg National Battlefield); Bert Dunkerly (Richmond National Battlefield Park); Joe Davis (Shiloh National Military Park); Bill Justice and Will Wilson (Vicksburg National Military Park); and Connie Langum (Wilson's Creek National Battlefield).

I also owe considerable thanks to state and private park managers, including Donny Taylor (Bentonville Battlefield State Historic Site); A. Wilson Greene (Pamplin Historical Park); Kurt Holman (Perryville Battlefield State Historic Site); and Charlie Crawford (Pickett's Mill Battlefield Historic Site).

For assistance with sites in the Shenandoah Valley Battlefields National Historic District, I owe considerable thanks to Terry Heder of the Shenandoah Valley Battlefields Foundation.

For their company, inspiration, and observations on numerous battlefield hikes, I owe thanks to my wife, Kathy Gilbert; to my Winchester, Virginia, neighbor Gene Schultz; and to my former National Park Service colleagues Jim Boyd, Rich Helman, and Jack Spinnler.

OPPOSITE: South Carolina State Monument, Chickamauga Battlefield, Chickamauga and Chattanooga National Military Park, Georgia.

# Suggested Reading List

Adelman, Garry E., ed. *The Civil War 150: An Essential To-Do List for the 150th Anniversary*. Guilford, CT: Lyons Press and the Civil War Trust, 2011.

Catton, Bruce. *The Centennial History of the Civil War, 1861–65*. 3 vols. New York: Doubleday, 1961.

_____. *Glory Road*. New York: Doubleday, 1952.

_____. *Mr. Lincoln's Army*. New York: Doubleday, 1951.

_____. *A Stillness at Appomattox*. New York: Doubleday, 1953.

Foote, Shelby. *The Civil War: A Narrative*. 3 vols. New York: Random House, 1974.

Keegan, John. *The American Civil War: A Military History*. New York: Knopf, 2009.

McPherson, James. *Battle Cry of Freedom: The Civil War Era*. New York: Oxford University Press, 1988.

_____. *For Cause and Comrades: Why Men Fought in the Civil War*. New York: Oxford University Press, 1997.

Potter, David M. *The Impending Crisis: 1848–1861*. New York: Harper & Row, 1976.

Shaara, Jeff. *Jeff Shaara's Civil War Battlefields: Discovering America's Hallowed Ground*. New York: Ballantine Books, 2006.

Smith, Timothy B. *The Golden Age of Battlefield Preservation: The Decade of the 1890s and the Establishment of America's First Five Military Parks*. Knoxville: University of Tennessee Press, 2008.

Stout, Harry S. *Upon the Altar of the Nation: A Moral History of the Civil War*. New York: Penguin, 2007.

Wiley, Bell Irvin. *The Life of Billy Yank: The Common Soldier of the Union*. Baton Rouge: LSU Press, 1952.

_____. *The Life of Johnny Reb: The Common Soldier of the Confederacy*. Baton Rouge: LSU Press, 1943.

# Photography Credits

© Jon Bilous/Shutterstock.com: pp. 202–203.

© Howard Clark: pp. 20, 182, 184 (top), 194, 205, 206–207, 211, 214–215, and 217.

© Cary Jones Crawford: p. 255.

© Michael Cynecki: pp. 322–323.

© Dave Getz: p. 321.

© David Gilbert: pp. 99, 170 (left), and 226–227.

© Bruce Guthrie: pp. 117, 161, 223, 258, 259, 291, 292, 297 (both), and 305.

© Rob Hainer/Shutterstock.com: p. 301.

© Chris Heisey: pp. 14–15, 16, 24–25, 44, 50, 72, 77 (right), 82, 84, 89, 94, 96–97, 120, 124–125, 141, 152–153, 159, 164–165, 177, 188, 198–199, 201, 204 (bottom), 208, 216, 282–283, 295, 298–299, 303, 311, 314–315, 316, and 327 (top).

© Tommy Kays: pp. 238–239.

Courtesy of Library of Congress: pp. 33, 49, 59, 73, 81, 101, 107, 116, 121, 131 (both), 169, 171, 179, 180, 195, 225, 257 (both), and 290.

© Eric Long: pp. 26, 110, 111, 129, 133 (bottom), 162–163, 167, 170 (right), 172, 173 (top), 175, 184 (bottom), 185, 189, 218, 263, 265 (both), 266–267, 277, 285, and 286–287.

© Jim Parkin/Shutterstock.com: p. 319.

© Theresa Rasmussen: pp. 10–11, 58, 60–61, 62–63, 66–67 (both), 68, and 108–109.

© Dane Reeves: p. 289.

© Shenandoah Sanchez: pp. 18–19, 28–29, 34, 37, 41, 42–43, 45, 47, 77 (left), 85, 100, 102–103, 134–135, 150–151, 157, 173 (bottom), 191, 193, 196–197, 204 (top), 213, and 219.

© Buddy Secor: pp. 2–3, 5, 7, 13, 22–23, 25, 31, 36, 39, 51, 52–53, 54, 57, 64–65, 69, 71, 74–75, 76, 79, 80, 83, 87, 90–91, 93, 105, 113, 137, 138–139, 147, 154–155, 200, 274–275, 331, and 334–335.

© Steven Stanley: pp. 143, 144–145 (both), 149, 156, 269, 308–309, 325, and 328–329.

© KennStilger47/Shutterstock.com: pp. 272–273.

© Mike Talplacido: pp. 1, 8, 34–35, 40, 55, 115, 118–119, 122–123, 127, 132, 133 (top), 136, 181, 182–183, 186–187, 209, 220–221, 229, 231, 232–233, 234–235, 236, 237 (both), 240, 241, 243, 245, 246–247, 248 (both), 249, 250–251, 252, 253, 260–261, 271, 272, 275, 280 (both), 281, 283, 284 (both), 293, 304–305, 306, 307, 313, 327 (bottom), 332, and 336.

Worm fencing on the Gaines' Mill Battlefield, Richmond National Battlefield Park, Virginia.

First published in the United States of America in 2017
by Rizzoli International Publications, Inc.  |  300 Park Avenue South  |  New York, NY 10010  |  www.rizzoliusa.com

© 2017 Rizzoli International Publications, Inc.  |  Foreword © 2017 Jeff Shaara

Associate Publisher: James O. Muschett  |  Project Editor: Candice Fehrman  |  Book Design: Susi Oberhelman  |  Maps: Steven Gordon, Cartagram, LLC

CIVIL WAR TRUST
*Saving America's Civil War Battlefields*

1156 15th Street NW  |  Suite 900  |  Washington, DC 20005  |  info@civilwar.org  |  www.civilwar.org

The Civil War Trust is the largest and most effective nonprofit organization devoted to the preservation of America's hallowed battlefields. Although primarily focused on the protection of Civil War battlefields, through its Campaign 1776 initiative, the Trust also seeks to save the battlefields connected to the Revolutionary War and War of 1812. To date, the Trust has preserved more than 43,000 acres of battlefield land in 23 states.

2017 2018 2019 2020 / 10 9 8 7 6 5 4 3 2

Printed in China  |  ISBN-13: 978-0-8478-5912-2  |  Library of Congress Catalog Control Number: 2016952489

PAGE 1: Georgia Monument, Chickamauga Battlefield, Chickamauga and Chattanooga National Military Park, Georgia; PAGES 2-3: Sunrise at Fort Stedman, Petersburg National Battlefield, Virginia; PAGE 5: Monument to Richard Rowland Kirkland of the 2nd South Carolina Volunteers along the Sunken Road, Fredericksburg Battlefield, Fredericksburg and Spotsylvania National Military Park, Virginia; PAGES 28-29: Stone House, Manassas National Battlefield Park, Virginia; PAGES 138-139: Sunrise on the Third Winchester Battlefield, Virginia; PAGES 164-165: Monument to the 96th Pennsylvania Volunteers near the Slaughter Pen, Gettysburg Battlefield, Gettysburg National Military Park, Pennsylvania; PAGES 220-221: Robertson's Alabama Battery, Shiloh Battlefield, Shiloh National Military Park, Tennessee; PAGES 260-261: Wiard Cannon near the Slaughter Pen, Stones River National Battlefield, Tennessee; PAGES 308-309: Bentonville Battlefield, Bentonville Battlefield State Historic Site, North Carolina; ABOVE: Shiloh Oak, Shiloh Battlefield, Shiloh National Military Park, Tennessee.